Year 6
Scottish Primary 7

50 Shared texts

Photocopiable texts for shared reading

- Fiction, non-fiction, poetry and drama
- Annotated versions
- Discussion prompts

Nikki Gamble

Credits

Author
Nikki Gamble

Illustrations
Angus Cameron

Series Consultants
Fiona Collins and
Alison Kelly

Series Designer
Anna Oliwa

Editor
Clare Gallaher

Designers
Anna Oliwa and
Allison Parry

Assistant Editor
Roanne Charles

Text © 2003 Nikki Gamble
© 2003 Scholastic Ltd

Designed using Adobe InDesign

Published by Scholastic Ltd
Villiers House
Clarendon Avenue
Leamington Spa
Warwickshire CV32 5PR

www.scholastic.co.uk

Printed by Bell and Bain Ltd, Glasgow

1 2 3 4 5 6 7 8 9   3 4 5 6 7 8 9 0 1 2

British Library Cataloguing-in-Publication Data
A catalogue record for this book is available from the British Library.

ISBN 0-439-98484-X

Contents

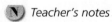 *Teacher's notes*    *Photocopiable*

 Teacher's notes    *Photocopiable*

Introduction

In 50 Shared texts you will find a range of texts for use in shared reading. In recent years shared text work has become the focal point of daily literacy work, and the success of such shared work is clearly linked to the quality and choice of text. Better understanding of children's reading and writing development has led to the realisation that a greater range of text types, or genres, is needed to enrich children's literacy development. For the busy classroom teacher, seeking out such a range of quality texts can be too time-consuming, which is why appropriate texts have been provided in this book.

Shared reading

Shared reading is at the heart of the activities in this book and is a cornerstone of the National Literacy Strategy, which states that through shared reading children begin to recognise important characteristics of a variety of written texts, often linked to style and voice.

First developed in New Zealand by Don Holdaway, shared reading has been a significant literacy routine for children since the 1980s. Holdaway's research and pioneering work in schools brought the benefits of sharing enlarged texts or Big Books to teachers' attention. From his observations of very young children attending to bedtime stories on a one-to-one basis he realised that a similar intimacy with print could be offered through sharing an enlarged text with a group or class of children. He showed how engagement with Big Books can teach children about the characteristics of different text types, their organisation and distinguishing features, as well as the finer details of print. For example, depending on the teacher's focus, an enlarged recipe could be used at text level to model the way a piece of instructional writing is structured, at sentence level to look at the use of imperative verbs or at word level to focus on a particular phoneme. In relation to literature, the meaning of a poem can be explored at text level, the poet's choice of verbs at sentence level and the rhyming pattern at word level. So, shared reading not only encourages the class to share the actual reading aloud of a text but also enables the teacher to discuss certain language features and support the children in both comprehending and responding to the text.

With younger children, shared reading involves following the text with a pointer to highlight key early concepts of print such as directionality and one-to-one correspondence. With such concepts securely in place, a rather different technique is needed for older children where the focus shifts more to understanding and responding to the text as well as discussing vocabulary and linguistic features. For all children, often the talk surrounding the reading is as important as the reading itself.

Finding the right quality texts for shared reading that will engage and interest the children, as well as meeting the many NLS objectives, can be a difficult task. Once a text is found, you need to identify salient features at word, sentence and text level.

Shared reading is also the springboard for shared writing, guided reading/writing and independent work. Both guided reading and writing provide opportunities for you to guide, support, model and comment on children's response to a text. Activities may involve reading aloud, role-play, performance or writing for a particular purpose. Independent activities may mirror these but need to be clearly structured to enable the children to work independently.

About this book

The texts in this book are organised term by term, following the NLS framework, so there are examples of fiction, poetry, plays and non-fiction.

For each text, both a blank and annotated version are provided. The former is for use with children and can either be enlarged or projected on an overhead projector; the latter is for teacher information and identifies the features of the text and links with NLS objectives.

Background

Background information is provided for each text. This will contextualise the extract, fill in any necessary details and give facts about its author as relevant. Information on themes, technical features or other related texts might also feature here.

Shared reading and discussing the text

This section offers guidance on ways of managing discussion around the text, as well as ways of organising the shared reading. Depending on the age of the children, and demands of the text, different strategies for working with the whole class on the text are given, as well as ways of triggering the children's responses. These include structured discussion suggestions, ideas for role-play, and performance techniques.

Activities

Building on the reading and discussion, this section suggests activities for both whole-class work and guided or independent group work. There are ideas for further textual analysis, sometimes involving shared writing. As in the previous section, talk is pivotal in developing the children's understanding.

Extension/further reading

Suggestions for taking activities into a broader context and ideas for linked reading are also provided, where appropriate. Reading may include books of the same genre, or texts that share the theme or the same author.

The texts

The choice of texts has been driven by the need to ensure that these are quality texts both in content and language. It is hoped that among the selection you will find a mixture of authors and texts, both familiar and new. Whole texts have been provided as far as possible so that children have the satisfaction of reading and appreciating a coherent and complete piece of writing.

Longer texts, such as novels, also need to feature in older children's reading, and sometimes more than one extract from the same carefully chosen novel has been included. Bearing in mind that children should experience as much of the novel as they can, it is recommended that you use the background notes to fill the children in on plot detail, and that you read the story to them or have copies, including a taped version, available for their own reading or listening. Other slots in the curriculum can be used for such reading: private reading, homework, independent group work or story time.

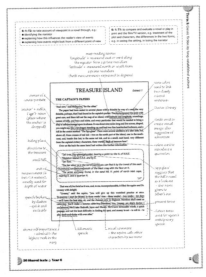
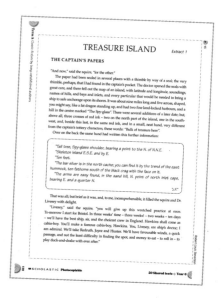

Range and objectives

Year 6 Term 1

Range	Text	NLS references
Classic fiction by long-established authors	**'Treasure Island'** (extract 1) from *Treasure Island* by Robert Louis Stevenson (Blackie)	T1, T2
	'Treasure Island' (extracts 2 and 3) from *Treasure Island* by Robert Louis Stevenson (Blackie)	S1, T2
Adaptations of classic drama by long-established authors	**'The story of Romeo and Juliet'** from *Shakespeare's Stories* by Leon Garfield (Victor Gollancz Ltd)	T1, T5
Classic poetry by long-established authors	**'Cargoes'** by John Masefield from *The Oxford Treasury of Classic Poems* edited by Michael Harrison and Christopher Stuart-Clark (Oxford University Press)	T3, T4
	'The Sea' from *Complete Poems for Children* by James Reeves (Classic Mammoth)	T3, T4, T10
	'Souvenir from Weston-Super-Mare' from *All Change* by Libby Houston (Oxford University Press)	T3, T4
Classic poetry	**'We'll Go To Sea No More'** from *Scottish Poems* chosen by John Rice (Macmillan Children's Books)	T3, T4
Classic drama by long-established authors	**'Romeo and Juliet'** (extract 1) from *Romeo and Juliet* by William Shakespeare at www.shakespeare.sk	T1, T6
	'Romeo and Juliet' (extract 2) from *Romeo and Juliet* by William Shakespeare at www.shakespeare.sk	W7, T1
Biography	**'Charles Darwin: The Early Years'** from *Science Discoveries: Charles Darwin and Evolution* by Steve Parker (Belitha Press)	T11, T14
Letters which recount experiences and events	**'A letter from Charles Darwin'** from *Charles Darwin's Letters: A Selection 1825–1859* (Cambridge University Press)	T11
Diaries and journals which recount experiences and events	**'Livingstone Discovers Victoria Falls, 1855'** from *Missionary Tales and Researches in South Africa* by David Livingstone (1858)	T11
	'Kensuke's Kingdom' from *Kensuke's Kingdom* by Michael Morpurgo (Heinemann)	T11
Autobiography	**'A Tiptoe Down Memory Lane'** (extracts 1 and 2) from *Freaks, Geeks and Asperger Syndrome* by Luke Jackson (Jessica Kingsley Publishers)	T11
	'The Village School' from *Cider with Rosie* by Laurie Lee (Penguin)	T11
Non-chronological reports	**'The Sources of Romeo and Juliet'** from *Romeo and Juliet* by Wendy Greenhill in the *Shakespeare Library* series (Heinemann Library)	T12, T13, T17
Journalistic writing	**'Power of the Ring too strong for boy wizard'** from the *Guardian Unlimited* website at www.guardian.co.uk	S1, S4, T12, T16

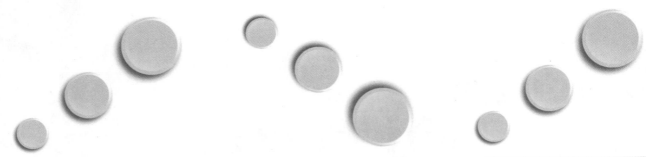

Year 6 Term 2

Range	Text	NLS references
Longer established fantasy novel	**'The Hobbit'** (extract 1) from *The Hobbit* by JRR Tolkien (HarperCollins)	T1, T7, T9, T10
	'The Hobbit' (extract 2) from *The Hobbit* by JRR Tolkien (HarperCollins)	T1, T7, T9
	'The Hobbit' (extracts 3 and 4) from *The Hobbit* by JRR Tolkien (HarperCollins)	T7, T8, T9
Longer established historical novel	**'The Eagle of the Ninth'** (extract 1) from *The Eagle of the Ninth* by Rosemary Sutcliff (Oxford University Press)	T1, T2, T7, T9
	'The Eagle of the Ninth' (extract 2) from *The Eagle of the Ninth* by Rosemary Sutcliff (Oxford University Press)	S3, T8, T9
	'The Eagle of the Ninth' (extract 3) from *The Eagle of the Ninth* by Rosemary Sutcliff (Oxford University Press)	T8, T9
Range of poetic forms: riddles	**'Riddles'** from *The Exeter Book of Riddles* translated by Kevin Crossley-Holland (Penguin), *The Hobbit* by JRR Tolkien (HarperCollins), *When I Dance* by James Berry (Hamish Hamilton Children's Books) and *The Red-All-Over Riddle Book* by George Szirtes (Faber & Faber)	T3, T4
Range of poetic forms: limericks	**'Limericks'** by Edward Lear from *The Lure of the Limerick* by William S Baring-Gould (Wordsworth Editions Ltd) and by PL Mannock and WS Gilbert from *The Kingfisher Book of Children's Poetry* (Kingfisher)	T3, T4, T9
Range of poetic forms: haiku	**'January to December'** from *Selected Poems* by Patricia Beer (Hutchinson)	T3, T5, T8
Range of poetic forms: sonnets	**'Sonnets'**: 'Ozymandias' by PB Shelley from *The Faber Book of Children's Verse* (Faber & Faber); 'Sonnet composed upon Westminster Bridge, 3rd September 1802' by William Wordsworth from *The Walker Book of Classic Poetry and Poets* selected by Michael Rosen (Walker Books)	T5, T6, T8, T9
Discussion texts	**'Rules – are they there to be broken?'** from *Citizenship and You* by Katrina Dunbar in the *What's At Issue?* series (Heinemann Library)	W8, T15, T16, T18
	'Performing sea creatures' from *Why Do People Harm Animals?* by Chris Mason (Hodder Wayland)	T15, T16
	'Why conservation?' from *Making a Difference* by Richard Spilsbury in the *What's At Issue?* series (Heinemann Library)	T15, T16, T18
Formal writing: public information documents	**'Packaging guidelines'** from *Code of Practice* by Parcelforce Worldwide (Consignia)	W5, S2, T17
	'Living well with allergies' from *Living with hayfever and other allergies* (Boots Group plc)	T17
Formal writing: notices	**'Fire instructions'** by Nikki Gamble	S2, T17

Year 6 Term 3

Range	Text	NLS references
Comparison of work by significant children's author	**'An Angel for May'** (extract 1) from *An Angel for May* by Melvin Burgess (Puffin)	T1
	'An Angel for May' (extract 2) from *An Angel for May* by Melvin Burgess (Puffin)	S1, T1
	'The Ghost Behind the Wall' (extracts 1 and 2) from *The Ghost Behind the Wall* by Melvin Burgess (Puffin)	S1, T1
	'The Ghost Behind the Wall' (extract 3) from *The Ghost Behind the Wall* by Melvin Burgess (Puffin)	S1, T1
Comparison of work by significant children's poet	**'Mum Dad and Me'** from *When I Dance* by James Berry (Hamish Hamilton Children's Books)	T3, T4
	'Sunny Market Song' from *When I Dance* by James Berry (Hamish Hamilton Children's Books)	S2, T3, T4
	'Mek Drum Talk, Man' from *When I Dance* by James Berry (Hamish Hamilton Children's Books)	S2, T3, T4, T12
Different authors' treatment of same theme	**'The Caged Bird in Springtime'** from *Collected Shorter Poems, Volume 1* by James Kirkup (Salzburg University Press)	T4
	'The Jaguar' from *The Hawk in the Rain* by Ted Hughes (Faber & Faber)	T2, T6
Explanations linked to work from other subjects	**'Forces'** from *Energy, Forces and Motion* by Alastair Smith and Corinne Henderson in the *Usborne Internet-linked Library of Science* series (Usborne Publishing Ltd)	S1, T15, T17, T20
	'How Things Work': extract 1 from *How Things Work* by Steve Parker (Kingfisher); extract 2 from *Eyewitness Guides: Force and Motion* by Peter Lafferty (Dorling Kindersley Ltd)	S1, T15, T17, T20
Non-chronological reports linked to work from other subjects	**'Meet the Wolf'** from *Wolf* by Michael Leach in the *Natural World* series (Hodder Wayland)	S1, S3, T16, T19
Non-chronological reports; poetry	**'Walk with a wolf'** from *Walk with a Wolf* by Janni Howker (Walker Books)	S1, T19
Explanations; reports	**'Why is the Grey Wolf an endangered species?'** from *Grey Wolf* (WWF-UK Ltd) at www.wwf.org.uk	S1, T19
Reference texts, range of dictionaries	**'Dictionary of phrase and fable'** from *Brewer's Dictionary of Phrase and Fable* (Cassell)	T17, T19
	'Origins of the word "wolf"': extract 1 from the *Oxford Dictionary of Word Origins* by John Ayto (Oxford University Press); extract 2 from *Chambers Dictionary of Etymology* (Chambers Harrap Publishers Ltd)	T17, T19
Reference texts, thesauruses	**'Thesaurus'** from the *Longman Synonym Dictionary* (Rodale Press)	T19

Treasure Island

by Robert Louis Stevenson

Extract 1

Background

Scottish novelist and poet Robert Louis Stevenson (1850–94) began writing his first full-length novel, *Treasure Island*, in 1881. It was written in serial form; Stevenson read the first 15 chapters aloud to his stepson Lloyd Osborne. It first appeared in book form in 1883. *Treasure Island* is considered a landmark book, being a forerunner of the psychologically complex novels of the 20th century and a prototype for many adventure stories. The plot is fast moving and Stevenson himself wrote: 'If this don't fetch the kids, why, they have gone rotten since my day.'

The story, mainly narrated by young Jim Hawkins, tells of the search for the buried treasure of the notorious pirate Captain Flint. When Jim discovers a bundle of papers in Billy Bones' sea chest he seeks advice from Squire Trelawney. Hidden among them is a document which the Squire verifies as Flint's treasure map. This extract depicts the moment of revelation when the captain's papers are opened. The first two paragraphs are descriptive, providing information about Treasure Island. There is a change of pace in the third paragraph, reflecting the Squire's excitement about the find.

Shared reading and discussing the text

● Provide contextual information about Robert Louis Stevenson and the writing of *Treasure Island*.

● Discuss the children's knowledge of the story. They may be familiar with film versions such as *Muppet Treasure Island* or *Treasure Planet*. If you are not reading the book as a class novel, explain what has previously happened in the story.

● Read the passage aloud. Give the children definitions for any words that are unfamiliar, or carry out a dictionary check.

● Re-read it a second time. Discuss why the doctor and the squire get excited when they open the Captain's document. How is the squire's excitement communicated?

● Ask the children what they imagine Jim to be thinking and feeling at this point.

● On a large copy of the text, highlight words and phrases that describe location and terrain, such as *hummock*, in the directions to the treasure.

Activities

● Ask the children to use the information in the passage – dimensions, shape and features – to draw a map on squared paper (they can do this in pairs); then mark features and the location of the buried treasure, and label their map.

● Can they write a description of what it might be like on the island, imagining what they might see, hear and feel? They could use pictures of islands from travel brochures to help visualise the scene.

● What might happen after the map has been discovered? Ask the children to plan and write their own versions of what may take place. Share and evaluate the stories in small groups.

● Ask the children to write Jim's diary, giving his thoughts on the prospective adventure.

● Suggest that they draw a treasure map and write a set of instructions explaining where the treasure can be located, using compass bearings to indicate directions.

Extension/further reading

Use the Internet and other sources to research Robert Louis Stevenson. Prepare a class display and collect together copies of his books. Include reviews of the books for other children to read.

Children may like to read the complete novel, *Treasure Island* (Puffin Classics). Other books include Robert Louis Stevenson's *Kidnapped* (Penguin) and *Dr Jekyll and Mr Hyde* (Evans Brothers); biographical material about Robert Louis Stevenson such as *Favourite Classic Writers* by Nikki Gamble (Hodder); abridged and illustrated versions such as Chris Mould's *Treasure Island* (OUP); sequels such as Francis Bryan's *Jim Hawkins and the Curse of Treasure Island* (Orion Children's Books).

6: 1: T2: to take account of viewpoint in a novel through, e.g.:
● identifying the narrator
● explaining how this influences the reader's view of events
● explaining how events might look from a different point of view

6: 1: T1: to compare and evaluate a novel or play in print and the film/TV version, e.g. treatment of the plot and characters, the differences in the two forms, e.g. in seeing the setting, in losing the narrator

map-reading terms:
'longitude' = measured east or west along the equator from a prime meridian
'latitude' = measured north or south from a prime meridian
(both measurements expressed in degrees)

owner of a country estate

'anchor' + suffix ('age'): noun (place where the anchor is dropped)

semi-colon used to link two closely related sentences

Doctor Livesey

TREASURE ISLAND

Extract 1

THE CAPTAIN'S PAPERS

"And now," said the squire, "for the other."

The paper had been sealed in several places with a thimble by way of a seal; the very thimble, perhaps, that I had found in the captain's pocket. The doctor opened the seals with great care, and there fell out the map of an island, with latitude and longitude, soundings, names of hills, and bays and inlets, and every particular that would be needed to bring a ship to safe anchorage upon its shores. It was about nine miles long and five across, shaped, you might say, like a fat dragon standing up, and had two fine land-locked harbours, and a hill in the centre marked "The Spy-glass". There were several additions of a later date; but, above all, three crosses of red ink – two on the north part of the island, one in the south-west, and, beside this last, in the same red ink, and in a small, neat hand, very different from the captain's tottery characters, these words: "Bulk of treasure here".

Over on the back the same hand had written this further information:

simile used to create visual image; also suggestive of adventure

colon used to introduce a quotation

hiding place

directions to the treasure

small hill

unit of measurement (6 feet/1.8 metres), usually used for depth of water

"Tall tree, Spy-glass shoulder, bearing a point to the N. of N.N.E.
"Skeleton Island E.S.E. and by E.
"Ten feet.
"The bar silver is in the north cache; you can find it by the trend of the east hummock, ten fathoms south of the black crag with the face on it.
"The arms are easy found, in the sand hill, N. point of north inlet cape, bearing E. and a quarter N.
"J.F."

'Spy-glass' suggests that the hill is used as a lookout – also name given to Silver's inn

That was all; but brief as it was, and, to me, incomprehensible, it filled the squire and Dr. Livesey with delight.

"Livesey," said the squire, "you will give up this wretched practice at once. To-morrow I start for Bristol. In three weeks' time – three weeks! – two weeks – ten days – we'll have the best ship, sir, and the choicest crew in England. Hawkins shall come as cabin-boy. You'll make a famous cabin-boy, Hawkins. You, Livesey, are ship's doctor; I am admiral. We'll take Redruth, Joyce and Hunter. We'll have favourable winds, a quick passage, and not the least difficulty in finding the spot, and money to eat – to roll in – to play duck-and-drake with ever after."

speech broken by dashes – quick and excitable

present tense

future tense used for squire's anticipatory speech

shows self-importance – admiral is the highest rank in the navy

idiomatic speech

social comment – the squire calls other characters by surname

Treasure Island

by Robert Louis Stevenson

Extracts 2 and 3

Background

One of the crew of the 'Hispaniola', the ship that the Squire hires to take him to Treasure Island, is the one-legged sea cook, Long John Silver, an original member of Captain Flint's crew. Silver is morally ambiguous; while the villain of the piece, he also possesses heroic qualities and is the most attractive character in the story. He becomes a surrogate father to Jim but he is also capable of brutal murder. Jim's initial liking for Silver turns to mistrust when, hidden inside an apple barrel, he overhears the cook's mutinous plot (Chapter 11).

The two extracts selected here show the contrasting sides of Silver's character. The first is from Chapter 8 where Jim first encounters Silver. The second comes from Chapter 14, entitled 'The first blow', in which Silver faces opposition from members of the crew.

Shared reading and discussing the text

● Read the first extract (extract 2) aloud. Ask the children to sketch Long John, labelling their drawing with any words or phrases from the passage that contribute to the image they have of him. This visualising activity enables the children to have independent responses before sharing them with the group. Allow a few minutes of concentrated activity.

● Share the sketches, picking out words from the extract that describe his physical appearance, for example *His left leg was cut off close by the hip, and under the left shoulder he carried a crutch.*

● Draw attention to the similes: *hopping about upon it like a bird; a face as big as a ham* (explain what a ham joint looks like – the pink colour and roundness are the salient features; this is how ham was cooked and served in the 19th century).

● Contrast the objective and subjective information we are given about Long John Silver. An example of the former is *a man came out of a side room.* But some information, such as the pleasant associations with the ham when his face is being described, influences what we think of Silver's personality. Adjectives (*merry, cheerful, clean, pleasant-tempered*) and verbs (*whistling*) also create a positive portrait.

● Read extract 3. Explain that the cook is Long John. Discuss what image we have of him from this passage, picking out influencing words and phrases. Compare the simile *agile as a monkey* with *hopping… like a bird.*

● Discuss whether it is authentic for a character to have more than one side to their personality. Draw on the children's experiences, asking them to think about their most positive traits and less favourable ones.

Activities

● Ask the children to divide a large sheet of paper in two, and write down phrases (or draw two pictures, one in each section) showing the two different sides of Long John Silver's character. If reading the book as a class novel, the children can find other examples of this ambiguity in the book.

● Similes are used in these extracts to create positive and negative associations (see above). Ask the children to choose a well-known fictional character and create similes to show the positive and negative sides of the character.

● The words that a writer selects to describe a character influence the reader's thoughts and feelings. For instance, we could say that *Long John smiled at Jim* – or *Long John smirked at Jim. Smirk* doesn't have the pleasant associations that *smile* has. Ask the children to use a thesaurus to find alternative words and phrases for *smile* and categorise the words into those that have positive associations and those that have negative ones. The children may discover that some are neutral.

● In these extracts we see Long John Silver through Jim's eyes but what story would Silver himself tell about these events? If you are not reading *Treasure Island* as a class novel, provide a synopsis of the story. Organise the children into small groups, each one a storytelling circle, and ask them to retell the story of Treasure Island from Long John Silver's point of view.

6: 1: T2: to take account of viewpoint in a novel through, e.g.:
● identifying the narrator
● explaining how this influences the reader's view of events
● explaining how events might look from a different point of view

6: 1: S1: to revise from Y5 the different word classes, e.g. prepositions

1st person narrator Jim Hawkins

introduced by physical appearance – this is what Jim would first notice

simile – comparison to bird creates image of quick, darting movements

quickness and skill in physical activity – has positive connotations

1st person narrator directly addresses reader

picks up bird imagery

adjectives used to describe Silver are positive

name of the inn where Jim lives with his mother

TREASURE ISLAND

LONG JOHN SILVER

At the Sign of the "Spy-glass" _Extract 2_

As I was waiting, a man came out of a side room, and, at a glance, I was sure he must be Long John. His left leg was cut off close by the hip, and under the left shoulder he carried a crutch, which he managed with wonderful dexterity, hopping about upon it like a bird. He was very tall and strong, with a face as big as a ham – plain and pale, but intelligent and smiling. Indeed, he seemed in the most cheerful spirits, whistling as he moved about among the tables, with a merry word or a slap on the shoulder for the more favoured of his guests.

Now, to tell the truth, from the very first mention of Long John in Squire Trelawney's letter, I had taken a fear in my mind that he might prove to be the very one-legged sailor whom I had watched for so long at the old "Benbow". But one look at the man before me was enough. I had seen the captain, and Black Dog, and the blind man Pew, and I thought I knew what a buccaneer was like – a very different creature, according to me, from this clean and pleasant-tempered landlord.

adjectives used to describe victim – reader is guided to sympathy for the victim

Long John Silver – he is the sea cook

clumsy in appearance

powerful image

The First Blow _Extract 3_

And with that this brave fellow turned his back directly on the cook, and set off walking for the beach. But he was not destined to go far. With a cry, John seized the branch of a tree, whipped the crutch out of his arm-pit, and sent that uncouth missile hurtling through the air. It struck poor Tom, point foremost, and with stunning violence, right between his shoulders in the middle of his back. His hands flew up, he gave a sort of gasp, and fell.

Whether he were injured much or little, none could ever tell. Like enough, to judge from the sound, his back was broken on the spot. But he had no time given him to recover. Silver, agile as a monkey, even without leg or crutch, was on top of him next moment, and had twice buried his knife up to the hilt in that defenceless body. From my place of ambush, I could hear him pant aloud as he struck the blows.

dexterity mentioned in 1st extract is now seen as a negative quality

simile contrasts with the above extract – monkey has negative connotations

character revealed through action

The story of Romeo and Juliet

by Leon Garfield

Background

Leon Garfield (1921–96) was born in Brighton. His first book, *Jack Holborn*, was published in 1964. This was followed by *Black Jack* (1968) and *Smith* (1967). The black humour in Garfield's stories is reminiscent of Dickens, and he writes with a distinctive style, incorporating his own archaic language to provide a period atmosphere. Garfield is also remembered for his splendid retellings, *Shakespeare's Stories*, and his brilliant adaptations for the *Animated Tales* that were shown on television (and are available in script versions).

This extract from Leon Garfield's *Romeo and Juliet* provides an interesting comparison with the extract from Act I Scene I of Shakespeare's play (see page 24).

Shared reading and discussing the text

● Read the passage, share first responses and check unfamiliar vocabulary.
● Identify and evaluate the effectiveness of the animal imagery that Garfield uses (*bright as wasps; at each other's throats like dogs*). Locate and discuss other instances of imagery in this passage (for example, *sweated knives*).
● Discuss the ways Garfield creates humour in this extract (for example, *doddering swords – that surely would have shaken more like straws in the wind than lightning in the sky*).
● Look at the ironic tone the writer uses (*in their valiant endeavours to cut each other into pieces*).
● Compare this text with the passage from Act I Scene I of Shakespeare's play. What are the similarities? (For example, events.) What are the differences? (For example, in script most of the information about character is carried through dialogue; in narrative, description provides information about character.)

Activities

● Ask the children to rewrite the scene as the opening for a story with a contemporary setting. They should include a balance between serious and humorous elements.

● The images that Garfield uses in this extract could be located and illustrated, the children captioning their illustrations with phrases from the text (*men were as bright as wasps and carried quick swords for their stings; Tybalt, a young Capulet so full of fury that he sweated knives*, and so on).
● Leon Garfield uses different words to describe anger (for example, *incensed, furiously*). Ask the children to extend a list of these, using a thesaurus, and make a collection of mood words for their personal word books. Encourage them to check the meaning of words and organise them along a scale of intensity from mild to strong.
● Using a plot synopsis, the children could continue writing the story of Romeo and Juliet in the style of Leon Garfield, using the extract as a model for language and tone.
● Prepare this text as a cloze passage. Delete the words that add colour to the description. Ask the children to work in pairs to suggest words to fill in the gaps. They should discuss possibilities and justify their vocabulary choices. It doesn't matter if they don't choose the original word. They can then work in fours, considering all suggestions before deciding on a group answer. Vary the challenge by carefully selecting the words for deletion.

Extension/further reading

Ask the children to read Garfield's *Romeo and Juliet*, select a scene and compare it with a film, dramatised or animated version of the story. They could use two headings: *Similarities* and *Differences*.

Books for further reading include *Shakespeare: The Animated Tales* abridged by Leon Garfield (Egmont); other adaptations of Shakespeare's plays such as Charles and Mary Lamb's *Tales from Shakespeare* (Puffin), Andrew Matthews' *The Orchard Book of Shakespeare Stories*, and Geraldine McCaughrean's *Stories from Shakespeare* (Dolphin); there is also Richard Brassey's *Shakespeare* in the *Brilliant Brits* series (Dolphin).

6: 1: T1: to compare and evaluate a novel or play in print and the film/TV version, e.g. treatment of the plot and characters, the differences in the two forms, e.g. in seeing the setting, in losing the narrator

6: 1: T5: to contribute constructively to shared discussion about literature, responding to and building on the views of others

narrative version of extract from Act 1 Scene 1

images of colours, sounds, heat

The story of Romeo and Juliet

exposition – place, character

animal imagery

exclamatory sentence

description of ordinary folk and Verona contrasts with the disturbance and anger, the 'uproar'

imagery

portent of events to come – from this point we are aware of the danger of someone disturbing the peace

simile – image of mad dogs

images extended through use of verbs

vocabulary is ironic

effective image conveyed by comparison

violent and emotive language

by means of

outward appearance

In old Verona, where the streets were hot and narrow and the walls were high, where men were as bright as wasps and carried quick swords for their stings, there lived two families – the Capulets and the Montagues – who hated each other worse than death. They had but to pass in the street and they were at each other's throats like dogs in the sun. Cursing and shouting and bawling, and crashing from civil pillar to post, they filled the good people of Verona with fear and anger to have their city's peace so senselessly disturbed.

They were at it again! In the buzzing heat of a July morning, two lazy no-good servants of the Capulets had spied two strolling men of the Montagues. Looks had been exchanged, then words, and in moments the peaceful market was in uproar as the four idle ruffians set about defending their masters' honour by smashing up stalls, overturning baskets, wrecking shops and wounding passers-by, in their valiant endeavours to cut each other into pieces.

Benvolio, a sensible young Montague, came upon the scene and tried to put a stop to it; Tybalt, a young Capulet so full of fury that he sweated knives, promptly went for Benvolio; old Montague and old Capulet appeared and tried to draw their doddering swords – that surely would have shaken more like straws in the wind than lightning in the sky. Men shouted, women screamed and rushed to drag wandering infants into safety… and bloody riot threatened to swallow up all the fair city, till the Prince of Verona, with soldiers, came furiously into the square.

"Rebellious subjects, enemies to peace!" he roared; and, by dint of stern anger and sterner threats, restored some semblance of peace. The vile destructive brawling between the Montagues and the Capulets incensed him beyond measure.

"If ever you disturb our streets again," he swore, "your lives shall pay the forfeit."

an oath

Cargoes

by John Masefield

Background

John Masefield (1878–1967, and Poet Laureate 1930–67) was born in Herefordshire. His mother died when he was young and he was put in the charge of a governess. At 13 he joined the merchant navy but suffered from acute seasickness and was discharged. The sea is a frequently occurring subject in his poetry.

'Cargoes' was first published in the collection *Ballads and Poems* (1910). It is a romantic poem about seafaring and maritime history. It comprises three stanzas representing three different periods in maritime history.

Shared reading and discussing the text

● Introduce the poem, giving brief information about John Masefield.

● Read the poem aloud at least twice, relishing the rich vocabulary and emphasising the contrasts in rhythm. Initially the children may not understand all of the words but they should be able to appreciate the musicality of the language. Share initial responses.

● Ask the children to identify unknown words, working in pairs. Take suggestions, list words in a prepared glossary and use a dictionary to check meanings. Now read the poem together.

● Discuss the contrasts in the three stanzas. Guide the children to consider the description of the cargoes (*ivory, apes, peacocks; diamonds, cinnamon, gold moidores; Tyne coal, firewood, cheap tin trays*). Highlight the three movement verbs (*rowing, dipping, butting*) and contrasts in weather and place (*sunny Palestine, the tropics by the palm-green shores, the Channel in the mad March days*). Consider the different effects created by these word choices.

● Notice that the assonance in the first two stanzas creates the impression of a leisurely pace. However, in the third stanza alliteration combines with the high incidence of monosyllabic words to create the onomatopoeic effect of a steamboat pushing through the water. Read and clap the last stanza together to emphasise this effect.

● Encourage the children to think about the images in this poem. What would the rowers be thinking on their journey? They are unlikely to have experienced the journey in the leisurely way that this poem suggests. Masefield presents a romanticised view of seafaring.

● Identify the rhyme scheme. The full rhyme at the end of the second and fifth lines provides a reassuring closure.

Activities

● Individually or in pairs, can the children write a fourth stanza, using the poem as a model? What kinds of cargo do ships carry today? (For example, military equipment, oil.) Encourage the children to use words that convey the cargo and the movement of the ship through the water. They could use the rhyme scheme of the original and then experiment by writing without a final end rhyme.

● The strong rhythms make this an ideal poem for learning by heart. Ask small groups to annotate copies of the poem and prepare a reading to emphasise the contrasts between the three stanzas.

● 'Cargoes' is a sensory poem that lends itself to a visual response. In groups, the children could create a poetry poster to depict one stanza, incorporating the lines from the poem.

● Provide the children with reference sources, including pictures of sailing vessels, to research seafaring in the periods that Masefield writes about in 'Cargoes'.

● After investigating the history of transport, as a class, ask the children to write a poem on a similar theme to 'Cargoes' (perhaps air, rail or road), using the language patterns identified in Masefield's poem.

Extension/further reading

Other writing by John Masefield includes *The Box of Delights* and *The Midnight Folk* (both Mammoth). There are also sea poems in anthologies such as *Down in the Marvellous Deep* compiled by Sophie Windham (Orchard Books).

6: 1: T3: to articulate personal responses to literature, identifying why and how a text affects the reader

6: 1: T4: to be familiar with the work of some established authors, to know what is special about their work, and to explain their preferences in terms of authors, styles and themes

scholars think that Ancient Ophir was probably India (peacocks came from India); name now commonly used for gold mines

ancient city in the Middle East

assonance creates leisurely impression

Roman war galley powered by 5 banks of rowers

Cargoes

Quinquereme of Ninevah from distant Ophir
Rowing home to haven in sunny Palestine,
With a cargo of ivory,
And apes and peacocks,
Sandalwood, cedarwood, and sweet white wine.

Central America

can be compared with locations in stanzas 1 and 3

sensory words focus on smells, colours and tastes

large sailing ship, heavily masted

Stately Spanish galleon coming from the Isthmus,
Dipping through the Tropics by the palm-green shores,
With a cargo of diamonds,
Emeralds, amethysts,
Topazes, and cinnamon, and gold moidores.

polysyllabic words add to leisurely impression

three verbs of movement, one in each stanza

spice trade

old Portuguese coin

cargo ship

Dirty British coaster with a salt-caked smoke stack
Butting through the Channel in the mad March days,[2]
With a cargo of Tyne coal,
Road-rail, pig-lead
Firewood, iron-ware, and cheap tin trays.[5]

alliteration

full rhyme at the end of lines 2 and 5 create closure

clipped, monosyllabic words work with alliteration to create onomatopoeic effect

John Masefield

6: 1: T5: to contribute constructively to shared discussion about literature, responding to and building on the views of others

The Sea

by James Reeves

Background

The English poet James Reeves was born in 1909 and died in 1978. His first collection of poetry for children, *The Wandering Moon*, published in 1950, was followed by *Blackbird in the Lilac* in 1952. In *From the Garden to the Street,* Morag Styles describes Reeves' poetry as 'full of delicate observations, the storyteller's taste for the strange and romantic and an almost childlike yearning at the wonder of the world'. These qualities are found in 'The Sea'. Reeves employs the device of an extended metaphor to illustrate the diversity of the sea's moods. The first two stanzas create images that are full of movement and accompanied by sounds of the sea; in contrast, the final stanza emphasises stillness and quiet.

Shared reading and discussing the text

● Read the poem aloud, emphasising the contrast in mood between the first two stanzas and the final stanza, and then ask for a volunteer to read the poem a second time.

● Read the poem a third time and ask the class to sketch any pictures that come to mind as they listen to the poem being read aloud. Allow five minutes for the children to complete their sketches. Discuss which lines of the poem evoked the strongest images.

● Ask what animal the sea is compared to and identify words and phrases that are used to make the comparison throughout the poem. It may be appropriate to revise the term *metaphor* and introduce the term *extended metaphor.* Adjectives and nouns attribute dog-like characteristics to the sea; and verbs indicate dog-like behaviour. Guide the children to see the contrast between the first two and the final stanzas. Encourage them to draw on their personal experiences to evaluate the observation of the dog's behaviour and to make judgements about how apposite the selected metaphor is for describing the sea.

● Ask the children if they can see any patterns in the language. Point out the rhyming patterns and look for contrasts in the way rhyme is used in the different stanzas. In what ways does James Reeves' use of rhyme help to express his ideas about the sea?

Activities

● Suggest that the children make a list of words and phrases from the poem that describe the different movements of the sea. They should then use a thesaurus to find new vocabulary, using dictionaries to find precise definitions, and add the list to their personal word books.

● Can the children create a visual poem by illustrating the metaphor *The sea is a hungry dog*? Some children may interpret this literally while others might be able to represent the idea symbolically. Discuss the different interpretations, drawing attention to literal and symbolic representations, where appropriate.

● Ask the children to write an extended metaphor poem comparing a natural phenomenon to an animal, for example a volcano might be compared with a lion, a snowstorm with a Siberian tiger, a thunderstorm with a bear. Children requiring more support with this idea can work in a group with an adult to play an association game (for example, *If a volcano were an animal, what animal would it be?* and so on).

● Let the children use their rough sketches produced in the shared reading session as the basis for artwork relating to the poem. Encourage independent selection of media and diversity of form. Artwork and text can be integrated to create illustrated picture book versions of the poem.

Extension/further reading

Listen to music inspired by the sea such as Debussy's *La Mer,* Elgar's *Symphony No 2* and Britten's *Four Sea Interludes.* Encourage the children to make notes of images, thoughts and feelings inspired by the music. They can use their jottings to write individual sea poems.

Further reading could include the poem 'The Wandering Moon' in *Complete Poems for Children* by James Reeves (Mammoth).

6: 1: T3: to articulate personal responses to literature, identifying why and how a text affects the reader

6: 1: T4: to be familiar with the work of some established authors, to know what is special about their work, and to explain their preferences in terms of authors, styles and themes

6: 1: T10: to write own poems experimenting with active verbs and personification

The Sea

The sea is a hungry dog. [a]
Giant and grey. [b]
He rolls on the beach all day. [b]
With his clashing teeth and shaggy jaws [c]
Hour upon hour he gnaws [c]

The rumbling, tumbling stones, [d]
And "Bones, bones, bones, bones!" [d]
The giant sea-dog moans, [d]
Licking his greasy paws. [c]

And when the night wind roars [e]
And the moon rocks in the stormy cloud, [e]
He bounds to his feet and snuffs and sniffs, [f]
Shaking his wet sides over the cliffs, [f]
And howls and hollos long and loud. [e]

But on quiet days in May or June, [g]
When even the grasses on the dune [g]
Play no more their reedy tune, [g]
With his head between his paws [c]
He lies on the sandy shores, [c]
So quiet, so quiet, he scarcely snores. [c]

James Reeves

extended metaphor and personification

dog-like behaviour expressed in these movement verbs

dog-like noises expressed in these verbs

connective used to make a contrast

dog at rest

effect of repetition: as though the sea is becoming increasingly quiet – echoes the gentle lulling of waves on the shore

complex rhyme scheme works subtly

internal rhyme contributes to the image of the waves; a repeating motion

in the final stanza, six lines are divided into two sets of three lines ending with full rhyme ('June'/ 'dune'/'tune'; 'paws'/ 'shores'/'snores'); this has a settling and reassuring effect which is consistent with the subject of the stanza

Souvenir from Weston-Super-Mare

by Libby Houston

Background

The subject of British poet Libby Houston's poem is a family trip to a British seaside resort, Weston-Super-Mare in Somerset, which became popular during the reign of Queen Victoria. Donkey rides are still a popular feature of seaside entertainment. The speaker of the poem decides to build a sand sculpture rather than a sandcastle. As the family leave the beach they look back and see another family stopping to look at the sand-cat. The young boy's secret response to it takes them by surprise.

Shared reading and discussing the text

● Read the poem at least twice, then share the children's favourite parts of it. Let them draw on their personal experiences; talk about visits to the beach and activities that they have enjoyed. Talk about sand sculptures they have built or seen.

● Ask the children who they imagine is speaking the poem. Draw their attention to parts of the poem that show the actions of the speaker (for example, *I scoop away. I build. I mould…*).

● Ask the children to visualise and talk about how they imagine the scene. Guide them to consider that although it is an overcast day (*cloud, tide, mud cement the scene grey*) the speaker is enjoying the visit and is reluctant to leave at the end of the day.

● Talk about the title. A souvenir is usually a gift that is bought as a memory of a holiday. What is the souvenir in this poem? (It is the stolen moment of seeing the boy unexpectedly stroke the cat.)

● Contrast the opening and closing stanzas. The poet has chosen to use hands as images in the opening and closing lines of the poem. The first stanza is slow-moving, the mood is reluctant (*creeping… prised… cross the day's backdrop again*), but the action in the final three lines is fast-moving (*Dodging… weaving… race*).

● Discuss some of the verb choices and evaluate their effectiveness (for example, *a family comes breasting the wind; prised from their hay; he strokes the sand fur*).

● Talk about the way in which stanzas 3 to 5 each end with an unfinished sentence (which is continued at the beginning of the following stanza). This acts as a literary intake of breath and provides tension.

Activities

● Ask the children to compare Libby Houston's depiction of the seaside with James Reeves' description of the sea (see page 18). They should consider the content of the poems, the patterns of language and layout. Encourage the children to discuss and justify their preferences.

● Suggest that the children write a poem about a remembered visit to a special place entitled 'Souvenir from…'.

● Libby Houston uses the verb *breasting* to describe what it is like to battle against the wind. Ask the children to generate a list of verbs that can be used to describe how people move in different weather conditions (for example wind, rain, snow), adding the words to their personal word books.

● 'Souvenir from Weston-Super-Mare' contains several images of time: time passing slowly and quickly. Dividing a page into two columns, the children could create some images that convey time passing slowly, in one column, and in the second column, create some images that convey time passing quickly.

Extension/further reading

The children could read and collect favourite sea poems. Make a class anthology incorporating these, together with poems written by the children. Notes explaining personal reasons for selecting the poems could be included.

'Maggie and Millie and Molly and May' by ee cummings in *Selected Poems 1923–1958* (Faber & Faber) and 'Storm At Sea' by Kevin Crossley-Holland in *Dark as a Midnight Dream* compiled by Fiona Waters (Evans Brothers) are both poems about the sea. Collections include Ann Turnbull and Michael Foreman's *The Sand Horse* (Andersen Press) and *The Puffin Book of Salt-sea Verse* compiled by Charles Causley.

usually an object bought in a shop; in this instance a memory of a stolen moment

Latin origin ('super' – on or above; 'mare' – sea)

Old English – 'West tun' ('tun' – settlement)

first stanza shows an uninspiring scene

action verbs – busy hands

making it hold together

verb created from a noun by adding 'ing' suffix (derivational morphology)

the sand-cat

last line of stanza flows smoothly into the line of the next without pause; enjambment

tenderness

shift in pace

SOUVENIR FROM WESTON-SUPER-MARE

Moving in a bunch like creeping hands
    the donkeys, prised from their hay,
cross the day's backdrop again: cloud, tide, mud
    cement the scene grey.

I scoop away. I build, I mould – the oil's
    good for adhesion. There, that
can do for the necessary moat,
    and look! A *sand-cat*!

Ears, nose, paws straight from Egypt. And still
    ten minutes before the bus.
We look back from the top of the wall
    Long drawn out after us

a family comes breasting the wind –
    it'll be right in their track.
The boy spots it first, running ahead.
    He goes running back

to fetch the others. They cluster and point,
    looking up and down the strand
before the wind detaches them again.
    He waits. Their backs turned,

he drops to his knees, he strokes the sand fur.
Come on – five past the bus leaves! [2]
Dodging the weaving cars we race the station
    clock's hands light as thieves. [4]

Libby Houston

simile

verb choice – shows donkeys are unwilling

repeated 'd' sounds punctuate the list

like a stage set

exclamatory – excitement (a sand-cat is unexpected)

metaphorical

the promenade wall

old word for 'beach'

striking image

rhyming words

race against the clock

patterned language – regular rhyme scheme (2nd and 4th lines)

hands are a recurring image: 'creeping hands', busy hands (which 'scoop', 'build' and 'mould'), 'clock's hands light as thieves', stroking hands

simile – time moves quickly; speaker engrossed in watching the boy, then suddenly comes to and has to run for the bus

We'll Go To Sea No More  Anon

Background

'We'll Go To Sea No More' is a simple ballad. Ballads are lyrical narratives that vary in length but have an exact metrical structure and regular rhyming pattern. Originally ballads would have been used as musical accompaniments to dance; the term comes from the Latin *ballare* meaning 'to dance'. 'We'll Go To Sea No More' is a folk ballad. Characteristically, it is anonymous, and would originally have been transmitted from singer to singer as part of the oral tradition. Folk ballads drew material from the lives of the ordinary people, their stories, superstitions and working lives. This ballad originates from the area around the Forth of Firth on the east coast of Scotland.

The features of 'We'll Go To Sea No More' that are common to the ballad form are the rhythm produced by the regular iambic metre (an iambic foot consists of an unstressed syllable followed by a stressed syllable); the regular abcb rhyme scheme (however, the stanzas in this poem consist of eight lines rather than the more conventional four lines); the incremental repetition of phrases; an envoi – a final verse which highlights the message and is usually addressed to the individual(s) for whom the ballad was sung or written.

Shared reading and discussing the text

● Read the poem aloud. Ask the children who they think is speaking the poem, and who is being spoken to. Pick up on the speaker mentioning *gude-man* (husband) and *bairns* (children). This indicates that the speaker is a fisherman's wife, who waits at home for her family to return from fishing. In this ballad, in which the woman is directly addressing her children, we can infer that they are worried about the dangers associated with a fisherman's life. She is telling them not to be afraid and to come home safely. These brave words may not reflect her true feelings.

● Ask the children to identify any words or phrases with which they are unfamiliar. List these under two headings: *New vocabulary* and *Accent and dialect words and phrases*. Explain *accent* (distinctive pronunciation) and *dialect* (grammar and vocabulary).

● Tell the children that the poem is a ballad. Ask them who wrote the poem. Explain that many ballads were anonymous and were passed down from singer to singer without being written down. Ballads were easy to memorise; they had a regular rhythm and rhyme scheme that increased their memorability. Clap the iambic rhythm together. Guide the children to identify the rhyme scheme in the poem and explain that this is typical of many traditional ballads.

Activities

● How does the fisherman's wife feel about her family going to sea? Discuss whether her words show her real feelings. A possible interpretation is that she too is worried about their safety but seeks to reassure them with her comforting words. Ask one of the children to take on the role of the fisherman's wife and be hot-seated to find out more about her thoughts and feelings. Then ask another child to take on the role, encouraging them to think about different ways the character might be feeling. Encourage the children to evaluate the authenticity of the responses to the questions.

● Look through local newspapers to find some stories that capture the imagination. Choose one story and help the children to turn it into a ballad, incorporating the features that have been identified (rhythm, rhyme, layout, incremental repetition and so on). Alternatively, the children could write a ballad about a historical local incident.

● Organise the children into small groups to prepare a dramatic reading and performance of the poem.

Extension/further reading

Further reading includes *Scottish Poems* chosen by John Rice (Macmillan Children's Books) and *The Oxford Book of Story Poems* edited by Michael Harrison and Christopher Stuart-Clark.

6: 1: T3: to articulate personal responses to literature, identifying why and how a text affects the reader

6: 1: T4: to be familiar with the work of some established authors, to know what is special about their work, and to explain their preferences in terms of authors, styles and themes

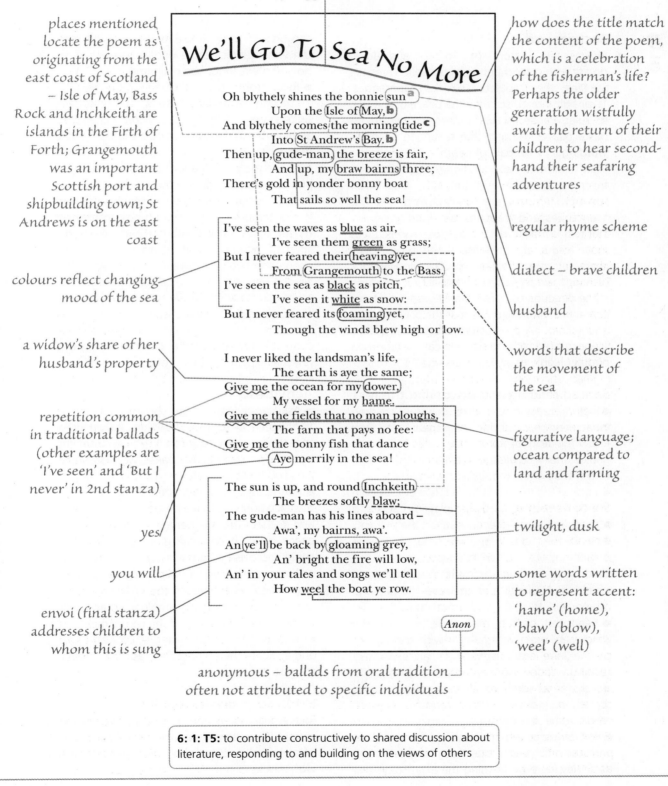

this is a ballad – a simple song from the oral tradition; who speaks the words of the poem? (vocabulary suggests fisherman's wife)

places mentioned locate the poem as originating from the east coast of Scotland – Isle of May, Bass Rock and Inchkeith are islands in the Firth of Forth; Grangemouth was an important Scottish port and shipbuilding town; St Andrews is on the east coast

colours reflect changing mood of the sea

a widow's share of her husband's property

repetition common in traditional ballads (other examples are 'I've seen' and 'But I never' in 2nd stanza)

yes

you will

envoi (final stanza) addresses children to whom this is sung

how does the title match the content of the poem, which is a celebration of the fisherman's life? Perhaps the older generation wistfully await the return of their children to hear second-hand their seafaring adventures

regular rhyme scheme

dialect – brave children

husband

words that describe the movement of the sea

figurative language; ocean compared to land and farming

twilight, dusk

some words written to represent accent: 'hame' (home), 'blaw' (blow), 'weel' (well)

We'll Go To Sea No More

Oh blythely shines the bonnie sun [a]
Upon the Isle of May, [b]
And blythely comes the morning tide [c]
Into St Andrew's Bay. [b]
Then up, gude-man, the breeze is fair,
And up, my braw bairns three;
There's gold in yonder bonny boat
That sails so well the sea!

I've seen the waves as blue as air,
I've seen them green as grass;
But I never feared their heaving yet,
From Grangemouth to the Bass.
I've seen the sea as black as pitch,
I've seen it white as snow:
But I never feared its foaming yet,
Though the winds blew high or low.

I never liked the landsman's life,
The earth is aye the same;
Give me the ocean for my dower,
My vessel for my hame.
Give me the fields that no man ploughs,
The farm that pays no fee:
Give me the bonny fish that dance
Aye merrily in the sea!

The sun is up, and round Inchkeith
The breezes softly blaw;
The gude-man has his lines aboard –
Awa', my bairns, awa'.
An' ye'll be back by gloaming grey,
An' bright the fire will low,
An' in your tales and songs we'll tell
How weel the boat ye row.

Anon

anonymous – ballads from oral tradition often not attributed to specific individuals

6: 1: T5: to contribute constructively to shared discussion about literature, responding to and building on the views of others

Romeo and Juliet

by William Shakespeare

Extract 1

Background

Shakespeare's story of Romeo and Juliet opens with a feud between two old Veronese families, the Capulets and the Montagues. Their fighting is disturbing the peace of the city. Its ruler, Prince Escalus, orders the families to make peace, warning that failure to heed his words will be on pain of death.

This extract, an action scene, is taken from the beginning of the play. It is a hot summer, tempers are running high and the Montagues and Capulets are fighting again. The text is mainly written in prose – which was most frequently the case when more lowly characters were speaking. The conventions of script writing used in this extract include stage directions, allocation of lines to different characters, and the division of the play into acts and scenes. (A prose story adaptation of this scene written by Leon Garfield can be found on photocopiable page 112, see page 14.)

Shared reading and discussing the text

● Before reading the text, ask the children what they know about Shakespeare. Do they know the story of Romeo and Juliet? Fill in the gaps in their knowledge or tell them the outline of the story if it is unfamiliar.

● Look at the text and how it is laid out. Explain the convention of dividing a play into acts and scenes, and stage directions. Read the extract.

● Read the text a second time, from the beginning to *Enter Benvolio*. Ask the children if there are any bits that they don't understand. Clarify and annotate the passage as appropriate.

● Read this part a third time, so that the children become very familiar with the rhythm of the language. Listening to an expressive reading will develop their understanding.

● Ask the children to allocate parts for this scene, in groups of four, and to practise reading the lines from the beginning up to *Enter Benvolio*. When the children are familiar with the lines, encourage them to speak them as if they were performing the play. Stage this section with some simple movements and mark the text to indicate the decisions made about how the text should be performed.

● Read from *Enter Benvolio* to the end for a second time and check the children's understanding, clarifying as appropriate. Look at how the older characters are used to add humour to the scene.

● Divide the class into two groups (Montagues and Capulets). Organise the children into two facing lines at about eight to ten paces apart. Use a tambour or other untuned instrument to set up a slow beat. On each beat, the lines of actors should alternately take one choreographed step towards each other as they say the phrases 1. *Clubs, bills and partisans!* 2. *Strike!* 3. *Beat them down!* 4. *Down with the Capulets!* 5. *Down with the Montagues!* The opposing sides should not make physical contact. This allows the children to gain a physical experience of the play.

Activities

● Ask the children to storyboard the opening fight scene in six pictures. They should draw speech bubbles and insert key lines from the extract (for example, *My naked weapon is out. Quarrel I will back thee*).

● Prince Escalus orders the families to cease their feuding and make peace with each other and declares that the penalty for breach of the peace is death. In small groups, the children could improvise a short scene in the Montague or Capulet household following the prince's declaration. How would the older members of the family react (for example, Lord and Lady Capulet)? And how would the young members of the family react (for example, Tybalt)? Share and evaluate the scenes. Then ask the children to write the scene, using the extract as a model for the conventions of scriptwriting.

● Ask the children to write a glossary of the Shakespearean vocabulary and phrases in this extract (for example, *No, marry* and *Is the law of our side?*) and add the list to their personal word books.

6: 1: T1: to compare and evaluate a novel or play in print and the film/TV version, e.g. treatment of the plot and characters, the differences in the two forms, e.g. in seeing the setting, in losing the narrator

6: 1: T6: to manipulate narrative perspective by producing a modern retelling

conventional way of writing act and scene – 5 acts in a Shakespearean play

common expression meaning 'no indeed!'

'as they wish' trying to instigate fight without taking responsibility

put your weapons away

biblical allusion ('Father forgive them for they know not what they do')

Sampson

conventions of writing scripted dialogue

pun: taken to mean 'turn my back' rather than 'support'

Gregory

in Elizabethan times this was an insulting gesture

wants to know if it is safe to say yes

playing a semantic game

I am ready to fight you

in Italian 'bene' means good – name literally means 'of good will', which describes his function in the play

stage directions in italic

reminds her husband of his age and folly

takes on peace-keeping role

the authority in Verona

pun: female deer (hinds) without male hart to protect them

broad-headed spears

axes with spikes at the back (long-handled)

crowd chant

hastily attired in dressing gown

domestic peace disrupted

keen to be involved in the fight

bold, sweeping gesture

attendants

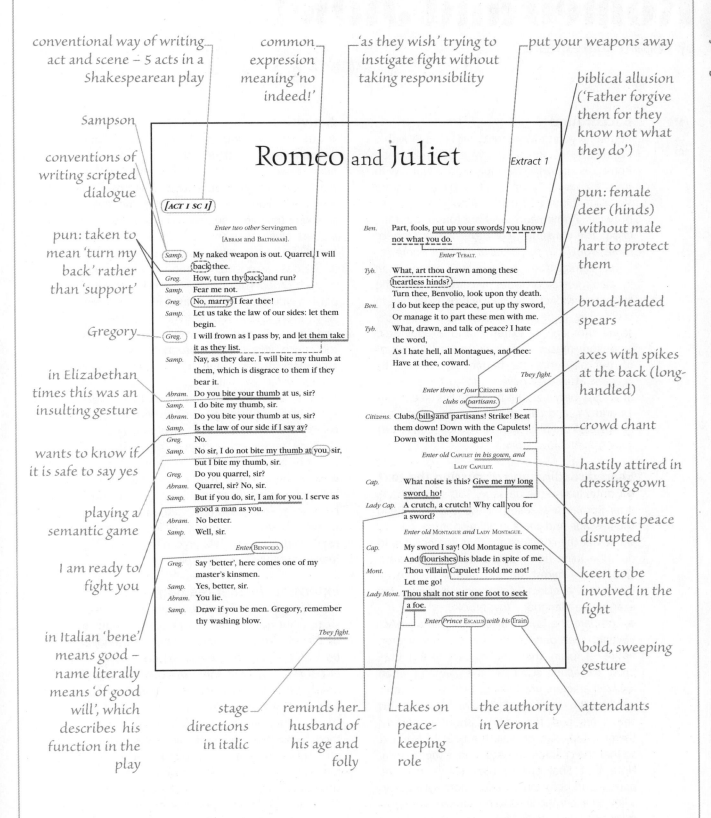

Romeo and Juliet

Extract 1

[ACT I SC I]

Enter two other Servingmen
[ABRAM *and* BALTHASAR].

Samp. My naked weapon is out. Quarrel, I will back thee.
Greg. How, turn thy back and run?
Samp. Fear me not.
Greg. No, marry! I fear thee!
Samp. Let us take the law of our sides: let them begin.
Greg. I will frown as I pass by, and let them take it as they list.
Samp. Nay, as they dare. I will bite my thumb at them, which is disgrace to them if they bear it.
Abram. Do you bite your thumb at us, sir?
Samp. I do bite my thumb, sir.
Abram. Do you bite your thumb at us, sir?
Samp. Is the law of our side if I say ay?
Greg. No.
Samp. No sir, I do not bite my thumb at you, sir, but I bite my thumb, sir.
Greg. Do you quarrel, sir?
Abram. Quarrel, sir? No, sir.
Samp. But if you do, sir, I am for you. I serve as good a man as you.
Abram. No better.
Samp. Well, sir.

Enter BENVOLIO.

Greg. Say 'better', here comes one of my master's kinsmen.
Samp. Yes, better, sir.
Abram. You lie.
Samp. Draw if you be men. Gregory, remember thy washing blow.

They fight.

Ben. Part, fools, put up your swords, you know not what you do.

Enter TYBALT.

Tyb. What, art thou drawn among these heartless hinds?
Turn thee, Benvolio, look upon thy death.
Ben. I do but keep the peace, put up thy sword,
Or manage it to part these men with me.
Tyb. What, drawn, and talk of peace? I hate the word,
As I hate hell, all Montagues, and thee:
Have at thee, coward.

They fight.

Enter three or four Citizens *with clubs or partisans.*

Citizens. Clubs, bills and partisans! Strike! Beat them down! Down with the Capulets! Down with the Montagues!

Enter old CAPULET *in his gown, and* LADY CAPULET.

Cap. What noise is this? Give me my long sword, ho!
Lady Cap. A crutch, a crutch! Why call you for a sword?

Enter old MONTAGUE *and* LADY MONTAGUE.

Cap. My sword I say! Old Montague is come,
And flourishes his blade in spite of me.
Mont. Thou villain Capulet! Hold me not! Let me go!
Lady Mont. Thou shalt not stir one foot to seek a foe.

Enter Prince ESCALUS *with his* Train.

Romeo and Juliet

by William Shakespeare

Extract 2

Background

Romeo, a young Montague, falls in love with a Capulet, Juliet. But their love is doomed when Romeo is drawn unwillingly into a fight with Juliet's cousin, Tybalt, and is banished from Verona. At the end of the play, after a series of twists, Romeo and Juliet are found together, dead. The play ends, *For never was a story of more woe/Than this of Juliet and her Romeo.*

This extract from Shakespeare's play, written in blank verse, provides a contrast with the extract from Act I Scene I which is largely in prose (see page 24). In the famous balcony scene, Romeo, in extreme and exaggerated language, muses on Juliet's beauty. This part of the play may be better experienced by children after they have explored the strength of enmity between the two families (see pages 14 and 24) and carried out some work on the synopsis of the play, so that it is not seen as just a sentimental love story.

Shared reading and discussing the text

● Contextualise the passage. This scene occurs after Romeo sees Juliet for the first time. Read the passage and share initial responses.

● Look at the comparisons that Romeo uses to describe Juliet (for example, *Juliet is the sun!; Two of the fairest stars in all the heaven...*). Evaluate the effect of Romeo's extreme and exaggerated language (hyperbole).

● Compare the layout of this extract with Act I Scene I (see page 24). What do the children notice? Explain that Shakespeare often uses prose for action scenes in the play and when lowly characters are talking, but verse (iambic pentameter – see page 22) for higher status characters and for writing about important themes. Tap, clap or walk the beat of the text so that the children can experience the rhythm. Note that Shakespeare uses subtle mid-line pauses and occasionally adds more syllables to a line to allow the lines to be spoken naturally.

● Discuss the oft-quoted lines: *What's in a name? That which we call a rose/By any other word would smell as sweet.*

Activities

● Cut the text into small meaningful units and give each child one section to read and learn. Check that each child understands their piece, and provide clarification where needed. Ask the children to walk around the room, speaking their lines quietly to themselves. After a short while, they should stop and introduce themselves to as many of the other children in the class as possible by repeating their lines to each other. They can then develop this into playing with the lines by saying them in different ways (in anger, sadness, impatience, excitement and so on). Enjoy this activity and don't worry too much about the appropriateness of the emotions at this stage. When the children are really familiar with their lines, come back together and read through the passage, with each child contributing their personal lines.

● Let the children pick their favourite lines, and illustrate and caption them. The illustrations might be abstract or literal.

● Help the children to identify examples of exaggerated language in this passage. Using a range of media resources (magazines, comics, television advertisements), collect examples used in advertising. Children can have great fun making up their own examples.

Extension/further reading

From an edition of the complete play, select six to eight quotes that will provide an outline of the story (for example, 1. *Two households both alike in dignity... break to new mutiny*; 2. *But soft, what light through yonder window breaks? It is the east and Juliet is the sun!* 3. *I am hurt. A plague o' both your houses. I am sped...*). Allocate lines to small groups and ask them to practise reading the lines, constructing a freeze-frame image to depict the action. Tell the story, pausing for each group to read their lines and present their freeze-frame images. This will provide an experience of most of the story and develop familiarity with some of the most powerful lines from the play as well as crystallising moments of dramatic tension.

6: 1: T1: to compare and evaluate a novel or play in print and the film/TV version, e.g. treatment of the plot and characters, the differences in the two forms, e.g. in seeing the setting, in losing the narrator

6: 1: W7: to understand how words and expressions have changed over time, e.g. old verb endings -st and -th and how some words have fallen out of use, e.g. yonder, thither

Romeo and Juliet

Extract 2

[ACT II SC II]

[Enter JULIET above.]

Romeo. But soft, what light through yonder window breaks?
It is the east and Juliet is the sun!
Arise fair sun and kill the envious moon
Who is already sick and pale with grief
That thou her maid art far more fair than she.
Be not her maid since she is envious,
Her vestal livery is but sick and green
And none but fools do wear it. Cast it off.
It is my lady, O it is my love!
O that she knew she were!
She speaks, yet she says nothing. What of that?
Her eye discourses, I will answer it.
I am too bold. 'Tis not to me she speaks.
Two of the fairest stars in all the heaven,
Having some business, do entreat her eyes
To twinkle in their spheres till they return.
What if her eyes were there, they in her head?
The brightness of her cheek would shame those stars
As daylight doth a lamp. Her eyes in heaven
Would through the airy region stream so bright
That birds would sing and think it were not night.
See how she leans her cheek upon her hand.
O that I were a glove upon that hand,
That I might touch that cheek.

Juliet. Ay me.
Romeo. She speaks.
Oh speak again bright angel, for thou art
As glorious to this night, being o'er my head,
As is a winged messenger of heaven
Unto the white-upturned wondering eyes
Of mortals that fall back to gaze on him
When he bestrides the lazy-puffing clouds
And sails upon the bosom of the air.

Juliet. O Romeo, Romeo, wherefore art thou Romeo?
Deny thy father and refuse thy name.
Or if thou wilt not, be but sworn my love
And I'll no longer be a Capulet.
Romeo. Shall I hear more, or shall I speak at this?
Juliet. 'Tis but thy name that is my enemy:
Thou art thyself, though not a Montague.
What's Montague? It is nor hand nor foot
Not arm nor face nor any other part
Belonging to a man. O be some other name.
What's in a name? That which we call a rose
By any other word would smell as sweet;
So Romeo would, were he not Romeo call'd
Retain that dear perfection which he owes
Without that title. Romeo, doff thy name,
And for thy name, which is no part of thee,
Take all myself.

Juliet comes to the window

Romeo is besotted – he compares her to the sun and accuses the moon of jealousy

melodrama

image of Juliet's eyes replacing the stars in the night sky

orbits

archaic form of 'does'

Romeo's excessive speech is indicative of teenage infatuation – he is passionate and idealistic

why

individuals are more than representatives of groups

extract contrasts with Act I Sc I; here the text is in blank verse rather than prose – it suits the elevated position of the characters and the content of the scene

allusion to Vestal Virgins – handmaids that attended Roman goddess Vesta

abbreviation for 'it is'

plead with

Juliet is more radiant than the stars

iambic pentameters split across three lines – the rhythm is maintained

Juliet is physically above Romeo on the balcony; he thinks she is like an angel in the heavens

Juliet does not know that Romeo is watching her; reveals that she loves him too

lines often quoted

owns

throw away

Charles Darwin: The Early Years
by Steve Parker

Background

Charles Darwin made a significant and lasting contribution to evolutionary science, although his theories were highly contentious in his day. In 1831, Darwin joined HMS *Beagle* on its scientific survey of South American waters as the expedition naturalist. The project lasted for five years, during which time Darwin acquired considerable knowledge about the flora, fauna and geology of the lands visited.

A biography is a form of recount, a written examination of the lives of others. Most frequently, biographies deal with lives of eminent people. They are often organised to cover the entire life of a subject from birth to death, as in the book from which this extract has been taken, but alternatively they can be structured thematically (relationships, career, travel, and so on). A biographer, like the writer of fiction, has to characterise the subject to develop empathy. The best biographies paint lively portraits and present a rounded subject, recognising personal strengths and weaknesses. A biographer must have a commitment to research – the reader expects factual accuracy; sources might include letters, journals, diaries, eyewitness accounts, news reports and interviews.

Shared reading and discussing the text

● Before reading the extract, explain that it is taken from the biography of Charles Darwin. Write the word *biography* on the board. Can anyone work out what it means? Demonstrate the morphology of the word: *bio* (life) *graph* (write) *y* (suffix).
● Ask the children what they would expect to find in a recount of someone's life, and make a list (for example, personal details, why the person is remembered, information about the person's thoughts, ideas, beliefs, the views of others who knew the person, and so on).
● Ask the children to read the passage independently. Ask them what they have learned about Darwin from reading this passage. Clarify any unfamiliar vocabulary.

● Discuss the difference between fact and opinion. Explain that a biography is dependent on factual information and that it is possible to distinguish between factual evidence and the opinion of the writer. Find examples of both in the text. (Facts: born in Shrewsbury, England, 12 February 1809; the quotation '*I believe that I was considered…*' and so on. Opinions: keener on shooting partridges than attending lectures, and so on.) Point out that expression of an opinion does not make it untrue. Explain that a quotation is the actual words spoken – often the source of a quotation will be cited to prove its authenticity.
● Look at how the text is structured, drawing out the features of biographical writing. For example, as biography reconstructs past experience it is characteristically written in the past tense, making use of temporal connectives (*then; later*) and adverbial clauses of time (*in 1825; at first*).

Activities

● Provide the children with a sheet of paper divided into two columns headed *Fact* and *Opinion*. Ask them to find and list examples in the passage, working individually or in pairs.
● In small groups, the children could use a range of resources, including the Internet, to further research the life and achievements of Charles Darwin. They could do this using a KWL grid (*What do we already <u>know</u>? What do we <u>want</u> to know? What have we <u>learned</u>?*). Use this information to write a class biography of Darwin, each group taking responsibility for a different aspect of his life.
● Ask the children to use the extract as a model to write biographies of other children in the school. They should first construct a list of questions that will help them to find out about their subject in an interview. Provide a writing frame, if needed, comprising introduction (name, date of birth, early life and the reasons for writing about the person), middle (significant experiences) and conclusion (What lasting contribution has the person made?).

6: 1: T11: to distinguish between biography and autobiography:
● recognising the effect on the reader of the choice between first and third person
● distinguishing between fact, opinion and fiction

6: 1: T14: to develop the skills of biographical writing: composing a biographical account based on research

possessive apostrophe subject to different conventions – some publishers prefer 'Charles's'

temporal connective

subordinate clause (demarcated by comma) within complex sentence

details of birth given in 1st paragraph

bracketing commas

terminology

connective

direct quotation introduced by colon and presented in double quotation marks

causal connective

outlines process of change and development

'-ist' suffix changes word to a noun, denoting an occupation; one who studies composition of the earth

one who studies plants

title in italic

means 'under the command of'

one who studies natural history in the environment

abbreviation for 'Her Majesty's Ship'

opinion – view held at the time

parenthesis used for enclosing additional contextual information

Charles Darwin:
The Early Years

Charles Robert Darwin was born in Shrewsbury, England, on 12 February 1809. His father Robert was a doctor, and his mother Susannah was daughter of the famous potteries owner, Josiah Wedgwood. Charles' grandfather was Erasmus Darwin, well known in his time as a scientist with unusual ideas. He wrote on a range of subjects such as travel by air, exploring by submarine, and evolution.

Despite his learned father and eminent grandfather, Charles' early years were not outstanding. He attended Shrewsbury School, where the main lessons were in the classics, such as Latin. Many years later, he wrote: "I believe that I was considered by all my masters and by my father as a very ordinary boy, rather below the common intelligence."

In 1825 Charles went to Edinburgh Medical School. He soon realized that medicine was not for him. He found the lectures dull, and he had to leave the operating theatre because he could not stand the horrors of surgery. (This was a few years before the first pain killer, chloroform, came into use.) So he gave up medicine, to the great disappointment of his father, who arranged the next best career. In 1828 Darwin went to Cambridge University, to study the

Bible and become a priest. Later, he wrote: "I did not then in the least doubt the strict and literal truth of every word in the Bible."

Despite being keener on shooting partridges than attending lectures, Darwin gained a Bachelor of Arts degree at Cambridge in 1831. He became friendly with two of the professors, geologist Adam Sedgewick and botanist John Henslow, and he continued to develop his interest in rocks, fossils, animals and plants.

Darwin then read *Personal Narrative* by the explorer Alexander von Humboldt. Rather than become a priest straight away, he decided to organize a natural history expedition to the Canary Islands. By chance at the same time the Royal Navy was arranging a round-the-world survey expedition under Captain Robert Fitzroy. Fitzroy asked Professor Henslow to recommend a naturalist for the expedition.

Henslow, knowing of Darwin's interest, recommended him for the job. At first Darwin's father refused to provide the money needed, but was eventually persuaded that this was an excellent opportunity for his son. On 27 December 1831, Charles Darwin set sail on the 235-ton sloop-brig HMS *Beagle*.

A letter from Charles Darwin by Charles Darwin

Background

On 27 December 1831, the *Beagle* set sail. The object of the expedition was to survey the territory of Patagonia and Tierra del Fuego; the naturalist on board was Charles Darwin. The *Beagle* visited the Cape Verde Islands, Rio de Janeiro, Buenos Aires, Patagonia, the Falkland Islands, Chile, Peru, the Galapagos archipelago, Tahiti, New Zealand, Australia and Mauritius, before returning to England in 1836. A full account is recorded in Darwin's journal *Voyage of the Beagle*.

This is an extract from a letter to his father – one of the many letters Darwin wrote. The tone is quite formal, but the letter does not have many of the features that are often included in formal letter writing – there is, for example, no sender's address and the layout does not conform to conventional guidance, although paragraphs are used.

Shared reading and discussing the text

● Supply the context of the letter, then read it. Check any unfamiliar vocabulary and supply definitions or conduct a dictionary search.
● Discuss what it must have been like to have been on board a ship when suffering from extreme sea-sickness. Consider what the sleeping quarters and living conditions would have been like. (A picture of the *Beagle* would be useful.) Pick out any words or phrases that convey Darwin's misery, and annotate the text. (Comparisons can be made with the extract from *Kensuke's Kingdom*, see page 34.) Trace Darwin's journey on a globe, and explain that the area around the Cape is notorious for extremely bad weather conditions.
● Ask the children how Darwin's letter compares to one they would send to parents, a close relative or friend. Look specifically at the tone signalled by the salutation (*My dear Father*) and the signing off (*Your most affectionate son Charles Darwin*).
● Consider why Darwin might have written this letter. Possibilities include: to share his experiences; because he might have felt homesick; out of duty; to let his family know that he was safe and well. Explain that there would have been no other form of communication.
● Identify older words and phrases that indicate that this letter was written over 150 years ago. (for example, *my dear-bought experience*). What alternative words and phrases might we use today? (For example, *I'll tell you what it was like for me.*)
● Look at the structure of the letter. There are three paragraphs – devise three headings that summarise what these paragraphs are about.

Activities

● Ask the children to imagine that they are Darwin's father and have just received this letter. They should write a reply, using the extract as a model for the formal language used. Information about Darwin's relationship with his father gathered when researching his biography (see previous extract) could be integrated into the letter they write.
● Comparing this letter with an example of a conventionally laid out letter, the children could annotate a copy of the text, highlighting the similarities and differences. They should then rewrite the letter as it would be written today.
● Ask the children to make a list of words from the text that describe the stormy and unsettled weather (for example *heavy gale*). They can then extend the list, using a dictionary and thesaurus, and write down definitions. They should add the list to their personal dictionaries.
● Suggest that the children use the words and phrases collected to write a poem about stormy weather at sea.

Extension/further reading

Use extracts from *Voyage of the Beagle* as a stimulus for drama work. Emphasise the themes of voyage and discovery. Use drama strategies such as forum theatre and freeze-frame to build tension and identify key moments and conflicts. Ask the children to record their drama experiences through letter writing.

6: 1: T11: to distinguish between biography and autobiography:
- recognising the effect on the reader of the choice between first and third person
- distinguishing between fact, opinion and fiction
- distinguishing between implicit and explicit points of view and how these can differ

ampersand not usually used in letter writing today

formal address to parent indicative of period

Cape Verde islands: off Senegal, west Africa

starts by explaining reasons for writing

shipping terms used for classifying weather

island in the Atlantic, south-west of Portugal, west of Morocco

north of Spain, west of France

large waves

A letter from Charles Darwin

The Voyage: South America

My dear Father

I am writing this on the 8th of February one day's sail past St. Jago, (Cape de Verd), & intend taking the chance of meeting with a homeward bound vessel somewhere about the Equator.— The date however will tell whether this opportunity occurs.— I will now begin from the day of leaving England & give a short account of our progress.—

We sailed as you know on the 27th of December & have been fortunate enough to have had from that time to the present a fair & moderate breeze: It afterward proved that we escaped a heavy gale in the Channel, another at Madeira & another on coast of Africa.— But in escaping the gale, we felt its consequence—a heavy sea: In the Bay of Biscay there was a long & continued swell & the misery I endured from sea-sickness is far far beyond what I ever guessed at.— I believe you are curious about it. I will give all my dear-bought experience.— Nobody who has only been to sea for 24 hours has a right to say that sea-sickness is even uncomfortable.— The real misery only begins when you are so exhausted—that a little exertion makes a feeling of faintness come on.— I found nothing but lying in my hammock did me any good.— I must especially except your receipt of raisins, which is the only food that the stomach will bear:— On the 4th of January we were not many miles from Madeira: but as there was a heavy sea running, & the Island lay to Wind ward it was not thought worth while to beat up to it.— It afterwards has turned out it was lucky we saved ourselves the trouble: I was much too sick even to get up to see the distant outline.— On the 6th in the evening we sailed into the harbour of Santa Cruz.— I now first felt even moderately well, & I was picturing to myself all the delights of fresh fruit growing in beautiful valleys, & reading Humboldt's descriptions of the Island's glorious views.— When perhaps you may nearly guess at our disappointment, when a small pale man informed us we must perform a strict quarantine of 12 days…

…The conviction that I am walking in the new world, is even yet marvellous in my own eyes, & I daresay it is little less so to you, the receiving a letter from a son of yours in such a quarter: Believe me, my dear Father Your most affectionate son

Charles Darwin

hanging bed made of net used on ships (minimises sway)

includes dates; records actual events

place in Canary Islands

ship kept in isolation from shore

concluding thoughts

description of sea-sickness

formality

Livingstone Discovers Victoria Falls, 1855

by David Livingstone

Background

In 1840, when he was just 27 years old, Scottish doctor and missionary, David Livingstone (1813–73) arrived in Africa. He spent most of his life there exploring the continent. Between 1852 and 1856 Livingstone conducted an expedition to explore the area around the Zambesi (also spelled *Zambezi*) river where he became the first European to witness the magnificent Victoria Falls. This account, taken from Livingstone's journal, is a record of that event. It is a descriptive scene-setting piece in which Livingstone tries to convey what he witnessed.

This example of journal writing is a form of recount, narrating personal experience and providing an eyewitness account. It is written in the first-person past tense and includes characteristic features such as adverbial clauses of time and place.

Shared reading and discussing the text

● Discuss the idea of writing a journal and the different types of journal that can be written (for example, those that articulate personal thoughts and feelings; record a voyage or travels; are intellectual or artistic). A journal can be personal – not intended to be read by anyone other than the writer – or an informative record. Consider who might write a journal and why. Ask whether any of the children keep a journal.

● Explain the context to this passage; provide some background information about Livingstone.

● Read the passage and clarify any unknown words. Make sure the children are familiar with geographical features mentioned (*ridge, lip*).

● Ask why Livingstone writes that the sight had never before been seen by European eyes.

● Explain that Livingstone did not have a camera so he had to make his reader see the scene by building a word picture. Ask the children to close their eyes and imagine the scene as you read the passage a second time. What sounds would there have been?

● Display some pictures of the Victoria Falls from travel brochures. (Or you can view pictures taken in 1891 on the website www.hoole.easynet.co.uk/views.html.) Compare the description in the text with the photographic images of the falls. Today we often record our visits to places with photographs. Consider whether writing about places can provide a different sort of information to the photographic image.

● Examine features of journal writing – a recount about past experiences written in first-person past tense (for example, *I left the canoe by which we had come down thus far...*).

Activities

● After re-reading the passage, the children could draw the scene that they imagine, paying close attention to Livingstone's description. In a plenary session, share the drawings and ask the children to explain which words and images helped them to visualise the scene (for example, the image of the vapour columns described as smoke).

● Ask the children to imagine that they are the first person to witness one of the wonders of the world (for example, the North Pole, the peak of Mount Everest). They should think about what it would look and feel like as well as the sounds that they might hear, and try to convey this in an eyewitness account.

● Using the passage and a range of narrative resources, pairs of children could find and list different clauses of time (for example, *After twenty minutes'...*). They should keep the list in their personal word books, to be used as a reference for their own writing.

● In pairs or small groups, the children could use holiday photographs as a stimulus for talking about places visited on holiday. The experiences can be written as recounts or recorded onto cassette as a class resource.

● Using a thesaurus and a good dictionary, develop a class vocabulary chart showing other words that could be used in place of *sylvan, adorned, eddies* and so on.

6: 1: T11: to distinguish between biography and autobiography:
- recognising the effect on the reader of the choice between first and third person
- distinguishing between fact, opinion and fiction
- distinguishing between implicit and explicit points of view and how these can differ

LIVINGSTONE
DISCOVERS VICTORIA FALLS, 1855

❖

place —

temporal connective in recount

positive language

powerful image

temporal connective

went on board

in 2nd paragraph Livingstone tries to give objective description of features

personal participant

give the appearance of smoke

comparison

take on the quality of smoke

woods

personal participant

small whirlpools

geographical feature – protruding overhang

After twenty minutes' sail from Kalai we came in sight, for the first time, of the columns of vapour appropriately called 'smoke' rising at a distance of five or six miles, exactly as when large tracts of grass are burned in Africa. Five columns now arose, and, bending in the direction of the wind, they seemed placed against a low ridge covered with trees; the tops of the columns at this distance appeared to mingle with the clouds. They were white below, and higher up became dark, so as to simulate smoke very closely. The whole scene was extremely beautiful; the banks and islands dotted over the river are adorned with sylvan vegetation of great variety of colour and form… no one can imagine the beauty of the view from any thing witnessed in England. It had never been seen before by European eyes; but scenes so lovely must have been gazed upon by angels in their flight. The only want felt is that of mountains in the background. The falls are bounded on three sides by ridges 300 or 400 feet in height, which are covered with forest, with the red soil appearing among the trees.

When about half a mile from the falls, I left the canoe by which we had come down thus far, and embarked in a lighter one, with men well acquainted with the rapids, who, by passing down the centre of the stream in the eddies and still places caused by many jutting rocks, brought me to an island situated in the middle of the river, and on the edge of the lip over which the water rolls. In coming hither there was danger of being swept down by the streams which rushed along on each side of the island; but the river was now low, and we sailed where it is totally impossible to do when the water is high. But, though we had reached the island, and were within a few yards of the spot, a view from which would solve the problem, I believe that no one could perceive where the vast body of water went; it seemed to lose itself in the earth, the opposite lip of the fissure into which it disappeared being only 80 feet distant. At least I did not comprehend it until, creeping with awe to the verge, I peered down into a large rent which had been made from bank to bank of the broad Zambesi, and saw that a stream of a thousand yards broad leaped down a hundred feet, and then became suddenly compressed into a space of fifteen or twenty yards.

river name (proper noun – capitalised)

Kensuke's Kingdom
by Michael Morpurgo

Background

Kensuke's Kingdom is a contemporary Robinson Crusoe story. When Michael's parents are made redundant, they buy a yacht and sail round the world. Later, during a violent storm, Michael is thrown overboard and washed up on a remote tropical island.

Kensuke's Kingdom is mainly a first-person narrative but Michael Morpurgo also uses the device of journal writing in the form of a ship's log, which Michael (in the story) completes. This entry for Christmas Day starts with an orientation (*Christmas Day at sea*). It is written largely in the first-person past tense (*Dad found…*) but shifts into the present when Michael moves from recounting the days' events to reflection (for example, *Mum says we're doing fine, just so long as we stay…*) or in bringing events up to date (*She's ahead now…*).

Shared reading and discussing the text

● Put this extract into context. Explain that it is a fictional journal entry and that Michael Morpurgo often uses similar devices to move the story on and to give an authenticity to the narration.

● Read the extract. Ask the children what they can learn about life at sea from the text. What would they like or not like about Michael's experience? (Comparisons can be made with Charles Darwin's letter, see page 30.)

● What impression do they have of Michael, the author of the ship's log? The children should support their views with evidence from the text. They may suggest that he has a sense of humour, he's lonely, anxious about his parents, and so on. His language is informal (he uses vocabulary such as *soggy* and *manky*, and contractions – *she's* and so on).

● Look at the way the paragraphs are structured (paragraph 1 – present exchange; paragraph 2 – reloading the *Peggy Sue*; paragraph 3 – passing St Helena; paragraph 4 – Stella and the Christmas pudding; paragraph 5 – sighting of the yacht; paragraph 6 – Mum and Dad's

chess rivalry). Each paragraph deals with a new subject.

● Re-read paragraph 4. When are these events happening? Demonstrate rewriting the whole paragraph in the past tense (*Stella was sulking…*). Ask the children how this rewriting affects the storytelling. Show how Michael Morpurgo moves from present (the time of writing the journal) to past and back to present again (see above).

Activities

● In small groups, the children could hot-seat the characters to explore their thoughts and feelings. This will allow the children to develop the context of the story. For example, how does Michael feel about the journey and spending Christmas aboard the *Peggy Sue*?

● It wouldn't be possible to take many personal possessions on the yacht. Ask the children what personal item they would choose to take with them if they could only take one thing. Ask them to draw the item and write their reasons for choosing it.

● Ask the children to write a diary entry for December 26th, using the extract as a model. They should make a paragraph plan before writing. Alternatively, they could plan and make a video diary.

Extension/further reading

Use an atlas to locate St Helena. Can the children find out why Napoleon was exiled there?

Have available a copy of *Kensuke's Kingdom* and other books by Michael Morpurgo, for example *The Wreck of the Zanzibar* (Heinemann) and *War Horse* (Egmont). When the children are familiar with the books, ask them to compare the similarities and differences between them, considering the settings, characters, plot and themes. They could also investigate narrative devices that Michael Morpurgo uses in his stories (for example, diaries and letters in *Wreck of the Zanzibar*).

6: 1: T11: to distinguish between biography and autobiography:
- recognising the effect on the reader of the choice between first and third person
- distinguishing between fact, opinion and fiction
- distinguishing between implicit and explicit points of view and how these can differ

vocabulary that would be used by narrator in his everyday speech

dated

dramatic effect of introductory sentence

variation in sentence length

apostrophes of contraction – they'd (they had), you're (you are), it's (it is), we're (we are), she's (she is), Stella's (Stella is), can't (cannot)

shift to present tense for reflective comment

interesting spelling – etymology of word shows it is derived from Norwegian

Kensuke's Kingdom

Ship's log

December 25

Christmas Day at sea. Dad found some carols on the radio. We had crackers, all of them a bit soggy so none of them cracked, and we had the Christmas pudding Gran made for us. I gave them a drawing each – my flying fish for Dad and one of the skipper, in her hat, at the wheel for Mum. They gave me a really neat knife they'd bought in Rio. So I gave a coin back. You're supposed to do that. It's for luck.

When we were in Rio we gave the *Peggy Sue* a good scrub down. She was looking a bit manky inside and outside, but she's not anymore. We took on a lot of stores and water for the long haul to South Africa. Mum says we're doing fine, just so long as we keep south, so long as we stay in the west-to-east South Atlantic current.

We passed south of an island called St Helena a few days ago. No need to stop. Nothing much there, except it's the place where Napoleon was exiled. He died there. Lonely place to die. So, of course, I had to do a history project on Napoleon. I had to look him up in the encyclopaedia and write about him. It was quite interesting, really, but I didn't tell them that.

Stella's sulking on my bunk. Maybe it's because no one gave her a Christmas present. I offered her a taste of Gran's Christmas pudding, but she hardly gave it a sniff. Can't say I blame her.

I saw a sail today, another yacht. We shouted Happy Christmas and waved, and Stella barked her head off, but they were too far away. When the sail disappeared, the sea felt suddenly very empty.

Mum won the chess this evening. She's ahead now, twenty-one games to twenty. Dad said he let her win because it was Christmas. They joke about it, but they both want to win.

contractions used for informal style

italic for boat name

moves from past into present tense here

abbreviation for 'Saint'

barred from his native country

pronoun used to refer to Mum and Dad

seafaring terminology

temporal connective

back to present tense – importance of final sentence (the end of the sentence carries the most weight)

A Tiptoe Down Memory Lane
by Luke Jackson

Extracts 1 and 2

Background

Autobiographical writing is as much about a search for self-identity as it is about the need to tell the facts, to write the truth; events are written from the subjective viewpoint of the author.

Luke Jackson was 13 when he wrote *Freaks, Geeks and Asperger Syndrome* (Jessica Kingsley Publishers). Luke has Asperger Syndrome (AS) and in his book he intersperses advice for young people, parents and carers with autobiographical vignettes that illustrate what life is like for someone with AS.

Characteristic features of autobiographical writing are: a structure that includes an introduction, main event and concluding statement; text written in the first-person past tense with some present tense interjections; a time sequence that is clearly signalled (for example, *once, meanwhile*).

Shared reading and discussing the text

● Read the text and ask the children who they think wrote it. Tell them about the author and explain that the extracts are autobiographical. If possible, have available a copy of *Freaks, Geeks and Asperger Syndrome*.

● Ask the children if they can recall the meaning of *biography* (see 'Charles Darwin: The Early Years', page 28). Split the word *autobiography* into its morphological components: *auto–bio–graph–y*. The prefix *auto* means 'to do oneself'. Ask the children to think of other words that have this prefix (for example, *automatic, autopilot, autograph*).

● Read the extracts. Ask the children what impression they get of the writer. Refer to the text and discuss what influences their views.

● Ask if the author uses any words or phrases that make the incident come alive. Guide the children to think about the use of descriptive detail to make the incident interesting and to add humour (for example, *As I walked and tolerated the disgusting feeling of wet sand between my toes… reed-type plants sticking out of the grass was too much for me*).

● Ask the children what tense the extracts are written in. Annotate the text to highlight verbs that indicate the past tense. Notice that the author sometimes interjects to explain things using the present tense (for example, *I have a strange kind of hearing and can only concentrate on listening to things if I know I am meant to*).

● Look at the concluding reflection (*Sometimes it is very hard to understand exactly what I have done wrong*). In what other ways might an autobiographical story conclude? (For example, a reflection: *Looking back, I think I should have told someone…*).

● Construct a list of the main features of autobiographical writing and display it as an aide-memoire for the children. (For example, *Autobiography is a recount of key moments in an individual's life; it is structured with an introduction, details of events and usually some concluding remarks; it is written largely in the past tense; most autobiographies are written in chronological order.*)

Activities

● Ask the children, in pairs, to identify in the extracts some facts (for example, *grass is like paper and can cut you*) and opinions (for example, *over what seemed to me like nothing*). Opinions can be explicit, like the example given, or implicit – that is, the author does not make it clear that what he is saying is opinion rather than fact.

● Individually, the children could write a short autobiographical piece about a moment when they were lost or their parents were worried about them. They should use the checklist of autobiographical features (see above) to help structure the writing. Point out that they should make the introduction interesting for the reader, check that events are described in a logical order, add descriptive detail to make the writing lively and interesting, and make sure the conclusion rounds the piece off well.

● Ask the children to rewrite this incident from Mum's point of view.

6: 1: T11: to distinguish between biography and autobiography:
- recognising the effect on the reader of the choice between first and third person
- distinguishing between fact, opinion and fiction
- distinguishing between implicit and explicit points of view and how these can differ

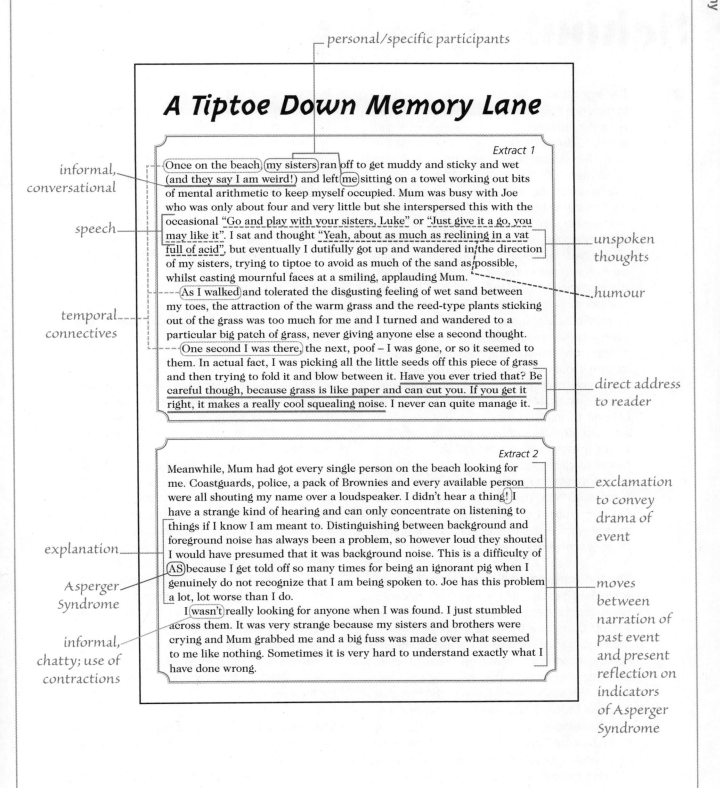

personal/specific participants

A Tiptoe Down Memory Lane

Extract 1

Once on the beach, my sisters ran off to get muddy and sticky and wet (and they say I am weird!) and left me sitting on a towel working out bits of mental arithmetic to keep myself occupied. Mum was busy with Joe who was only about four and very little but she interspersed this with the occasional "Go and play with your sisters, Luke" or "Just give it a go, you may like it". I sat and thought "Yeah, about as much as reclining in a vat full of acid", but eventually I dutifully got up and wandered in the direction of my sisters, trying to tiptoe to avoid as much of the sand as possible, whilst casting mournful faces at a smiling, applauding Mum.

As I walked and tolerated the disgusting feeling of wet sand between my toes, the attraction of the warm grass and the reed-type plants sticking out of the grass was too much for me and I turned and wandered to a particular big patch of grass, never giving anyone else a second thought. One second I was there, the next, poof – I was gone, or so it seemed to them. In actual fact, I was picking all the little seeds off this piece of grass and then trying to fold it and blow between it. Have you ever tried that? Be careful though, because grass is like paper and can cut you. If you get it right, it makes a really cool squealing noise. I never can quite manage it.

informal, conversational

speech

temporal connectives

unspoken thoughts

humour

direct address to reader

Extract 2

Meanwhile, Mum had got every single person on the beach looking for me. Coastguards, police, a pack of Brownies and every available person were all shouting my name over a loudspeaker. I didn't hear a thing! I have a strange kind of hearing and can only concentrate on listening to things if I know I am meant to. Distinguishing between background and foreground noise has always been a problem, so however loud they shouted I would have presumed that it was background noise. This is a difficulty of AS because I get told off so many times for being an ignorant pig when I genuinely do not recognize that I am being spoken to. Joe has this problem a lot, lot worse than I do.

I wasn't really looking for anyone when I was found. I just stumbled across them. It was very strange because my sisters and brothers were crying and Mum grabbed me and a big fuss was made over what seemed to me like nothing. Sometimes it is very hard to understand exactly what I have done wrong.

explanation

Asperger Syndrome

informal, chatty; use of contractions

exclamation to convey drama of event

moves between narration of past event and present reflection on indicators of Asperger Syndrome

The Village School

by Laurie Lee

Background

English poet, and novelist, Laurie Lee (1914–97) is best remembered for his autobiographical trilogy *Cider with Rosie* (1959), *As I Walked Out One Midsummer Morning* (1969) *and A Moment of War* (1991), which depict his childhood in the country, his quest to seek his fortune in London, and his experiences in the Spanish Civil War. Lee was born in Stroud, Gloucestershire, where life had remained unchanged for centuries: rural families were large, they lived in overcrowded cottages and the incidence of child mortality was high. But Lee's depiction of his boyhood is nostalgic in its recollection of aspects such as home-made wine and church outings.

Although autobiographies are accounts of one's own life, they are not necessarily any more 'true' than other kinds of writing. Sometimes a writer will deliberately conceal or omit things that they think will embarrass or cause offence, and memory is not infallible. Direct speech is almost always an invention – few of us can remember the exact words used in a conversation many years ago. Speaking on Radio 4 in 1985, Lee said he made *Cider with Rosie* as true as he could but admitted that memory and time play tricks on the writer, and his sister's memory of events was different.

Shared reading and discussing the text

● Read the passage and share initial responses. What did Laurie feel about his first day at school? Check that the children understand the source of Laurie's confusion arising from the homonym *present*. Encourage them to share their own memories of their first day at school.
● Who wrote the text? Tell the children that it comes from a book called *Cider with Rosie*, the autobiography of Laurie Lee. Consider why someone might choose to write their autobiography. Guide the children to think of different reasons (to record events before they are forgotten, for enjoyment, to hand on family history to children and grandchildren, to make money, and so on).

● Ask the children to identify words and phrases that convey Laurie's thoughts and feelings about his first day at school (for example, *roared like a rodeo; I was encircled; grit flew in my face like shrapnel*). Discuss the effectiveness of the word choices. Laurie Lee's similes compare the playground to a battle arena. Draw attention to and revise the use of similes.
● Look at Lee's use of speech. Revise the conventions of writing direct speech. Lee largely uses direct untagged speech (without tags such as *said*), but you can tell who is speaking and how the words are spoken from the contextual information. Too much tagging of speech can sound overwritten.

Activities

● Ask the children to write an individual recount entitled 'My first day at school'. Encourage them to include some reflection – looking back at how significant something was at the time and their attitude towards it now.
● In small groups, the children could improvise a scene called 'In the playground'. They could then develop their sketch into a short piece of dialogue, using tagged and untagged speech.
● Ask the children to rewrite this passage from the point of view of one of Laurie's sisters. They should consider what she would have thought of Laurie's resistance to going to school and his misunderstanding about the present.
● In pairs, the children could compare this text with the extract from *Freeks, Geeks and Asperger Syndrome* (see page 36), identifying similarities and differences. Ask the children which extract they prefer and to give reasons for their choice.

Extension/further reading

Prepare a radio programme called 'Memories of first school days' which includes interviews with children talking about their memories. One child should be an introducer and the children should consider how to link different memories together to create a cohesive programme.

6: 1: T11: to distinguish between biography and autobiography: distinguishing between fact, opinion and fiction

The Village School

context – potato for lunch but also to keep warm

The morning came, without any warning, when my sisters surrounded me, wrapped me in scarves, tied up my bootlaces, thrust a cap on my head and stuffed a baked potato in my pocket.

verbs create visual image of the scene

tagged speech

"What's this?" I said.

"You're starting school today."

direct speech (untagged)

"I ain't. I'm stopping 'ome."

"Now come on, Loll. You're a big boy now."

pet name

"I ain't."

"You are."

non-standard speech; rural dialect

"Boo-hoo."

They picked me up bodily, kicking and bawling, and carried me up to the road.

"Boys who don't go to school get put into boxes, and turn into rabbits, and get chopped up Sundays."

reflection, looking back, commenting

I felt this was overdoing it rather, but I said no more after that. I arrived at the school just three feet tall and fatly wrapped in my scarves. The playground roared like a rodeo, and the potato burned through my thigh. Old boots, ragged stockings, torn trousers and skirts, went skating and skidding around me. The rabble closed in; I was encircled; grit flew in my face like shrapnel. Tall girls with frizzled hair, and huge boys with sharp elbows, began to prod me with hideous interest. They plucked at my scarves, spun me round like a top, screwed my nose, and stole my potato.

vocabulary choice (verbs, nouns and adjectives) depicts Laurie's bewildering first day at school:

I was rescued at last by a gracious lady – the sixteen-year-old junior-teacher – who boxed a few ears and dried my face and led me off to The Infants. I spent that first day picking holes in paper, then went home in a smouldering temper.

"What's the matter, Loll? Didn't he like it at school, then?"

homophone – misunderstanding arises from dual meaning (understanding the joke is contingent upon knowing both meanings)

"They never gave me the present!"

"Present? What present?"

"They said they'd give me a present."

"Well, now, I'm sure they didn't."

"They did! They said: 'You're Laurie Lee, ain't you? Well, just you sit there for the present.' I sat there all day but I never got it. I ain't going back there again!"

But after a week I felt like a veteran and grew as ruthless as anyone else. Somebody had stolen my baked potato, so I swiped somebody else's apple.

~~~~~ = verbs

_____ = nouns

------ = adjectives

concluding observation; Laurie has adjusted to his new environment

The Sources of Romeo and Juliet
by Wendy Greenhill

Background

In this historical report about Shakespeare's sources for *Romeo and Juliet*, the first paragraph is in recount mode, providing biographical information but also making connections between Shakespeare's personal life and the play he was about to write (his eldest child Susannah was 13, about the same age as Juliet).

The content is about past times, so the past tense is used (for example, *Shakespeare was a master at choosing the most interesting ideas and developing them into something more complex than the originals*). But the tense shifts into the present to focus on what the contemporary reader will find in the plays (for example, *In Romeo and Juliet we find a wider range of attitudes to love than in any of the stories on which it was based*).

The overall structure of the piece is non-chronological – if we identify headings for each of the paragraphs this becomes evident (1. Shakespeare's life; 2. His knowledge and understanding of audience; 3. Pre-existent sources for *Romeo and Juliet*; 4. The Elizabethan tradition of using well-known stories; 5. The language of Shakespeare's *Romeo and Juliet*). Each of these paragraphs begins with a topic sentence, which signposts the introduction of a new topic to the reader (for example, *The Story of Romeo and Juliet was well known in several forms before Shakespeare made it his own*).

Shared reading and discussing the text

● Read the extract, then identify the topic for each of the paragraphs, annotating the text. Notice how the first sentence in each paragraph acts as a signpost to the content of the paragraph (topic sentences).

● Re-read paragraph 3 – identify fact and opinion, underlining text in different colours. For example, fact: *There had been poems, plays and stories in Italian and French*; Opinion: *it is likely that Shakespeare had the poem in front of him as he wrote.* We have no evidence to prove this. It is an explicit opinion because the author

has used the words *it is likely.* Sometimes opinions are implicit, for example *Shakespeare had a shrewd understanding of the subjects which would be popular…* This can be surmised from his success, but whether this was a lucky accident or shrewd understanding cannot be proved. Opinion is presented implicitly as fact.

Activities

● Ask the children to divide a sheet of paper into three columns. In the first column they should make a list of facts found in the extract; in the second column, a list of opinions; and in the third column, information that is difficult to categorise. Compare the results as a class.

● Using a range of reference sources, the children could research facts about a topic, for example Shakespeare's theatre or Elizabethan playwrights. They should write down each fact on a Post-it Note, then amalgamate their facts into a non-chronological report. Suggest that they do this by drawing a picture of the subject of their report in the middle of a large sheet of paper and arrange the Post-it Notes around the picture. They can then group facts together and write a topic sentence that covers each group. This can act as a planning sheet for a report on their chosen topic.

● To help the children with difficult vocabulary, ask them to make a list of unfamiliar words from the passage, for example *shrewd, lamentable.* In their personal word books they should write what they think the word means from the context; check in a dictionary and write the definition; check in a second dictionary and write that definition. They should then re-read the sentence in which the word occurs to make sure they understand it.

Extension/further reading

Suggestions for further reading include Michael Rosen's *Shakespeare* (Walker Books), *Welcome to the Globe!* and Peter Chrisp's *Shakespeare* (both Dorling Kindersley) and Anita Ganeri's book and CD pack *The Young Person's Guide to Shakespeare* (Pavilion Books).

6: 1: T13: to secure understanding of the features of non-chronological reports:
- introductions to orientate reader
- use of generalisations to categorise
- language to describe and differentiate
- impersonal language
- mostly present tense

6: 1: T17: to write non-chronological reports linked to other subjects

paragraph 1: where Shakespeare was in his life at the time of writing Romeo and Juliet

italic for title

specific dates given

temporal connective

pronoun – objective case of 'who'

historical, therefore written in past tense

on the verge of

use of colon to provide name for the 'new form of entertainment' – stands for 'that is'

discerning, clever

opinion

ellipsis shows that more was said

topic sentence introduces the subject of the paragraph

THE SOURCES OF ROMEO AND JULIET

1 By 1594 or 1595 when *Romeo and Juliet* was most probably written, Shakespeare had already begun to make his mark in the London theatre. Since about 1590 he had been working there as an actor and playwright. Back home in Stratford upon Avon he had left behind a wife, whom he had married when he was eighteen, and three children. His eldest child Susannah was thirteen, around the age of Juliet. Shakespeare himself was 30 years old. He was an experienced man, poised for success in what was still an exciting new form of entertainment: the theatre.

2 Shakespeare had a shrewd understanding of the subjects which would be popular with audiences and the theme of tragic young love was no exception. A version of *Romeo and Juliet*, printed and sold in London in 1599, was described as 'an excellent and lamentable tragedy…'. Romeo and Juliet was a success right from the start.

3 The story of Romeo and Juliet was well known in several forms before Shakespeare made it his own. There had been poems, plays and stories in Italian and French. In 1567, borrowing from these European originals, William Painter had included 'The goodly history of Rhomeo and Julietta' in a volume of short stories. Even earlier, in 1562, another writer, Arthur Brooke, had turned the story into a long poem, 'The Tragical History of Romeus and Juliet'. There are many similarities between Brooke's poem and Shakespeare's play, and it is likely that Shakespeare had the poem in front of him as he wrote.

4 It was quite normal for Elizabethan playwrights to use existing stories as the basis for their plays. Shakespeare was a master at choosing the most interesting ideas and developing them into something more complex than the originals. In *Romeo and Juliet* we find a wider range of attitudes to love than in any of the stories on which it was based…

5 …Shakespeare's use of language, too, is much more interesting. The contrasts in the play are expressed in many different styles. These range from formal poetry to witty puns, from the angry outbursts of Juliet's father to the passionate idealism of the lovers. We feel the atmosphere of the play through its language.

paragraph 3: specific information about Romeo and Juliet sources

present tense, comment

paragraph 4: Shakespeare's Romeo and Juliet in comparison to previous versions

move from historical past to present tense

existential verbs common in report writing

paragraph 5: the language of Romeo and Juliet

paragraph 2: knowledge of his audience

this is evident in the extract from Act II Scene II (see page 26)

6: 1: T12: to comment critically on the language, style, success of examples of non-fiction such as periodicals, reviews, reports, leaflets

Power of the Ring too strong for boy wizard

Background

This Internet news report is taken from the *Guardian*'s website. News reports are structured differently from stories. Rather than working to a structure that includes an exposition (beginning), developing conflict (middle), and climax/denouement/resolution (ending), a news story usually seeks to answer six questions *who*, *when*, *where*, *what*, *why* and *how*. The answers to these questions are often given in the first paragraph; this is called the *lead*. The following paragraphs elaborate on the main points. This example does not adhere strictly to the format but the principle can generally be seen; the most important information is given at the beginning of the report and elaboration is evident in the later paragraphs.

Shared reading and discussing the text

● Before reading the text ask the children whether they have seen the films *Harry Potter and the Chamber of Secrets* and *The Two Towers*. Discuss which they preferred and why.

● Read the report, masking the headline. Discuss the content.

● Ask the children to write a headline. Reveal the original. Evaluate the headlines, thinking about appropriate match to the story, eye-catching appeal and quality of language. Notice how the two films are linked through shared content in the original headline.

● Explain that news reports often aim to answer the six *W* questions in the first paragraph. Divide a large sheet of paper into two columns. List the six *W*s in the first column. In the second column find and write the relevant information. In this example the *Who* is really a *What* (*Who/What*: *The Two Towers* film; *When*: yesterday (December 18); *What*: broken UK advance ticket sales; *Where*: general release (nationwide); *Why*: better than current *Harry Potter* and an improvement on *The Fellowship of the Ring*; *How*: implied rather than stated – people are buying tickets. Evaluate the quality of the information.

● Look at the information in paragraphs 4 and 5. Show how some of this information can be cut without altering the main story.

● Find the names of the newspapers mentioned. Consider why newspapers are given these names – what does the word *Globe* or *Star* suggest? Ask the children if they know the names of any other newspapers. Consider the significance of newspaper names (*Observer, Independent, Mirror* and so on).

● Find and talk about the connecting words and phrases (for example, *also, Last year, In the meantime, added*).

● Identify comparative words and phrases used in the report to compare *The Two Towers* with *Harry Potter and the Chamber of Secrets* and *The Fellowship of the Ring* (*better, tighter, smarter, funnier, bigger, higher*). Generate a list of comparatives. Explore the difference between comparatives and superlatives (*best, tightest, smartest, funniest, biggest, highest*). Draw attention to inflectional endings (*-er* indicates comparative; *-est* indicates superlative).

Activities

● Give individuals or pairs a selection of headlines that have been cut out of newspapers. Ask them to invent their own answers to the six *W* questions and then use their ideas to write a short news report. The first paragraph should contain all the necessary information and the second and third paragraphs more detail and elaboration.

● Photocopy the extract and cut it into sentences (but not the headline). The children could reconstruct the text and explain their preferred order. Encourage them to share and discuss their views. Prompt them to think about the appropriate order of the content and cohesive ties.

● In pairs, the children could highlight the connecting words and phrases used in the report. They can then generate a list of linking words that can be used in writing news reports and add them to their personal word books.

6: 1: T12: to comment critically on the language, style, success of examples of non-fiction such as periodicals, reviews, reports, leaflets

6: 1: S1: to revise from Y5 the construction of complex sentences

film's director

linked by common content in two films – magic and wizardry

part

headline

| News | # Power of the Ring too strong for boy wizard |

three related films

complex sentence

Thursday December 19, 2002

The second instalment in Peter Jackson's Lord of the Rings trilogy has broken the UK box office record for advance ticket sales.

tickets sold before film release date

James Bond

The Two Towers, which went on general release yesterday, racked up a mammoth £1.7m in advance sales, well ahead of the likes of Harry Potter and the Chamber of Secrets and the recent Bond outing, Die Another Day. The figure also trumps the £1.2m in advance sales amassed by its predecessor, The Fellowship of the Ring.

gathered together a large figure

~~~ = indicators of quantity

The figures have prompted the Odeon cinema chain to predict that The Two Towers will go on to beat Harry Potter over the long run at the box office. Last year, The Fellowship of the Ring grossed $860m worldwide, yet lost out to Harry Potter and the Philosopher's Stone, on $965m. Odeon predicts the positions will reverse this time round.

proper noun capitalised

one coming before

total amount earned (before taxes etc)

great enthusiasm

In the meantime, The Two Towers opened yesterday to rave reviews in North America. The New York Daily News hailed it as "a masterpiece of epic film-making", while Newsday dubbed it a "stirring epic and an adventure of old-fashioned substance and eye-popping visuals".

newspapers

connective

quotations

long film usually portraying heroic deeds

The general consensus was that The Two Towers was both better than the current Harry Potter excursion and an improvement on the first film in Jackson's trilogy. The Boston Globe said that chapter two was "better: tighter, smarter, funnier". The Toronto Star added that "the movie plays like a true blockbuster follow-up: the action is bigger, the characters far more numerous and the stakes are much higher".

agreement

newspapers

quotation marks

quotations

comparatives

6: 1: S4: to investigate connecting words and phrases:
● collect examples from reading and thesauruses
● classify useful examples for different kinds of text – for example, by position (*besides, nearby, by*); sequence (*firstly, secondly…*); logic (*therefore, so, consequently*)

6: 1: T16: to use the styles and conventions of journalism to report on e.g. real or imagined events

The Hobbit

by JRR Tolkien

Extract 1

P

127

Background

JRR Tolkien (1892–1973) was Professor of English language and literature at Oxford. In 1937 he wrote a fantasy story for children: *The Hobbit.* This was followed by *The Lord of the Rings* (1954–56), which has become the archetype of the heroic fantasy. Tolkien was painstaking in his creation of an alternative world and even developed a prehistory for it in the Prologue to *The Lord of The Rings* and in the *Silmarillion.* The inspiration for the Shire was drawn largely from the Midlands countryside that Tolkien knew and loved.

Shared reading and discussing the text

● Ask the children if they have read *The Hobbit* or seen *The Lord of the Rings* films, and briefly discuss their responses.

● Read the text aloud (don't show the children the text at this stage). Ask for initial responses. Follow up with guided questions, for example *Can you tell from the opening paragraphs what kind of story this is?* (Fantasy fiction.) *What clues helped you?*

● The opening passage quickly establishes Bilbo as a home-loving creature, fond of small luxuries and comforts. Even before we meet him an image is created by the description of his home. In the third paragraph we are led to expect that his way of life is about to change. We learn that he *never had any adventures or did anything unexpected.* But of course it wouldn't be much of a story if he continued this uneventful established routine, so we surmise that he is about to embark on an exciting, if unexpected, adventure. Evaluate the opening: does it make you want to read on?

● Explain to the children that you are going to read the passage a second time and that afterwards they will sketch the hobbit-hole. Share the sketches and discuss any key words and phrases that the children picked up from listening to the passage. This visualisation validates the children's individual responses to the text and facilitates a discussion on the effects of the language.

● Identify and highlight the different ways in which Tolkien presents the hobbit-hole (for example, he describes what the hole *is not*; uses simile; supplies some details). Look at how the hobbit-hole is viewed as if the reader is taking a tour – entering the front door, moving through the hall and then into the rooms. Construct a prompt sheet to aid the children's writing.

● Read from *The tunnel wound on and on…* to *sloping down to the river.* Look at the use of parentheses: *(lots of these), (he had whole rooms devoted to clothes), (going in).* Discuss the effect that this has on the way the passage is read aloud. The text in parenthesis supplies additional information which is read like an aside or an afterthought. It gives the narration a conversational tone, setting up an informal relationship between the narrator and the reader. The storyteller's voice is also evident in the last line – *well, you will see whether he gained anything in the end.*

Activities

● Ask the children to create their own imaginary settings, using some of the same techniques as Tolkien (for example, use of similes, interesting details). They can refer to the prompt sheet (see above) to assist their writing.

● Organise the children into small groups and ask them to tell a story using Tolkien's beginning. Each member of the group tells part of the story and then passes the story on by tapping the person on their left. The next person picks up the story and continues.

● Can the children devise a storyboard to show the adventure that Bilbo might have, including an orientation, initiating event, complication and resolution?

● In shared writing construct a framework for a character profile for Bilbo Baggins. Think of the headings that you should include (name, type of creature, description, likes, dislikes, and so on). Then ask the children to use the clues from this passage to complete the profile, working independently. They could draw a passport style 'photograph' on their profile sheet.

6: 2: T1: to understand aspects of narrative structure, e.g.:
● how chapters in a book (or paragraphs in a short story or chapter) are linked together
● how authors handle time, e.g. flashbacks, stories within stories, dreams
● how the passing of time is conveyed to the reader

6: 2: T7: to identify the key features of different types of literary text, e.g. stock characters, plot structure, and how particular texts conform, develop or undermine the type, e.g. through parody

homely vocabulary

describes the hobbit-hole by telling us what it is <u>not</u>

THE HOBBIT *Extract 1*

1 In a hole in the ground there lived a hobbit. Not a nasty, dirty, wet hole, filled with the ends of worms and an oozy smell, nor yet a dry, bare, sandy hole with nothing in it to sit down on or to eat: it was a hobbit-hole, and that means comfort.

2 It had a perfectly round door like a porthole, painted green, with a shiny yellow brass knob in the exact middle. The door opened on to a tube-shaped hall like a tunnel: a very comfortable tunnel without smoke, with panelled walls, and floors tiled and carpeted, provided with polished chairs, and lots and lots of pegs for hats and coats – the hobbit was fond of visitors. The tunnel wound on and on, going fairly but not quite straight into the side of the hill – The Hill, as all the people for many miles round called it – and many little round doors opened out of it, first on one side and then on another. No going upstairs for the hobbit: bedrooms, bathrooms, cellars, pantries (lots of these), wardrobes (he had whole rooms devoted to clothes), kitchens, dining-rooms, all were on the same floor, and indeed on the same passage. The best rooms were all on the lefthand side (going in), for these were the only ones to have windows, deep-set round windows looking over his garden, and meadows beyond, sloping down to the river.

3 This hobbit was a very well-to-do hobbit, and his name was Baggins. The Bagginses had lived in the neighbourhood of The Hill for time out of mind, and people considered them very respectable, not only because most of them were rich, but also because they never had any adventures or did anything unexpected; you could tell what a Baggins would say on any question without the bother of asking him. This is a story of how a Baggins had an adventure, and found himself doing and saying things altogether unexpected. He may have lost the neighbours' respect, but he gained – well, you will see whether he gained anything in the end.

paragraph 1: exposition – place and character introduced

paragraph 2 details the hobbit-hole

capitalisation of proper nouns

food important – childlike comfort

paragraph 3 details Bilbo

colon: introduces a clause which demonstrates the previous clause

2 similes used to describe aspects of the hobbit-hole

narrator's voice

colon use as above

parentheses used to add more information which is bracketed off to give the impression of an afterthought in conversation

pastoral vocabulary

the last 4 lines are a direct address to reader

humour in pluralisation of 'Baggins'

6: 2: T9: to increase familiarity with significant poets and writers of the past

6: 2: T10: to use different genres as models to write, e.g. short extracts, sequels, additional episodes, alternative endings, using appropriate conventions, language

The Hobbit

by JRR Tolkien

Extract 2

P

128

Background

Gandalf the Grey, a wizard noted for his spectacular fireworks, knocks on Bilbo's door and is soon joined by a company of dwarves. After a feast of raspberry jam, apple tart, mince pies, cheese, coffee and ale followed by music and song, the band gather round to discuss business: a plot to raid the treasure hoard of Smaug and reclaim the dwarves' inheritance. In this extract the narrative is carried largely through dialogue. The examination of the treasure map in this scene makes it an exciting, tension-filled episode.

Shared reading and discussing the text

● Contextualise the passage. Read the text aloud and ask for initial responses. Is the passage exciting? Why? Consider the importance of the map in leading the reader into the story. Show how the map works as a device to explain past events as well as looking forward to the forthcoming quest. (This passage can be linked to *Treasure Island*, see pages 10 and 12.)

● Look at Tolkien's use of dialogue as a narrative device. From what the characters say to each other we hear about places that the expedition will visit: the Mountain; Mirkwood; the Withered Heath. We discover that they will need to uncover a secret door into the Mountain and that Smaug the dragon is a fierce man-eater.

● Ask the children to imagine what the different characters' voices sound like. They should try to justify their opinions by referring to the text. Read some of the dialogue aloud, experimenting with different voices for the characters. Discuss what works well and why.

● Highlight some of the dialogue to illustrate the varied presentation. Identify examples of detailed tagging (for example, *he said in answer to the dwarves' excited questions*) as well as untagged speech. The tags give important contextual information, but this is not overdone; excessive tagging would slow the pace of the story, disrupt the rhythm and be unnecessarily detailed. Notice also that Tolkien frequently uses the verb *said* rather than more specific speech verbs; overuse of descriptive verbs would draw attention to the manner of speech rather than focusing on the content of what is spoken. Draw attention to the correct punctuation for writing direct speech, including the insertion of a tag.

● Names are very important in alternative-world fantasies and Tolkien was skilled at finding the perfect names for his characters and settings. *Mirkwood* and *Withered Heath* can only be unpleasant and terrifying places. Here are some other names that Tolkien invented; what do the children imagine these places to be like: *Lothlorien, Rivendell, Misty Mountains*? And what about these characters: *Elrond, Gollum, Tom Bombadil, Beorn, Warg*?

● Revisit features of narration that were noted in the first extract (such as the use of parentheses and direct address to the reader – *He was only a little hobbit you must remember*). This is an opportunity to draw attention to some of the features of the author's distinctive style.

Activities

● The children could use a thesaurus to make a collection of speech verbs that can be used judiciously instead of *said*. They should classify them according to mood (angry words, happy words, and so on). If they insert the verbs in their personal word books, they can use them for reference when writing.

● To encourage understanding of inference of character through speech, ask the children to write on strips of paper something one of the characters from this extract would typically say (not words from the extract). They can do this in small groups. They should then place the strips of paper in a container, and take it in turns to take a slip of paper from the container and read it aloud. Can they decide who would say those words and why?

● Ask the children to select one character and write a journal entry for the character's day before he sets out on the quest. What might the character be thinking and feeling?

6: 2: T1: to understand aspects of narrative structure, e.g.:
● show chapters in a book (or paragraphs in a short story or chapter) are linked together
● how authors handle time, e.g. flashbacks, stories within stories, dreams
● how the passing of time is conveyed to the reader

6: 2: T7: to identify the key features of different types of literary text, e.g. stock characters, plot structure, and how particular texts conform, develop or undermine the type, e.g. through parody

6: 2: T9: to increase familiarity with significant poets and writers of the past

fantasy fiction names

material from animal skin used as paper

plural of 'dwarf' (rules of pluralisation)

characters of an ancient alphabet, especially in carved inscription, often with magical association

'said' is the speech verb most frequently used

untagged direct speech; narrative is carried through dialogue

presentation of speech: direct tagged speech – use of adverb ('disappointedly') and action ('after a glance') to add detail

fantasy fiction names

inserted tag shows punctuation conventions in direct speech: comma before close of speech marks and after tag

fantasy fiction names

THE HOBBIT *Extract 2*

On the table in the light of a big lamp with a red shade he spread a piece of parchment rather like a map.

"This was made by Thror, your grandfather, Thorin," he said in answer to the dwarves' excited questions. "It is a plan of the Mountain."

"I don't see that this will help us much," said Thorin disappointedly after a glance. "I remember the Mountain well enough and the lands about it. And I know where Mirkwood is, and the Withered Heath where the great dragons bred."

"There is a dragon marked in red on the Mountain," said Balin, "but it will be easy enough to find him without that, if we ever arrive there."

"There is one point that you haven't noticed," said the wizard, "and that is the secret entrance. You see that rune on the West side, and the hand pointing to it from the other runes? That marks a hidden passage to the Lower Halls." (Look at the map at the beginning of this book, and you will see there the runes.)

"It may have been secret once," said Thorin, "but how do we know that it is secret any longer? Old Smaug has lived there long enough now to find out anything there is to know about those caves."

"He may – but he can't have used it for years and years."

"Why?"

"Because it is too small. 'Five feet high the door and three may walk abreast' say the runes, but Smaug could not creep into a hole that size, not even when he was a young dragon, certainly not after devouring so many of the dwarves and men of Dale."

"It seems a great big hole to me," squeaked Bilbo (who had no experience of dragons and only of hobbit-holes). He was getting excited and interested again, so that he forgot to keep his mouth shut. He loved maps, and in his hall there hung a large one of the Country Round with all his favourite walks marked on it in red ink. "How could such a large door be kept secret from everybody outside, apart from the dragon?" he asked. He was only a little hobbit you must remember.

"In lots of ways," said Gandalf. "But in what way this one has been hidden we don't know without going to see. From what it says on the map I should guess there is a closed door which has been made to look exactly like the side of the Mountain."

contrast between Bilbo's maps, which are like local ramblers' maps, and the treasure map, which signals the start of a quest – nevertheless, the fact that Bilbo displays an interest in maps hints at an underlying adventurous spirit

direct address to the reader

The Hobbit

by JRR Tolkien

Extracts 3 and 4

Background

The writer of fantasy fiction has to create places and characters that readers can believe in, to write in a way that enables readers to visualise them. In these extracts Tolkien uses contrasting techniques to introduce Bilbo and his adversary Gollum. The first passage (extract 3) is warm and light in tone, the second (extract 4) is poetic and written in an elevated style.

Shared reading and discussing the text

● Revisit extract 1 (see page 44) and summarise ideas about Bilbo drawn from the description of the hobbit hole.
● Read extract 3. Ask the children whether this description confirms or challenges the image of Bilbo derived from the first extract.
● Ask the children to read extract 4 independently and highlight any words or phrases that give information about the character. Ask them to circle clues that give literal information about Gollum's appearance (for example, *a small slimy creature*) and underline clues from which they can infer things about his appearance (for example, *never a ripple did he make* suggests that he is stealthy). Tell them to annotate the passage with any comments they want to make about Gollum's appearance, then sketch a picture of him using the marked extract. Read the passage aloud to the class. Compare, discuss and evaluate the children's sketches, highlighting different responses to the text. Look at how the same information allows readers to imagine in different ways.
● Encourage the children to comment on the language, picking out any words or phrases that they find interesting or powerful. Look at the poetic language Tolkien uses to introduce Gollum. There are repeated patterns of sound (*d, l*) and words (<u>down</u> *there,* <u>down</u> *at the very roots of the mountain*).
● Draw attention to the varied sentence length and structure. Long sentences joined by a semi-colon add descriptive colour: *He had a little boat, and he rowed about quite quietly on the lake; for lake it was, wide and deep and deadly cold.* Contrasting short sentences create suspense and carry a lot of weight through the implied meaning: *He liked meat too.* Look at the elevated syntax: *He paddled it with large feet dangling over the side, but never a ripple did he make.* Rewrite this sentence in everyday language (for example, *but he never made a ripple*). What difference does this make to the effect created?
● Summarise the different ways in which Tolkien builds Gollum's character: his home, his appearance, what he does and how he moves.

Activities

● In extract 4 the narrator says, *I don't know where he came from nor who or what he was.* Ask pairs of children to draw up a list of questions to ask Gollum (*Why does he live deep underground? Where did he come from?* and so on). Then they should role-play an interview, with one child as the interviewer and the other taking the role of Gollum. Interviews can be recorded and written up as a news story (for example, 'Gollum, the true story' or 'Where he came from nobody knows').
● Ask the children to compare these two extracts, picking out similarities and differences in the way Tolkien describes hobbits and Gollum. Share observations in a plenary session.
● Can the children create their own fantasy character? Provide them with a series of questions and prompts in note form before they write an introduction to their character. For example: *What type of creature is your character? Where does it live? Describe the outside of its home. What does it like to eat? What does it like doing? What makes your character laugh? What makes your character cry? What does it look like? What problems does this character have in its life?*
● In the centre of a sheet of paper, the children could draw a picture of Gollum or Bilbo. Encourage them to select key words and phrases from the passage (either extract 3 or 4) that describe the character, and use them to accompany the illustration.

6: 2: T7: to identify the key features of different types of literary text, e.g. stock characters, plot structure, and how particular texts conform, develop or undermine the type, e.g. through parody

6: 2: T8: to analyse the success of texts and writers in evoking particular responses in the reader, e.g. where suspense is well built

characterisation in fantasy fiction shown in both extracts

narration – storyteller's voice is used

humour provides a light tone in this extract

physical attributes

use of parenthesis (also see extract 1)

THE HOBBIT

Extract 3

I suppose hobbits need some description nowadays, since they have become rare and shy of the Big People, as they call us. They are (or were) a little people, about half our height and smaller than the bearded Dwarves. Hobbits have no beards. There is little or no magic about them, except the ordinary everyday sort which helps them to disappear quietly and quickly when large stupid folk like you and me come blundering along, making a noise like elephants which they can hear a mile off. They are inclined to be fat in the stomach; they dress in bright colours (chiefly green and yellow); wear no shoes, because their feet grow natural leathery soles and thick warm brown hair like the stuff on their heads (which is curly); have long clever brown fingers, good-natured faces, and laugh deep fruity laughs (especially after dinner, which they have twice a day when they can get it).

Extract 4

Deep down here by the dark water lived old Gollum, a small slimy creature. I don't know where he came from, nor who or what he was. He was Gollum – as dark as darkness, except for two big round pale eyes in his thin face. He had a little boat, and he rowed about quite quietly on the lake; for lake it was, wide and deep and deadly cold. He paddled it with large feet dangling over the side, but never a ripple did he make. Not he. He was looking out of his pale limp-like eyes for blind fish, which he grabbed with his long fingers as quick as thinking. He liked meat too. Goblin he thought good, when he could get it; but he took care they never found him out. He just throttled them from behind, if they ever came down alone anywhere near the edge of the water, while he was prowling about. They very seldom did, for they had a feeling that something unpleasant was lurking down there, down at the very roots of the mountain.

physical attributes

adjectives add detail to characters being depicted

hobbits are associated with food; links to extract 1 (see page 44) – 'pantries (lots of these)'

storyteller's voice

sentence structure: the effect is lost if the pronoun 'he' is moved to read 'but he never made a ripple'

movement verbs that describe Golllum

alliterative qualities in the passage (repetition of 'd', 'm', 's'); will echo Gollum's speech

physical attributes

unusual, effective simile – avoids more obvious clichés (also suggests that Bilbo should remain alert and not let his guard down)

location as an indicator of character – allusion to an underworld or hell

patterned language – repetition of 'down' emphasises the literal and metaphorical depth of Gollum's lair

6: 2: T9: to increase familiarity with significant poets and writers of the past

The Eagle of the Ninth

by Rosemary Sutcliff

Extract 1

Background

Rosemary Sutcliff (1920–92) was diagnosed at the age of two with a crippling illness, Still's Disease, and consequently spent much of her life wheelchair bound. Disability is a theme that recurs in her novels and many of her characters gain new strength through their struggles. Sutcliff is admired for her historical novels for children and particularly for her trilogy set in Roman Britain.

The first book in the trilogy, *The Eagle of the Ninth* (1954), tells the story of Marcus Flavius Aquila, a young Roman soldier wounded in battle who fought against the Celtic tribesmen. Invalided out of the Roman army, he sets off to find out what happened to his father's lost legion, the Ninth Hispana, and to recover the legion's Standard, a golden eagle. It is an undertaking so hazardous that no one expects him to return; his only companion is a Celtic tribesman, Esca, an ex-gladiator turned slave before Marcus grants him his freedom.

In this extract, Sutcliff introduces the reader to Roman Britain and its inhabitants.

Shared reading and discussing the text

● Provide some background on Rosemary Sutcliff and the historical context for *The Eagle of the Ninth*.

● Read the passage. After reading, ask each child to suggest one question to ask about the passage. They might ask about definitions of specific words; background to Roman customs; predictions as to what might happen in the story; or questions about the author. List their questions without comment and then review the list. Consider which questions can be answered quickly and how the answer can be located; which questions require more research and which might be answered by reading of the story.

● Point out that the exposition establishes the time and place and introduces the main character. Ask the children how the description helps them visualise the landscape and people of Roman Britain. Highlight the text and discuss the effectiveness of the words and phrases that the children suggest (for example, the image *corduroys of logs*).

● Look at how the text is structured. The four paragraphs move from a wide-angle view of the road to a mid-distance focus on the travellers and the Roman legion, and then into a close-up of the centurion. Link this to the way films often begin. Highlight the opening line of each paragraph to emphasise the point.

● Draw attention to the legion's march through diverse terrain and how this suggests great distance and the passing of time.

● Identify the moment that moves this passage from a description of Roman Britain to the beginning of a story. The last two sentences make the reader wonder about how the test will come in the story and how the honours will be achieved.

Activities

● Let the children use this extract as a model for writing an introduction to a historical story. Suggest some ideas for the story, for example a group of archaeologists are excavating an ancient tomb in the pyramids of Egypt. Their introduction could start with a wide-angle view of the landscape, move into mid-shot and then finally to a close up of a character.

● Ask the children to add a glossary of specialist Roman terminology (*centurion, legion, Standard, garrison, laurel wreath, auxiliaries* and so on) to their personal word books.

● In pairs, the children could develop a list of criteria for evaluating historical fiction (for example, believable characters; time and place brought alive for the reader). Suggest that, in fours, they compare and evaluate each other's list of criteria, then make a composite list.

● Ask the children to imagine that they are one of the soldiers in the legion or a Briton travelling along the Fosseway. Ask them to talk, in small groups, about what life would have been like. They can use reference materials for further information, then construct a monologue for their chosen character.

6: 2: T1: to understand aspects of narrative structure, e.g.:
● how chapters in a book (or paragraphs in a short story or chapter) are linked together
● how authors handle time, e.g. flashbacks, stories within stories, dreams
● how the passing of time is conveyed to the reader

6: 2: T2: to analyse how individual paragraphs are structured in writing, e.g. comments sequenced to follow the shifting thoughts of a character, examples listed to justify a point and reiterated to give it force

Roman name for city now called Exeter

colon used before illustration of previous clause

one of the main Roman roads

visual and textural image

paragraph 2 focuses on the types of travellers found on the road

division of legion

paragraph 3 zooms in to focus on the cohort

patterned language – repetition of 'on' emphasises unceasing marching

changes in landscape show distance travelled

stop

long view, setting the scene like establishing shot in film

fake opticians

Celts

department of the army that organises food supplies

description of landscape

wild boar found in Britain in Roman times

literally, in charge of 100 men, but in this case 600

importance of the last line – at this point we are expecting something to happen in the story: will the honours be won? at what cost?

foreign soldiers serving the Roman Empire; Gaul is in modern-day France

emblem carried into battle at the top of a pole

The Eagle of the Ninth

Extract 1

On the Road

From the Fosseway westward to Isca Dumnoniorum the road was simply a British trackway, broadened and roughly metalled, strengthened by corduroys of logs in the softest places, but otherwise unchanged from its old estate, as it wound among the hills, thrusting further and further into the wilderness.

2 It was a busy road and saw many travellers: traders with bronze weapons and raw yellow amber in their ponies' packs; country folk driving shaggy cattle or lean pigs from village to village; sometimes a band of tawny-haired tribesmen from further west; strolling harpers and quack-oculists, too, or a light-stepping hunter with huge wolf-hounds at his heel; and from time to time a commissariat wagon going up and down to supply the Roman frontier post. The road saw them all, and the cohorts of the Eagles for whom all other travellers must make way.

3 There was a cohort of leather-clad auxiliaries on the road today, swinging along at the steady Legion's pace that had brought them down from Isca Silurium at twenty miles a day; the new garrison coming to relieve the old one at Isca Dumnoniorum. On they went, following the road that now ran out on a causeway between sodden marsh and empty sky, now plunged into deep boar-hunted forest, or lifted over bleak uplands where nothing grew save furze and thorn-scrub. On with never a halt nor a change of rhythm, marching century by century, the sun bright on the Standard at their head, and the rolling dust-cloud kicked up over the pack-train behind.

At the head of the column marched the Pilus Prior Centurion, the cohort Commander, the pride that shone from him showing clearly that this was his first command. They were, he had long since decided, a command worthy of anyone's pride; six hundred yellow-haired giants recruited from the tribes of Upper Gaul, with the natural fighting power of mountain cats, drilled and hammered into what he firmly believed to be the finest auxiliary cohort ever to serve with the Second Legion. They were a newly joined cohort; many of the men had not yet proved themselves in action, and the spearshaft of their Standard had no honours on it, no gilded laurel wreath nor victor's crown. The honours were all to win – perhaps during his command.

6: 2: T7: to identify the key features of different types of literary text, e.g. stock characters, plot structure, and how particular texts conform, develop or undermine the type, e.g. through parody

6: 2: T9: to increase familiarity with significant poets and writers of the past

The Eagle of the Ninth

by Rosemary Sutcliff

Extract 2

P

131

Background

This extract depicts a scene at a gladiatorial contest where Marcus first sees Esca (the swordsman) whom he later purchases as his slave. Like many gladiators, Esca, a Celtic tribesman, was captured after losing in battle against the Romans. Gladiators were trained in a similar manner to professional athletes today. As part of their training they learned how to use a range of weapons including the net, trident, sword, war chain, dagger and lasso. If a gladiator survived five years of combat he was freed, though this was a rare occurrence. A gladiator defeated in the arena was subject to a popular vote granting him life or death.

In this passage Rosemary Sutcliff recreates the tense atmosphere of the gladiatorial arena with a combination of long and short sentences. She uses a high proportion of movement verbs which create an action scene almost like a choreographed scene from a film or play.

Shared reading and discussing the text

● Read the passage aloud, emphasising the build up of tension and variation in pace. Ask the children how the passage makes them feel when they listen to it.

● Ask the children to read the passage a second time, in pairs, underlining any unfamiliar words and using dictionaries to locate meanings. (Explain that the *Fisher* is the gladiator with a three-pronged spear and a net.) Ask for any new words that have been learned. Put the words into new sentences (for example, *exquisite*: *Her handwriting was exquisite.*). Check that the children understand the meaning of a new word in the context of the extract.

● Ask for suggestions as to how Rosemary Sutcliff builds tension. Highlight the sentence *Never taking his eyes from his adversary...* What effect does this long sentence have? (It maintains the slow pace.) Look at how the sentence is constructed and punctuated.

● Sutcliff employs a range of different movement words to help create tension in the extract. Prepare a cloze version of the passage, with the movement verbs covered. Read through the text and ask the children to suggest words to fill in the gaps. Take more than one suggestion for each gap and ask the children to justify which substitution is most apposite. Look at the original word used by Sutcliff and discuss its effectiveness.

● Consider the appropriateness and effectiveness of the images, for example *The net whipped out like a dark flame; it licked round the running swordsman* and *helplessly meshed as a fly in a spider's web.*

Activities

● Ask the children to make a collection of verbs of movement and classify them according to speed (fast or slow words). They should add the list to their personal word books.

● *Never taking his eye from his adversary, he slipped one foot in front of the other; crouching a little, covering his body with the round buckler, inch by inch he crept forward, every muscle tensed to spring when the time came.* Ask the children to write each of these clauses on a separate strip of paper. How many different ways can be found to order the sentence? What happens when the sentence is ordered in a different way? (For example, does the emphasis occur in a different place?) See if the children can generate a new sentence, using the same structure as the original. This activity will encourage them to use sentences from the extract as models for writing.

● Ask the children to write a short tension-building scene for a story; suggest that they include some long sentences and short ones to vary the pace.

● Can the children write some images to describe the movement of a ballet dancer, a footballer and so on?

Extension/further reading

Further reading includes Jon Scieszka's *See You Later Gladiator* (Puffin) and Richard Ross Watkins' *Gladiator* (Houghton Mifflin).

6: 2: T8: to analyse the success of texts and writers in evoking particular responses in the reader, e.g. where suspense is well built

6: 2: S3: to revise work on complex sentences:
● identifying main clauses
● ways of connecting clauses
● constructing complex sentences
● appropriate use of punctuation

contrast between noise and silence

delicacy of this operation contrasts with action and violence that follows

semi-colon used to join two closely related sentences

gladiator with weapons of trident and net

throw (in modern usage a fishing line or net is 'cast')

object of hunt

change of pace – quick movement contrasts with previous stillness

as if time is almost standing still

slow movement verbs (maintains the slow pace)

ready for action; scene is charged with tension

three-pronged spear

fast movement verbs

mark of a slave

fast movement verbs

like baying of hunting hounds

continued hunting image

powerful image

The Eagle of the Ninth

Extract 2

Gladiators

The roar which greeted the pair of fighters had fallen to a breathless hush. In the centre of the arena the two men were being placed by the captain of the gladiators; placed with exquisite care, ten paces apart, with no advantage of light or wind allowed to either. The thing was quickly and competently done, and the captain stepped back to the barriers. For what seemed a long time, neither of the two moved. Moment followed moment, and still they remained motionless, the centre of all that great circle of staring faces. Then, very slowly, the swordsman began to move. Never taking his eyes from his adversary, he slipped one foot in front of the other, crouching a little, covering his body with the round buckler, inch by inch he crept forward, every muscle tensed to spring when the time came.

The Fisher stood as still as ever, poised on the balls of his feet, the trident in his left hand, his right lost in the folds of the net. Just beyond reach of the net, the swordsman checked for a long, agonising moment, and then sprang in. His attack was so swift that the flung net flew harmlessly over his head, and the Fisher leapt back and sideways to avoid his thrust, then whirled about and ran for his life, gathering his net for another cast as he ran, with the young swordsman behind him. Half round the arena they sped, running low; the swordsman had not the other's length and lightness of build, but he ran as a hunter runs – perhaps he had run down deer on the hunting trail, before ever his ear was clipped – and he was gaining on his quarry now. The two came flying round the curve of the barrier towards the Magistrates' benches, and just abreast of them the Fisher whirled about and flung once more. The net whipped out like a dark flame; it licked round the running swordsman, so intent on his chase that he had forgotten to guard for it; the weight carried the deadly folds across and across again, and a howl burst from the crowd as he crashed headlong and rolled over, helplessly meshed as a fly in a spider's web.

6: 2: T9: to increase familiarity with significant poets and writers of the past

The Eagle of the Ninth

by Rosemary Sutcliff

Extract 3

Background

When Marcus decides to go in search of his father's lost legion he feels that he cannot compel his slave, Esca, to accompany him, so he offers him his freedom. In this passage the narrative is carried through dialogue. However, just as in life, what a character says and their inner feelings may not be congruent. Some insight into Marcus's feelings is given (*And watching him, Marcus remembered suddenly and piercingly the moment… but Esca?*). Esca's thoughts, on the other hand, can only be inferred from his expression (*Esca smiled, the slow grave smile that always seemed to come a little unwillingly to his face*) and his words. This allows for some difference of interpretation although there may be a dominant reading of the text.

Shared reading and discussing the text

● Read the extract to the children and clarify any unfamiliar vocabulary.

● Discuss what is happening in this passage. Why does Marcus feel that he can't ask a slave but he can ask a friend? There are two main ideas here. First, in reality Marcus wouldn't need to ask a slave. A slave couldn't make a choice from free will and Marcus wants to test Esca's friendship to see if he will freely go with him. Secondly, there are things that we ask of our friends but would not ask of anyone else. Ask the children to think of parallel situations in their own lives in which they have been able to ask a friend to do something for them that they would not have been able to ask of anyone else.

● Discuss what is meant by the saying *If you really love something you must set it free*. Discuss this in relation to the two examples in the extract, and broaden the discussion to take account of the children's personal experiences where appropriate.

● Consider how effectively Rosemary Sutcliff evokes empathy for the characters in this passage. Discuss whether she tells the reader what the characters are thinking or whether the reader has to work it out from other clues and hints. Note that there is room for a difference of interpretation here and it is important to allow individual responses.

● Write out the dialogue on a large sheet of paper. Leave space for writing between each line. Select two children, one to take on the role of Marcus and one to take on the role of Esca. Ask the children to read the dialogue, stopping after each utterance. Prompt the children to think beyond what is actually said in the extract to infer what the character might be feeling based on clues in the text and understanding of the context. Feelings are likely to be mixed rather than clear-cut. Encourage the children to consider the complexity and authenticity of the situation. Use a contrasting colour to write thoughts underneath the dialogue.

● Revise the conventions for setting out dialogue.

Activities

● Organise the children into groups of three to practise reading the extract to each other (narrator, Marcus, Esca). Encourage them to convey the feelings experienced by the characters in their reading.

● In pairs, the children could rewrite this scene as a poem for two voices (for example, verse 1, Marcus; verse 2, Esca; verse 3, Marcus; verse 4, Esca). Allow free choice of form.

● Remind the children that Esca was a Celtic tribesman and after losing in battle against the Romans was taken prisoner and trained as a gladiator. He was bought as a slave by Marcus before being given his freedom. Ask the children to write a diary entry for Esca in which he reflects on the events that have led to him being given his freedom.

● The children could recreate this scene as a comic strip. Dialogue can be written in speech bubbles and thoughts in thought bubbles. The work can be supported by looking at comics to see how speech and thoughts are conventionally represented in these texts.

● Ask the children to write a poem entitled 'Friendship'.

temporal connective in narrative

polishing

material for writing made from papyrus plant

release from slavery

we can infer from this observation that this action is highly unusual and therefore not readily understood; that he is being released causes confusion

untagged speech

indication of Marcus's character – kind, moral, warm-hearted

reader is shown the scene but there is no indication of the character's thoughts

reader given access to Marcus's thoughts – he is worried that he will lose Esca if he sets him free

an official

portentous – animals used to create atmosphere (their sensory perception)

this action indicates a friendly approach; perhaps a signal that they are equals

importance of these words

uncertain

The Eagle of the Ninth

Extract 3

Esca's Freedom

When Marcus, with Cub at his heels, entered his sleeping-quarters that night, Esca, who was waiting for him as usual, laid down the belt whose clasps he had been burnishing, and asked: "When do we start?"

Marcus closed the door and stood with his back against it. "Probably the morn's morning – that is, for myself, at least. The details can wait awhile; but first you had best take this," and he held out a slim papyrus roll he had been carrying.

Esca took it with a puzzled glance at his face, and unrolling it, he held it to the lamplight. And watching him, Marcus remembered suddenly and piercingly the moment that afternoon when he had taken off Cub's collar. Cub had come back to him; but Esca?

Esca looked up from the papyrus, and shook his head. "Capitals are one thing," he said, "but I can make nothing of this script. What is it?"

"Your manumission – your freedom," Marcus said. "I made it out this evening, and Uncle Aquila and the Legate witnessed it. Esca, I ought to have given it to you long ago; I have been a completely unthinking fool, and I am sorry."

Esca looked down at the thing in his hands once more, and again back to Marcus, as though he was not sure that he understood. Then he let the roll spring back on itself, and said very slowly: "I am free? Free to go?"

"Yes," Marcus said. "Free to go, Esca."

There was a long dragging silence. An owl cried somewhere afar off, with a note that seemed at once desolate and mocking. Cub looked from one to the other, and whined softly in his throat.

Then Esca said, "Is it that you are sending me away?"

"No! It is for you to go, or stay, as you wish."

Esca smiled, the slow grave smile that always seemed to come a little unwillingly to his face. "Then I stay," he said, and hesitated. "It is perhaps not only I who think foolish thoughts because of the Tribune Placidus."

"Perhaps." Marcus reached out and set both hands lightly on the other's shoulders. "Esca, I should never have asked you to come with me into this hazard when you were not free to refuse. It is like to prove a wild hunt, and whether or not we shall come back from it lies on the knees of the gods. No one should ask a slave to go with him on such a hunting trail; but – he might ask a friend." He looked questioningly into Esca's face.

Riddles

by Kevin Crossley-Holland, JRR Tolkien, James Berry and George Szirtes

Background

Riddles have a long history. In Greek mythology, Oedipus had to answer a riddle set by the Sphinx: *What animal goes on four feet in the morning, two at noon and three in the evening*? (Answer: *man* because he crawls on hands and knees in babyhood, walks upright in adulthood and must use a stick in old age.) *The Exeter Book* (c940) translated by Kevin Crossley-Holland from Old English lists over 100 riddles. These traditional riddles usually concealed the identity of an object and would often end with the words *Say what I mean* or *Guess what I am.*

The first of these examples is from a translated Anglo-Saxon riddle; the puzzle is presented as a metaphor. The second example is from *The Hobbit*. Many readers will recall the chapter entitled 'Riddles in the Dark' in which Gollum and Bilbo challenge each other in a life-and-death contest of wits. It is believed that young Anglo-Saxon men may have engaged in similar verbal duelling – testing each other without resorting to acts of physical aggression. The third example comes from the Caribbean tradition of riddling and asks the reader to solve the mystery of the concealed object, inviting them to guess the answer. The opening lines have a lively song-like rhythm. The last example written by contemporary poet George Szirtes uses some of the elements of traditional riddles.

Many jokes told by children take the form of guessing an object, for example *What is black and white and red all over?* (*A newspaper*) and they may also be familiar with spelling riddles (*My first is in dark and also in day,* and so on).

Shared reading and discussing the text

● Before reading the text have a joke-telling session. Ask the children if they know any jokes of the type *What is yellow and extremely dangerous?* (Answer: *shark-infested custard.*) Ask them why this kind of joke is appealing. The children may also have come across other forms of riddles in fantasy computer games.

● Conceal the answers to the riddles. Read the first riddle and work out the answer together. In pairs, ask the children to read the other riddles to each other and see if they can determine the solutions. Discuss the answers. Which was the easiest riddle to solve? Which was the most difficult?

● Look at the techniques that the writers employ in their riddling:

– Introduce or recap the term *metaphor.*

– Identify and talk about the effects of the rhyming patterns.

– Notice that some riddles invite the reader to work them out.

Activities

● Ask the children to write riddles employing some of the techniques discussed above. Then organise a riddle contest like Bilbo and Gollum have in *The Hobbit*. Some simple one-sentence examples can be provided to help children requiring more support: for example, *What has hands but no arms?* (Answer: *a clock.*)

● The children could find out about Anglo-Saxon riddles using the Internet and other sources (see below). Ask them to read and select some favourite riddles to share.

● Read the Oedipus myth to the children and help them to find out about the riddle of the Sphinx. Suggest that they write a scene for an adventure film in which the hero/heroine has to answer a riddle before reaching the goal of his/her quest.

● Make a class anthology of collected riddles, including those written by the children. The book should be produced so that answers to the riddles are on a different page.

Extension/further reading

The children could read further extracts from Kevin Crossley-Holland's *The Exeter Book of Riddles* (Enitharmon Press). Other books which may be of interest are Phil Cousineau's *A World Treasury of Riddles* (Conari Press) and JRR Tolkien's 'Riddles in the Dark' from *The Hobbit* (HarperCollins).

6: 2: T3: to recognise how poets manipulate words:
● for their connotations
● for multiple layers of meaning, e.g. through figurative language

6: 2: T4: to investigate humorous verse: how poets play with meanings

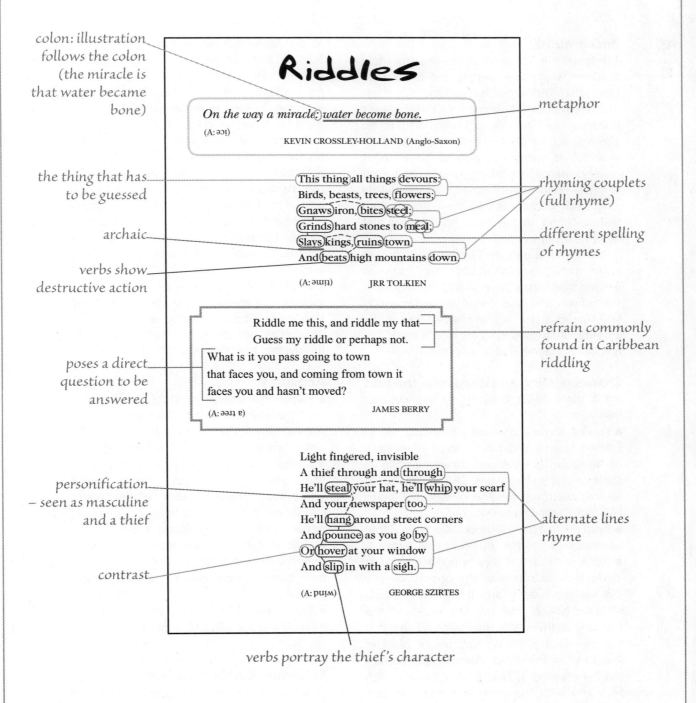

colon: illustration follows the colon (the miracle is that water became bone)

Riddles

On the way a miracle: water become bone.

(A: ice)

KEVIN CROSSLEY-HOLLAND (Anglo-Saxon)

metaphor

the thing that has to be guessed

This thing all things devours:
Birds, beasts, trees, flowers;
Gnaws iron, bites steel;
Grinds hard stones to meal;
Slays kings, ruins town
And beats high mountains down

(A: time)   JRR TOLKIEN

rhyming couplets (full rhyme)

different spelling of rhymes

archaic

verbs show destructive action

Riddle me this, and riddle my that—
Guess my riddle or perhaps not.
What is it you pass going to town
that faces you, and coming from town it
faces you and hasn't moved?

(a tree :A)   JAMES BERRY

refrain commonly found in Caribbean riddling

poses a direct question to be answered

personification – seen as masculine and a thief

Light fingered, invisible
A thief through and through
He'll steal your hat, he'll whip your scarf
And your newspaper too.
He'll hang around street corners
And pounce as you go by
Or hover at your window
And slip in with a sigh.

(A: wind)   GEORGE SZIRTES

alternate lines rhyme

contrast

verbs portray the thief's character

Limericks

by Edward Lear, PL Mannock and WS Gilbert

P

134

Background

The limerick is a humorous five-line story told in verse which was popularised by Edward Lear (1912–88) with the publication of his illustrated *Book of Nonsense* (1846). Lear's unhappy childhood is well documented; he was subject to bouts of depression and ill-health, and was particularly sensitive about his appearance, describing himself as having 'a most elephantine nose' and 'singularly long' neck. Characters with these exaggerated features occur frequently in his limericks and other humorous verse.

The name apparently derives from an old party game; guests would take turns to extemporise nonsense verse and conclude with the refrain 'Will you come up to Limerick?' The limerick has a regular rhyme scheme and patterns of stressed syllables (see below). The humour is exaggerated and absurd.

Shared reading and discussing the text

● Ask the children to share any limericks that they know.

● Provide some contextual information about Edward Lear. If you have a copy of *A Book of Nonsense* (Routledge), show the children some of Lear's illustrations. Or use web-based sources which you can find by typing *"Edward Lear"* into a search engine.

● Read the first three limericks. Ask the children whether they find the limericks funny. Why?

● Ask the children if they notice any patterns in the look or sound of the poems. Identify the five-line pattern and the rhyming aabba scheme. Notice that the last word of the first and fifth lines is the same in the first two examples – this is characteristic of older limericks. In the third example the pattern has been varied so that the second and fifth lines end with the same word. Explain that sometimes Lear would invent a nonsense word if he couldn't find a good rhyming word. Most of Lear's limericks were about a person from a specific place – *There was a young lady from Ryde, There was an old man from Calcutta* and

so on. Many subsequent writers of limericks followed this tradition.

● The children will implicitly recognise the rhythm pattern of the limerick. Use percussion instruments, such as wood blocks, to tap out the rhythm, so that in lines 1, 2 and 5 they can experience the stress falling on the second, fifth and eighth syllables. In limericks the stress occurs on the last syllable of each line; this is called a masculine ending.

● Read the fourth example. Additional humour is supplied by the alliteration here. Mannock has combined two forms – the tongue-twister and the limerick – to produce this humorous verse.

● Read the fifth limerick – the humour in this example is dependent upon already knowing how a limerick is constructed as it subverts the rhyming conventions of the form. Discuss with the children how this works.

Activities

● Prepare some cloze passages from limericks with the rhyming words deleted. Show the children how to use a rhyming dictionary to find appropriate words to fill in the gaps.

● Create some rhyming maps for places, names and common objects (for example, *horse, sauce, source, course, coarse, gorse, Morse*). Encourage the children to use a rhyming dictionary to extend the rhyme maps.

● Children can write and illustrate their own limericks incorporating the features identified from reading. (Avoid using names of children in the class.)

● See if the children can write a tongue-twisting limerick using Mannock's limerick as a model.

Extension/further reading

Books for further reading include *The Complete Nonsense of Edward Lear* (Faber & Faber), *Loopy Limericks* edited by John Foster (Collins), *The Wordsworth Book of Limericks* edited by Linda Marsh (Wordsworth Editions) and Rosalind Fergusson's *The Penguin Rhyming Dictionary*.

6: 2: T3: to recognise how poets manipulate words for their quality of sound, e.g. rhythm, rhyme

6: 2: T4: to investigate humorous verse: where the appeal lies.

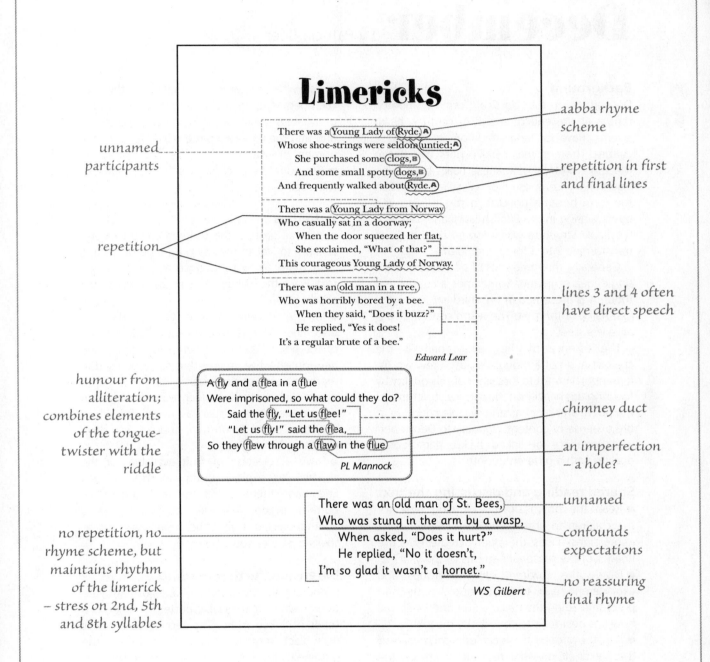

Limericks

aabba rhyme scheme

unnamed participants

There was a Young Lady of Ryde, **A**
Whose shoe-strings were seldom untied; **A**
She purchased some clogs, **B**
And some small spotty dogs, **B**
And frequently walked about Ryde. **A**

repetition in first and final lines

repetition

There was a Young Lady from Norway
Who casually sat in a doorway;
When the door squeezed her flat,
She exclaimed, "What of that?"
This courageous Young Lady of Norway.

There was an old man in a tree,
Who was horribly bored by a bee.
When they said, "Does it buzz?"
He replied, "Yes it does!
It's a regular brute of a bee."

Edward Lear

lines 3 and 4 often have direct speech

humour from alliteration; combines elements of the tongue-twister with the riddle

A fly and a flea in a flue
Were imprisoned, so what could they do?
Said the fly, "Let us flee!"
"Let us fly!" said the flea,
So they flew through a flaw in the flue

PL Mannock

chimney duct

an imperfection – a hole?

no repetition, no rhyme scheme, but maintains rhythm of the limerick – stress on 2nd, 5th and 8th syllables

There was an old man of St. Bees,
Who was stung in the arm by a wasp,
When asked, "Does it hurt?"
He replied, "No it doesn't,
I'm so glad it wasn't a hornet."

WS Gilbert

unnamed

confounds expectations

no reassuring final rhyme

6: 2: T9: to increase familiarity with significant poets and writers of the past

January to December
by Patricia Beer

Background

Derived from the classical form of poetry, renga, at the end of the 17th century, haiku poems have a long tradition in Japanese culture. The first major haiku poet was Basho Matsuo (1644–94). Japanese haiku have been traditionally composed of 17 syllables; when the form became popular in the 1950s, with poets writing in the English language, the 5, 7, 5 syllable structure was adopted by them and transformed into a three-line poem.

Generally, the three lines of a haiku express a single idea or image. Sometimes a contrasting thought is presented in the third line, as in the first haiku of this text: *The warm cows... Dead-alive like steel.*

The essence of the haiku poem is the crystallisation of a thought in just a few words. It is important not to lose sight of this quality by focusing too heavily on the surface structures of the poem and emphasising syllable counting at the expense of content. 'January to December' is a sequence of linked haiku, each poem dealing with a different month.

Shared reading and discussing the text

● Read the poem slowly, allowing time for the children to absorb the ideas. Discuss first impressions. Does the poem create effective images of the seasonal patterns of the year?
● Divide the children into 12 groups and allocate one haiku to each group. Ask them to practise reading the haiku aloud and to decide how it is best read to convey the meaning.
● Ask the groups to select one child to read the haiku. (It is easier to concentrate on the meaning if the children are not trying to read in unison.) If more children want to participate, the text can be read a third time with different voices. Each time a haiku is read aloud by different voices, new nuances of meaning become apparent.
● Encourage each group to say something about the images, thoughts and feelings generated by their haiku and to talk about any word choices they particularly like.

● Ask what patterns they notice in the way the poem is set out. Tell them that the number of syllables (beats) in each stanza is patterned and that the repeated pattern is 5, 7, 5. Tap the number of syllables.
● Conclude the discussion with a re-reading of the poem.

Activities

● In small groups, the children could interpret January to December using a range of art and craft materials, paying close attention to the text. Place the haiku poems at the centre of the artwork.
● In shared writing, use the 'January to December' theme to write an urban version of the poem. Ask the children to suggest and develop effective images that could be used to represent each of the months.
● Write a class haiku sequence poem based on a particular theme, such as water (for which the focus could be on rain, puddles, ice, dew, clouds and so on).
● Have a selection of fruit available for the children to explore using all their senses. Encourage them to cut the fruit and notice patterns inside. Ask them to write a haiku about a piece of fruit. Other collections such as shells or stones could be used.

Extension/further reading

Encourage the children to read, enjoy and write poems with other syllabic patterns. Renga is a series of linked haiku. The second verse takes its subject from something touched on in the last line of the first verse; the third verse takes its subject from something touched on in the last line of the second verse and so on. Tanka is another Japanese form which has five lines of 31 syllables (5, 7, 5, 7, 7). The cinquain form is five lines of 22 syllables (2, 4, 6, 8, 2).

Relevant further reading on haiku includes the *Haiku Picturebook for Children* by Keisuke Nishimoto and Kozo Shimizu (Shen's Books) and *The British Museum Book of Haiku* by David Cobb.

no life left in the field

haiku:
5 syllables
7 syllables
5 syllables

oxymoron

hard effect of this image

emphasis on the word 'novel' by placing it first

combines image of flowers and snow

word order – greater emphasis on both words by having adjective after noun

mid-line full stop makes a strong statement

evocative sounds of summer

in haiku 3rd line often presents a contrasting image or a shift in perspective

deceptive – time moves on regardless of outward appearances

the onset of autumn and inevitable death

'dog' used here means 'follow persistently', but also creates image of people walking their dogs

pruned and trimmed

January to December

The warm cows have gone
From the fields where grass stands up
Dead-alive like steel.

Unexpected sun
Probes the house as if someone
Had left the lights on.

Novel no longer
Snowdrops melt in the hedge, drain
Away into spring.

The heron shining
Works his way up the bright air
Above the river.

Earth dries. The sow basks
Flat out with her blue-black young,
Ears over their eyes.

The early lambs, still
Fleecy, look bulkier now
Than their shorn mothers.

In this valley full
Of bird song, the gap closes
Behind the cuckoo.

Fields of barley glimpsed
Through trees shine out like golden
Windows in winter.

Though nothing has changed –
The sun is even hotter –
Death is in the air.

Long shadows herald
Or dog every walker
In the cut-back lanes.

A crop of mist grows
Softly in the valley, lolls
Over the strawsacks.

Meadows filmed across
With rain stare up at winter
Hardening in the hills.

Patricia Beer

return to image of hardness encountered at the beginning of the poem

Sonnets

by PB Shelley and William Wordsworth

Poems 1 and 2

Background

A sonnet is a poem consisting of 14 lines of ten syllables. Sonnets are often love poems but the form has also been used for reflective and for comic purposes. The rhyme schemes of sonnets vary; Shakespeare used a particular pattern which is now called the Shakespearean sonnet. The final six lines of a sonnet often provide a contrast in tone and meaning to the first eight lines.

Ozymandias, the Greek name for Ramases II, was pharaoh of Egypt at the time of Moses, according to the book of Exodus. Shelley's (1792–1822) poem, written in 1818, describes a traveller's encounter with a ruined statue of the pharaoh. The last six lines (sestet) include the words of the inscription found on the pedestal of the colossus. Ironically, the intention had been for the statue to subdue and intimidate Ramases' rivals but ultimately it is reduced to dust and fragments.

Wordsworth's (1770–1850) 'Sonnet composed upon Westminster Bridge, 3rd September 1802' also pictures a scene – less exotic, but one that Wordsworth directly experienced. It describes the city early in the morning before the daily bustle begins. In the first eight lines he pictures the scene and in the final six lines he offers his thoughts about what he sees.

Shared reading and discussing the text

● Read Shelley's poem. Clarify unfamiliar vocabulary, then read it a second time. Ask the children to jot down one thought about the poem.

● Ask the children to share their thoughts. Extend discussion about the poem, drawing attention to the contrast between the inscription and the reality – introduce the term *irony* if appropriate. Provide some contextual information about the poem.

● Read Wordsworth's poem. Clarify unfamiliar vocabulary. Highlight old verb forms (*doth*, *glideth*) and tell the children the modern equivalents. Establish that the poem is written in the first-person present tense. Read it a second time and explore the children's initial responses.

● Ask guided questions about the second poem. What time of day is it? From what viewpoint is the scene seen? (From the bridge, where it is possible to see the tops of buildings.)

● To Wordsworth the city is like a living being. What words and phrases does he use to convey this idea? (For example, *This City now doth, like a garment, wear; The very houses seem asleep*. Introduce the term *personification*.

● Ask the children if they can see any similarities between the two poems. They will notice that both poems consist of 14 lines. Introduce the term *sonnet* and give the children some background about the form. Note that neither Wordsworth nor Shelley uses the more traditional rhyme scheme of the Shakespearean sonnet (abab, cdcd, efef, gg).

Activities

● Organise the children into small groups. Ask them to talk about their experiences of special places they have seen or visited, and describe the scene to each other. Encourage them to share some of these experiences with the whole class. Independently the children can write descriptions of their special places. They may choose to write about the place in the early hours of the morning, as Wordsworth did, and then think of a contrasting time to describe it. Or they might think of contrasting times of the year, for example spring and winter.

● Take a trip outside the classroom and ask the children to describe what they see. They should now try personifying the scene. For example, is the sun male or female? Young or old? If it could speak what would it want to say? What would it enjoy? Ask the children to think of their own questions and write down the answers. They should then use their ideas to write a description of the view. On returning to the classroom, these ideas can be used as the basis for shared writing.

6: 2: T6: to read and interpret poems in which meanings are implied or multi-layered; to discuss, interpret challenging poems with others

6: 2: T5: to analyse how messages, moods, feelings and attitudes are conveyed in poetry

person reporting what he has been told – a traveller's tale

broken face

Sonnets

OZYMANDIAS

14 lines, with 10 syllables in each line

can imagine what he was like from the sculpture

Ramases II

irony now that the statue is crumbling and his works are gone

only the desert remains

I met a traveller from an antique land A
Who said: Two vast and trunkless legs of stone B *
Stand in the desert… Near them, on the sand, A
Half sunk, a shattered visage lies, whose frown B *
And wrinkled lip, and sneer of cold command, A
Tell that its sculptor well those passions read C
Which yet survive, stamped on these lifeless things, D
The hand that mocked them, and the heart that fed: C
And on the pedestal these words appear: E *
'My name is Ozymandias, king of kings: D
Look on my works, ye Mighty, and despair!' E *
Nothing beside remains. Round the decay F
Of that colossal wreck, boundless and bare E
The lone and level sands stretch far away. F

PB SHELLEY

rhyme scheme does not conform to Shakespearean sonnet – note use of half-rhyme (*) which is more subtle

quotation on the statue's pedestal

huge (a colossus is a gigantic statue often from antiquity, such as the Colossus of Rhodes)

Sonnet composed upon Westminster Bridge, 3rd September 1802

14 lines, with 10 syllables in each line

word choice shows positive emphasis on appearance

sun is personified (male)

river is personified (male)

invocation of God is in keeping with the majestic picture that has been created

Earth has not anything to show more fair: A
Dull would he be of soul who could pass by B
A sight so touching in its majesty: C *
This City now doth, like a garment, wear A
The beauty of the morning; silent, bare, A
Ships, towers, domes, theatres and temples lie B
Open unto the fields, and to the sky; B
All bright and glittering in the smokeless air. A
Never did sun more beautifully steep C *
In his first splendour, valley, rock or hill; D
Ne'er saw I, never felt, a calm so deep! C
The river glideth at his own sweet will: D
Dear God! The very houses seem asleep; C
And all that mighty heart is lying still! D

WILLIAM WORDSWORTH

rhyme scheme not conventional but more reassuring than Shelley's, especially in the regularly alternating last 6 lines – note use of half-rhyme (*)

personification: the city of London is wearing the morning's beauty

before fires have been lit

awareness that the peaceful scene will soon change when everyone wakes and starts to go about their business

6: 2: T9: to increase familiarity with significant poets and writers of the past

6: 2: T8: to analyse the success of texts and writers in evoking particular responses in the reader, e.g. where suspense is well built

Rules — are they there to be broken?

by Katrina Dunbar

Background

This discussion text opens with a summary of two contrasting attitudes towards rules and laws. It asks lots of questions which can serve to stimulate thinking and oral discussion about the topic. Nevertheless bias can be detected in the discussion; in spite of the provocative title, the writer is clearly in favour of rules and leads the reader towards this conclusion. The factual evidence supplied supports the view that rules are essential for a safe and orderly society.

Shared reading and discussing the text

● Before reading the text, open with a discussion about rules in school. Who makes them? Are they necessary? Why do the children think we have rules? What rules would they choose to change and why? Can they think of any instances when rules should be broken? Encourage them to consider whether laws and rules can be unjust.

● Read the text. Ask whether the writer of the piece thinks rules are a good idea or not. Encourage the children to justify their opinions with evidence from the text.

● Explain that this extract has some of the features of a discussion text. Highlight the two opening opinions linked by the oppositional connective *but*. Ask the children if there are any other connectives that could be used which enable the text to retain its original meaning (for example, *however, nevertheless*).

● Look at how the discussion is organised. Sub-headings are used and each section starts with an orientating opening either in the form of a question or a topic sentence. The text concludes with a question to stimulate further thought and discussion. Factual evidence is provided in a box format to support the conclusion that rules are necessary but this isn't overtly stated in a concluding remark.

● Look at the quotation in the second paragraph and the use of the modal verb *should*. Experiment by replacing it with other modal verbs (for example, *could, might, must*) and discuss the effect that this has.

● List the main features of a discussion text and give examples, using the extract as a model: statement of a contentious issue; two sides of an argument presented; ends with questions or conclusions; uses sub-headings; uses topic sentences to orientate the reader; uses oppositional, additional and logical connectives; uses the simple present tense; includes modal verbs. Construct a prompt sheet to aid the children's writing.

● Evaluate this extract as a discussion text. Summarise the strengths and weaknesses of the argument in favour of rules and the argument in favour of fewer rules.

Activities

● In pairs or small groups, the children could make a list of reasons that support an argument in favour of rules and a list of possible reasons for breaking rules. Encourage them to refer to specific situations to support their ideas.

● With the whole class, construct a survey about rules. Ask the children to draft some questions, working in pairs (for example, *Who should make school rules?*). List the questions on the board and evaluate them (for example, do they require full answers or just a *yes/no* response?). Agree on a final set of questions, then the children can ask a range of people to complete the survey, either in written or oral form. When the evidence has been collected, ask the children to write a discussion text, individually. They could use headings to help plan their writing, such as *Issue: whether rules are there to be broken; Arguments for; Arguments against; My conclusion based on a survey of people's opinions*.

● Invite the children to write an additional paragraph to insert in their discussion text with the sub-heading *The occasions when rules should be broken*. They should write a concluding statement to replace the concluding question.

● Ask the children to compile a bank of useful words that can be used to present an argument – *therefore, whereas, similarly* and so on.

6: 2: T15: to recognise how arguments are constructed to be effective, through, e.g.:
● the expression, sequence and linking of points
● the provision of persuasive examples, illustrations and evidence
● pre-empting or answering potential objections
● appealing to the known views and feelings of the audience

6: 2: T16: to identify the features of balanced written arguments which, e.g.:
● summarise different sides of an argument
● clarify the strengths and weaknesses of different positions
● signal personal opinion clearly

present tense

1st paragraph (orientation): statement of a contentious issue, with 2 sides of an argument presented

idiomatic expression

opening question

sub-headings used for clarity of presentation

contrasting questions used to stimulate thinking and discussion

modal verb

quotation is offered as a position to be discussed

topic sentence to orientate reader

title given in the form of a question

oppositional connective

explanation

this question addresses only one side of the discussion (the alternative question, 'Can you think of a situation where you think fewer rules or laws are needed?' could have been asked)

statistical information adds weight to discussion text, but does not necessarily present impartial view (other information may have been found out in the survey and omitted)

colon used before quotation

source stated for authentication of facts

Rules – are they there to be broken?

The media often describes a new band or fashion as 'breaking all the rules'. This means they think it is exciting, refreshing and rebellious. The word 'rules' suggests boring and restricting regulations, but a healthy society needs some rules and laws so that citizens can live harmoniously together. Citizens over the age of 18 are responsible for voting in the government, whose job it is to create the laws.

Why have any rules at all?
Are rules at home and school just adults' way of bossing children about and stopping them from being individuals? Or can rules be helpful? Do you agree with this young person's opinion, which comes from the National Children's Bureau's *Young Opinions, Great Ideas* survey: "I think that the children should have a say in the rules and it shouldn't just be the parents' point of view of what you should and shouldn't do. I think that children should put down some rules for them as well."

Keeping you safe
Both in school and outside, rules and laws are intended to protect you from yourself and others. Sometimes they are really a warning, for example shops are not allowed to sell cigarettes to anyone under the age of sixteen because they are so bad for your health. There are always big lists of rules at swimming pools, which aim to prevent accidents. Speed restrictions on roads and rules about not driving if you have drunk alcohol are there to save lives and avoid accidents.

If everybody had enough money, and everything they needed to have a good quality of life, do you think we would still need laws? The only thing that seems to stop some people from breaking the rules and committing crimes is a fear of going to prison. Can you think of a situation where you think more rules or laws are needed?

FACTS
● *75% of 12–25 year-olds are afraid of being physically attacked, and boys are more worried about it than girls.*
● *39% of 11–16 year-olds declare disruptive classmates as the most common cause of problems at school.*
2020 Vision *survey by the Industrial Society, 1997*

6: 2: T18: to construct effective arguments:
● developing a point logically and effectively
● supporting and illustrating points persuasively
● anticipating possible objections
● harnessing the known views, interests and feelings of the audience

6: 2: W8: to build a bank of useful terms and phrases for argument, e.g. *similarly… whereas…*

Performing sea creatures

by Chris Mason

Background

This discussion text presents the case for and against marine theme parks and centres. The first paragraph sets up an orientation to the subject, the second paragraph looks at the role of sea life centres and the third and fourth paragraphs describe the facilities of a larger marine theme park; the 'for' and 'against' arguments for these attractions are merged together in the final paragraph. The case study picks up the theme of education and entertainment. It is not, however, clear whether or not the writer of this text supports sea life centres as there is no concluding statement or question. Participants are generalised – *Critics of this kind of park; very popular with schools and young people* – with the exception of the named interviewee in the case study.

Shared reading and discussing the text

● Briefly talk about children's experiences of visiting aquaria or marine parks. Tell them you are going to read a non-fiction text called 'Performing sea creatures'. Write the heading on the board. What do the children predict the passage will say? Read the text and ask them to compare the content with their predictions.

● Ask the children whether they think the writer is in favour of sea life centres and marine parks or not. Encourage them to justify their views by referring to evidence in the text. List their suggestions under the headings *In favour of...* and *Not in favour of...*

● Ask the children why they think a case study has been included. Consider whether a balanced discussion would need more than one case study to illustrate different points of view.

● Look at the organisation and topic of each of the paragraphs. Ask whether there is a concluding statement or question at the end of the text. Tell the children to write a suitable concluding statement for the text, then share and evaluate the statements.

● Highlight the sentence *Critics of this kind of park say that it is cruel to keep large marine animals captive; they need more space than the park can offer.* Explain the use of the semi-colon to link two sentences that are very closely connected. Look at other ways in which this could be written, for example *Critics of this kind of park say that it is cruel to keep large marine animals captive because they need more space than the park can offer.* Discuss any differences in emphasis that emerge.

Activities

● Set up and record a small-group discussion on the subject 'Should zoos be banned?'. The children can nominate a member of the group to be the 'chair'. Explain that the chair's role is to make sure that the discussion remains focused on the question and that everyone has a chance to express a point of view. Let the children play back the recorded discussion and identify important points. These can be written out as quotations and displayed (see the quotation in the case study). Ask the children to evaluate the discussion (*How well did we listen? Did we express our points of view clearly enough?* and so on).

● Give the children a series of statements from the text, on a prepared sheet, and ask them to write a contrasting point of view for each one. For example:

1. It is cruel to keep large marine animals in captivity <u>but</u> you can see animals at close quarters.

2. Standards of care are high at sea world adventure parks <u>but</u>...

3. Animals live in a version of their natural habitat <u>but</u>...

4. Sea life centres are entertaining <u>but</u>...

Children who need more support can be given contrasting statements to match.

● Ask the children to write several 'for' and 'against' statements on the topic of zoos. Provide a writing frame, if needed. For example, *The issue is: do we need zoos in the 21st century?, Arguments for..., Arguments against..., My thoughts on this issue are...* Encourage the children to use their statements in a class discussion.

6: 2: T15: to recognise how arguments are constructed to be effective, through, e.g.:
- the expression, sequence and linking of points
- the provision of persuasive examples, illustrations and evidence
- pre-empting or answering potential objections
- appealing to the known views and feelings of the audience

Performing sea creatures

opening statement

A new trend in animal entertainment is the growth of centres and theme parks devoted to sea life. These twenty-first century aquaria attract the same type of criticism as zoos because they use captive animals, but they defend themselves by pointing out the high standard of care that they provide for their animals.

two contrasting viewpoints joined by connective

figure of speech in single speech marks

Sea life centres in Britain are very popular with schools and young people. The 'walk through' layout takes visitors past and even under glass tanks that allow them to see marine animals in a version of their natural habitat. The centres are primarily for entertainment but they also offer a great deal of information and education. The sea life centres do not keep larger marine animals captive as they feel that this would be cruel.

presents facts

The sea world adventure parks in the USA are much larger. Sea World Florida covers 81 hectares and is home to some of the largest marine mammals including the famous orca (killer whale) Shamu. Sea World focuses on entertainment, offering rides, shows and attractions that star 800 different creatures including whales, walruses, seals, polar bears, sea lions, otters, dolphins and many others.

animals are often given proper names in captivity (all the orcas at Sea World have been called Shamu)

common alternative name in parenthesis

opinion

semi-colon to join two closely related sentences

Critics of this kind of park say that it is cruel to keep large marine animals captive; they need more space than the park can offer. Sea World says that its animals enjoy what they do, they are looked after well by experts and are happy living in the company of others in large tanks. In addition, Sea World is actively involved in education, rescue rehabilitation and captive breeding work.

opinion

chosen adverb has a positive effect

reintroducing animals to the wild

· case study · case study ·

Catharine Mason and her Brownie group visited her local sea life centre in Tynemouth, UK for a sleepover.

"It was great, we slept in the hotel next to the centre and were allowed in to the centre at night. They switched all the lights off except in the tanks – it was beautiful. We learned a lot about fish and they even let us stroke the rays."

· case study · case study ·

an alternative case study could have been presented to ensure balanced discussion

writing in this paragraph is well balanced – difficult to detect writer's viewpoint

quotation (no concluding statement or question given)

case study adds authenticity – persuasive device

6: 2: T16: to identify the features of balanced written arguments which, e.g.:
- summarise different sides of an argument
- clarify the strengths and weaknesses of different positions
- signal personal opinion clearly

Why conservation? by Richard Spilsbury

Background

This extract argues for the developed world taking responsibility for environmental conservation. Persuasive statements are included (for example, *only two of the top ten copper-producing countries use large amounts of copper*) and potential objections are pre-empted (for example, *Although all this may seem far removed from you…*). The points raised are made in a logical sequence, and key questions are used to structure the writing. Bullet points are used for presenting statistical information clearly.

Shared reading and discussing the text

● Show the children the title and ask if anyone knows what conservation means. Do they know of any conservation projects? What do they think this piece of writing will be about?

● Read the passage aloud. Ask the children to summarise what they think is the writer's point of view. Guide them to justify their opinions with evidence from the text.

● Ask whether they find the piece persuasive. Do they agree with the writer? Does anyone have an alternative point of view? If so, what?

● What persuasive techniques does the writer use? (For example, including questions and answers; pre-empting alternative viewpoints; providing statistical information; using emotional appeal.) Draw attention to the writer's attempt to present his text from the point of view of the reader: the second person is used as a direct address, and the can of cola given as an example is intended to make an appeal to a young readership.

● Look at how the bullet points are presented, and the use of a colon to introduce the list.

● Draw attention to the language of discussion. Passive sentence construction is a typical feature of discussion texts. Look at the sentence *The people living near mines are <u>actually exposed to</u> increased pollution…* The use of comparative adjectives is another characteristic feature (for example *<u>higher</u> standard of living than their own…; from the world's <u>poorest</u> countries*).

Activities

● Use role-play to explore the issues. Divide the children into groups of three (mining company representatives, local residents and conservationists). Set up a meeting in which representatives of the mining company are holding a residents' meeting to outline plans for the development of a new mine. Conservationists opposed to the plans are also attending the meeting. In groups the children can prepare arguments prior to the role-play. Support the discussion by chairing the meeting in role.

● Ask pairs of children to re-read the text and write down questions generated from their reading (for example, *Are there other more environmentally friendly ways of generating money in developing countries?*). They can then share and discuss their questions with another pair or with the class. Explain that you would like them to use the questions to initiate library research and note-taking. When the information has been gathered, it can be shared and discussed in a plenary session.

● Prepare the text by cutting it up into meaningful chunks and mixing up the chunks. Ask the children to restructure the text, making notes of the clues used (for example, content, development of the argument, cohesive devices).

● Let the children use this text as a model to write a persuasive discussion. The subjects can be varied and relate to the children's own interests. Children can be in small groups or pairs to discuss their initial ideas and then work independently on the writing. Encourage them to refer to a wide range of secondary resources for factual information to support their discussion pieces.

Extension/further reading

Books related to this theme include Roger Few's *Blue Peter: The Young Person's Guide to Protecting the Planet* (Dorling Kindersley), Gloria Rand's *Fighting for the Forest* (Henry Holt) and Jeannie Baker's *Window* (Red Fox).

6: 2: T15: to recognise how arguments are constructed to be effective, through, e.g.:
● the expression, sequence and linking of points
● the provision of persuasive examples, illustrations and evidence
● pre-empting or answering potential objections
● appealing to the known views and feelings of the audience

6: 2: T16: to identify the features of balanced written arguments which, e.g.:
● summarise different sides of an argument
● clarify the strengths and weaknesses of different positions
● signal personal opinion clearly

opening question to orientate discussion

persuasive discussion: the viewpoint of the writer is evident – conservation is primarily the responsibility of those living in the developed world

preservation, protection, usually of the environment and world's resources

decentres to possible viewpoint of the reader – a persuasive device

Why conservation?

What does conservation have to do with us?

mining – to take out of the earth

supplementary question

It is not always easy to see why we should get involved in conservation. After all, in the UK most people have enough food, computers are everywhere and most homes have a television, washing machine and telephone. What are the links between our standard of living and events in other parts of the world?

operations to extract the metals cause wide-scale damage to their environment. Developing countries cannot afford to put the damage right and very often mining companies extracting the metals think that the environmental damage is not their responsibility. They argue that the economy of the countries concerned benefit from mining activities.

statement made by writer – aligns himself with the developing countries

answers the question above

opinion of mining companies

physical surroundings

Our standard of living depends on using resources taken from the environment. The resources may not be from our immediate environment – indeed many of the goods we need and want are made from metals that come from the world's poorest countries. For example:

In fact, the money a country earns from sending its resources to other countries to be turned into manufactured goods is rarely enough to improve the living standards of its people. The people living near mines are actually exposed to increased pollution which can lead to health problems such as lead poisoning and respiratory diseases. In addition, turning resources into goods uses up valuable fuel energy.

reasons why developing communities do not benefit

colon before bulleted list

superlative

statistics provide impression of authenticity

● only two of the top ten copper-producing countries use large amounts of copper, the rest is exported to other countries
● only four of the top ten lead-producing countries use large amounts of lead
● of the ten top tin-producing countries, five are not leading tin users.

bold for terminology

use of 2nd person makes text personal and dramatic

asks questions on behalf of the reader

So, what do the figures mean? Developing countries that need resources (in this case, metals) for their own development are selling the resources to other countries that already have a far higher standard of living than their own. At the same time, the large-scale mining

Although this may seem far removed from you, the copper wires that carry electricity to your house to power your television could well have come form a developing country. That is just one of many examples. What can you do to make a difference? By recycling your can of cola you are helping reduce the amount of new aluminium that needs to be mined. Can you think of other ways to make a difference? Every small action helps.

question to involve reader in discussion

parenthesis contains additional information

concludes by taking argument back to the reader

concluding question and encouraging statement

example implies a young audience being addressed

6: 2: T18: to construct effective arguments:
● developing a point logically and effectively
● supporting and illustrating points persuasively
● anticipating possible objections
● harnessing the known views, interests and feelings of the audience

Packaging guidelines

Background

This extract is taken from the Parcelforce guidelines for sending parcels through the post. The information is presented in table format for clarity. Connections can be made with the text on rules (see page 64). However, the rules listed here are made only for safety and practical reasons rather than ethical ones.

Shared reading and discussing the text

● Ask whether anyone has ever received a parcel through the post. Did the contents arrive safely or not? If not, what happened? Explain that Parcelforce prepares guidance for customers to try to ensure that parcels arrive safely and that post office workers are protected from hazards.

● Look at the text and ask the children who might need this information and where it might be displayed.

● Why is the guidance set out in table form? Read the list of *dos* and ask the children what they think the reasons are for each of the rules. For example, sealing cartons at the bottom with an 'H' seal will prevent the bottom from falling open. This is to ensure that the item being sent doesn't break but also to protect workers. If a glass item were to fall out of the bottom of a box the splinters of glass could cause injury.

● Read through the *don'ts* and ask the children to consider the reasons for them. For example, *Don't send consignments without the full address...* is to make sure that items don't go missing. Explain that these instructions are written in the imperative.

● Have a look at the table of recommended carton grades. Check that the children are familiar with the abbreviations. Point out that *gsm* is explained in a note underneath the table. Explain that clarity is important in public information documents and it cannot be assumed that all readers will know what the abbreviations mean.

● Identify the technical words and investigate their meaning. For example, *polystyrene* – from *poly* (many) and *styrene* – made from oil and coal tar, a plastic substance that is both strong and lightweight; *polyethylene* – from *poly* (many) and *ethylene* – a strong plastic that can be used as a light packing material.

● Read the last paragraph and check that the meaning has been understood (for example, *compensation*). Explain the legal implications and the reasons for companies having to explain liability.

● Evaluate the clarity of the information. Is the guidance easy to use? Is the information easily understood? Could the information be presented in more effective ways? Consider whether different groups of people (for example, the visually impaired) might need the information presenting in different formats.

Activities

● Ask the children to write a set of guidelines for safe play in the playground. They should set out a list of dos and don'ts in table form. They can then test and evaluate the instructions by asking different users (for example, children of different ages, playground supervisors, teachers, the headteacher) for their opinions on the appropriateness of the information and clarity of the presentation.

● In shared writing discuss how you would write a letter asking for compensation for damaged parcel contents. Construct the letter providing details of how the parcel was packaged and addressed. Also state that the packaging has been retained as proof that the parcel was appropriately packaged.

● After checking any unfamiliar vocabulary in a dictionary, the children could add the words and definitions to their personal word books.

● Can the children pack and label a parcel appropriately with the name of the addressee and a return address?

● Ask the children to make a list of other known vocabulary for man-made materials, for example *nylon, polyester, Gortex*, and find out what these terms mean.

● Compile and display a class list of abbreviations used for different measurements.

6: 2: T17: to read and understand examples of official language and its characteristic features, e.g. through discussing consumer information, legal documents, layouts, use of footnotes, instructions, parentheses, headings, appendices and asterisks

informal, non-threatening headings

anything forbidden or limited

technical vocabulary (strong but light packing materials)

very specific information

information tabulated for easy reading

explicit

abbreviation

Packaging guidelines

PARCEL—FORCE WORLDWIDE

Dos	Don'ts
Do check on any prohibitions or restrictions on goods.	Don't send dangerous or prohibited goods as you may be liable to prosecution.
Do use a strong outer container such as a corrugated fibreboard carton with a good quality kraft outer liner.	Don't use substandard or damaged cartons.
Do put protective wrapping around each individual item.	Don't allow movement of contents.
Do use expanded polystyrene chips, polyethylene foam, bubble plastic or shredded paper to cushion fragile items.	Don't allow fragile items inside parcel to touch each other.
Do seal cartons top and bottom with an 'H' seal using 38mm or 50mm wide plastic or reinforced carton sealing tape.	Don't use domestic adhesive tape.
Do strap (with non metallic strapping if possible) and tape large or heavy items, use an outer carton strong enough to withstand fully tensioned strapping.	Don't use string around boxes (it can be used around other wrapping).
Do include the sender's address on the outer carton/wrapper, as well as inside the parcel.	Don't send consignments without the full address, the postcode or zip code, or telephone number of the addressee.

Suggested content and carton grades

It is important that the outer packaging is of sufficient grade in relation to the weight of the contents. Please see table:

Weight of Contents (up to)	Grade of Carton
5kg	200gsm
10kg	300gsm
15kg	150gsm double wall
20kg	200gsm double wall
25kg	200gsm double wall
30kg	300gsm double wall

Please note: gsm (grammes per square metre) is a standard measure for the weight of paper.

Suitable cushioning material, of which a minimum thickness of 50mm is recommended, should be used for inner packaging to protect contents from damage.

Claims for compensation in the event of damage will be refused if the contents are inadequately packaged and may be refused if the packaging is not retained. For further information and guidance about packaging, please phone the Parcelforce Worldwide Enquiry Centre free on **08708 50 11 50**.

vocabulary indicates legal responsibility

easily broken

American for 'postcode'

abbreviation for 'millimetres'

legal claim for money to make up for (or partially make up for) goods that have been damaged

kept

capital letters denote company name

contact number for enquiries

6: 2: W5: to extend work on word origins and derivations from previous term. Use personal reading, a range of dictionaries and previous knowledge to investigate words with common prefixes, suffixes, word roots

6: 2: S2: to understand features of formal official language through, e.g.:
● collecting and analysing examples, discussing when and why they are used
● noting the conventions of the language, e.g. use of the impersonal voice, imperative verbs, formal vocabulary
● collecting typical words and expressions, e.g. *'those wishing to...' 'hereby...' 'forms may be obtained...'*

Living well with allergies

P

141

Background

This is an extract from a leaflet provided by a high street chemist chain for public information purposes. It gives information on recognising an allergic reaction, the causes of allergies and a contact address if further information is needed. Leaflets such as this one provide information in an easily digestible format and make it accessible to the public. It is a form of explanation text and also uses some persuasive devices: by implication, in answering the question *Why are so many people suffering from allergies today?* it urges the reader to adopt a lifestyle that avoids the points listed.

Shared reading and discussing the text

● Before reading the text, make a display of a variety of public information documents (from doctors' surgeries or libraries, for example) and discuss with the children the range of topics covered by them. You could encourage the children to collect their own leaflets to add to the display.

● Read this leaflet and ask the children who they think the intended audience is. Establish that the leaflet is aimed at the allergy sufferer or perhaps the parent or carer of a child who has an allergy; note that the second person is used to address the reader directly (as *you*). Ask why an address is given. Explain that this is in case the reader wishes to obtain further information on how to deal with allergies.

● Look at the structure of the leaflet. There is a logical progression of questions and statements: 1. an opening statement about who suffers from allergies; 2. an explanation of what an allergy is; 3. an explanation of the causes; 4. an explanation for the increase in the number of sufferers. Consider why sub-headings are used and why in this extract they are written in the form of questions. (This can be related to work on explanation texts, see pages 94 and 96).

● Look at other aspects of layout including the use of bullet points. Point out the use of the colon before a bulleted list.

● Consider whether the information is fact, opinion or fiction. Look at the use of the modal verb *may* in the last section (*Modern lifestyles may have an effect on our immune systems*). What does its use indicate? Consider the purpose served by the inclusion of statistical information: it authenticates the information.

● Pick out other language features, including the use of the present tense (in common with other explanation texts) and the inclusion of causal connectives, demonstrating cause and effect (*They tend to run in the family so if one of your parents…*). List other causal connectives that could be used (for example, *because, as a result, therefore*).

Activities

● Ask the children to design a public information leaflet about an aspect of health (for example, healthy eating, looking after your teeth, sun safety). Encourage them to think about who the audience for the leaflet is (children, parents, school staff?), and where their leaflet would be distributed (perhaps at the doctor's surgery, the dentist's surgery, the supermarket, playgroup and so on). Let the children use this text as a model, providing information about their chosen health issue (explanation) as well as some suggestions for prevention (persuasion). They should try to include sub-headings and bullet points.

● In pairs, the children could choose a leaflet from the collection on display and evaluate its effectiveness as a public information document. They should consider the clarity of the information, the layout, and the appeal of the design. Encourage them to annotate the leaflet, highlighting positive features in red and negative features in blue.

Extension/further reading

Make a class chart showing the topics covered by public information leaflets, and where and how they are distributed.

Nancy Brigham's *How to do Leaflets, Newsletters and Newspapers* (Writer's Digest Books) provides useful advice.

6: 2: T17: to read and understand examples of official language and its characteristic features, e.g. through discussing consumer information, legal documents, layouts, use of footnotes, instructions, parentheses, headings, appendices and asterisks To understand the importance of purpose and audience in communication and evaluate text in relation to these ideas.

1 in 4, or 25 per cent

conditional connective

addresses audience

terminology in inverted commas and followed by common alternative word ('trigger')

colon to introduce list

items in list separated by semi-colons

causal connectives common in explanation texts

2nd person used in direct address to reader

fact – statistic as a percentage (5 in every 100)

informal tone – use of contractions

colon to introduce bulleted list

abbreviation for 'for example'

layout: bulleted lists used for clarity

questions as sub-headings posed on behalf of reader

opinion signalled by use of modal verb 'may'

statistics included to authenticate information

Living well with allergies

A quarter of the UK population will experience an allergic reaction at some point in their lives. This number is increasing by 5% every year, and children now make up half the total number of sufferers.

While hayfever is probably the most common condition, there are many more, each with a wide range of effective treatments. So, once you've found the best way to manage your allergy, it needn't stop you from leading a full, comfortable and enjoyable life.

What is an allergy?

An allergy or allergic reaction is caused when your body's immune system reacts to a particular 'allergen' or trigger. This trigger gets into your body through your skin or eyes, but you can also eat it or breathe it in.

The most common allergies are: hayfever, with 9 million sufferers; eczema, 6 million; asthma, 5.1 million; and year round hayfever-like symptoms, triggered by dust mites, known as perennial rhinitis. They tend to run in the family so if one of your parents has an allergy you have a one in three chance of being affected too. This rises to a two in three chance if both your parents have allergies.

What causes an allergic reaction?
The most common triggers are pollen, the house dust mite and pets. Others include:
- Bee and wasp stings
- Latex
- Mould spores
- Particular foods, e.g. nuts and shellfish

Why are so many people suffering from allergies today?
Modern lifestyles may have an effect on our immune systems:
- Warm, well-sealed homes encourage common triggers like the house dust mite.
- We now spend on average 90% of our time indoors.
- Most people's diets are high in fat and low in fruit and vegetables.
- Fluctuating levels of air pollution.

Further information and advice
British Allergy Foundation
Deepdene House
30 Bellegrove Road
Welling
Kent DA16 3PY

contact address for further information; conventional layout for postal address

sub-headings in bold text stand out and allow reader to scan text for relevant information

Fire instructions

Background

Instructions as to what should be done in an emergency or fire are to be found in most public places. Children should be made aware of how to locate this information and what to do in the event of an emergency.

Fire instructions are a form of instructional text. They are organised in a logical and stepped sequence; sentences are written in the imperative; they are short and to the point; participants are generic; bullet points are often used for additional clarity.

Shared reading and discussing the text

● In the week before you use this text in shared reading, ask the children to notice safety and emergency instructions in public places (trains, buses, shops). Stress that emergencies are rare but it is important to know what to do should one arise, and taking the correct course of action can save lives. Also encourage them to notice signs for emergency exits.

● Ask the children to brainstorm in pairs a list of the things they would need to include in a set of fire instructions. Discuss their ideas.

● Show the children the text and read it through. Get them to reassess their list – which features did they include? Did they leave out any crucial points? Structuring the activity so that they are working from prior understandings and experience will make the children more active in noticing vital information.

● Ask if they have any questions about the content (for example, why you must not use lifts in the event of a fire). Stress that they should never put themselves at risk to deal with a fire – personal safety always comes first.

● Look at the way the instructions are laid out with numbered headings. Capital letters are used to stress the most important information. In section 1, *If you discover a fire*, the precise words that should be given on the telephone are displayed in quotation marks. Note that it is important to give the instructions clearly and precisely. Bullet points are used for brevity and clarity in section 2.

● Look at the language: verbs are written in the imperative form (*press, pick, say, give, leave, act, do not use* and so on). Discuss why it doesn't say *you can press the nearest fire alarm button* or *you might leave the building*. Look at the adverbs that are used (*immediately, distinctly, quietly*). The manner in which people act during an emergency such as a fire is really important (remind the children that taking note of this can save lives).

● Discuss where the best place to display a notice like this would be (for example, by a door; in stairwells, where it will not be obstructed). Consider what colours should be used and how large the font needs to be.

● Summarise the discussion.

Activities

● In shared writing, construct a checklist of how to write a set of instructions for an emergency.

● Individually or in pairs, the children could write a set of fire instructions for the classroom, using the checklist for support. Encourage them to explore different ways of presenting the instructions. Different coloured paper and text can be used as well as different font styles and sizes. The children can conduct a survey to see which notice is the most effective.

● Cut up the instructions given in section 1, *If you discover a fire*. Ask the children to sequence them in the correct order. In a plenary session, discuss why such instructions must be ordered in a logical sequence.

● Prepare a cloze passage of a different set of safety instructions in which the verbs and adverbs have been deleted. Ask the children to fill in the gaps and then share their ideas in pairs, giving reasons for the choice of words they have inserted.

Extension/further reading

Organise a visit from a local fire safety officer, who could talk to the children about emergency procedures.

Provide the children with other safety notices to read.

6: 2: T17: to read and understand examples of official language and its characteristic features, e.g. through discussing consumer information, legal documents, layouts, use of footnotes, instructions, parentheses, headings, appendices and asterisks

headings numbered for clarity

adverb: manner in which action must be taken

imperative verb for instructions

put out

capitalisation for emphasis

temporal connective

bullet points for clarity

conditional ('If... then...')

heading provides information about following content; introduced with colon

words that must be spoken are given in quotation marks to be repeated verbatim to operator

clearly

imperative verb

adverb

note spelling of homophone 'draft'

FIRE INSTRUCTIONS

1. IF YOU DISCOVER A FIRE:

a. Immediately press the nearest fire alarm button – causing the fire alarm bells to ring.

b. Pick up the nearest telephone and dial 999 – the operator will ask you which service you require. Say:

"Fire Brigade"

Give this telephone number:

01234 56789

Then say distinctly:

FIRE AT NAME OF BUILDING AND STREET.

c. Try to extinguish the fire by using the nearest suitable fire extinguishers but DO NOT take any personal risks.

2. EVACUATION OF THE BUILDING

On the sounding of the alarm leave the building and assemble away from the building leaving all approach roads clear to enable the fire brigade to reach the building.

- Act quietly.
- Use the nearest available exit.
- Do not use lifts or elevators.

3. ADVICE FOR DEALING WITH A FIRE

a. If a person's clothing is on fire, use an overcoat, rug or other similar article and wrap it around the person, who should be laid on the ground to prevent the flames reaching the head.

b. If electrical fittings are involved in a fire, be sure that the current is switched off before touching them or dealing with the fire.

c. Shut the doors and, if possible, the windows of the room in which the fire is discovered. This will prevent draughts and reduce the risks of the fire spreading.

6: 2: S2: to understand features of formal official language through, e.g.:

● collecting and analysing examples, discussing when and why they are used

● noting the conventions of the language, e.g. use of the impersonal voice, imperative verbs, formal vocabulary

An Angel for May

by Melvin Burgess

Extract 1

Background

Melvin Burgess was born in 1954 in Sussex. He achieved critical acclaim with the publication of *Cry of the Wolf* which was shortlisted for the Carnegie Medal. Burgess' hard-hitting books for teenage readers such as *Junk* and *Lady* have attracted controversy as well as accolades and awards.

An Angel For May (1992) is one of Burgess' books for Key Stage 2 readers. In this time-slip story, Tam travels back from the present to the Second World War through a portal in the fireplace of an old derelict farmhouse. Here he befriends May, an orphaned war evacuee, who is being cared for by Sam Nutter, the farm owner. Sam provides a refuge for Tam on his farm. Tam's guide between the two worlds is Rosey, a homeless vagrant, and her dog, Winnie. Tam later realises that Rosey is the adult May. When Tam learns that Sam's farm was destroyed during a bombing raid and that the occupants died in the fire, he returns to the past to take care of May.

In this extract taken from the first chapter of the book, the main character, Tam, is introduced. We learn that he is unhappy at home (his parents are divorcing) and see him take refuge in the derelict farm that is the focal setting for the story. Burgess creates this setting by evoking the senses (sight, touch and sound), and there are references to the past and the future that anticipate the time-travelling element of the narrative. The point of view is Tam's; the reader experiences what he sees, feels and hears.

Shared reading and discussing the text

● Read the extract aloud. To help the children visualise the text, ask them to close their eyes and imagine the scene as if they were watching a film. Then ask them to re-read it independently and to suggest one word that describes the feelings evoked by the text. (List the words on the board.) Look closely at how Melvin Burgess does this. In particular focus on ways in which different sensations contribute to the atmosphere of the piece: what does Tam see, hear and feel?

● What are Tam's feelings at this point in the story? Ask the children to suggest what they think might be the cause of his unhappiness.

● What might happen next in this story? Guide the children to consider the significance of the last two sentences.

Activities

● Ask the children to choose their own setting for a story and describe it. They might like to try one of these: a derelict school, a department store at night, a lighthouse in a storm, an old mine shaft. Atmospheric scenes let the reader experience what it feels like to be in a particular place at a particular time. To create atmosphere, they should imagine the sights, sounds, sensations, smells and even tastes that a character might experience. They could also consider the weather and lighting (for example, bright, dim, dark); the weather is an important indicator of atmosphere in this extract.

● The children could build a sound collage, or soundtrack, to recreate the atmosphere in this scene. Realistic or stylised sounds can be used to convey a sense of place; voices can create different sounds, the children speaking key words and phrases from the passage. If each child suggests a different sound, you (or a child) can take on the role of 'conductor', orchestrating the sounds by giving signals (for loud, soft, intermittent sounds, and so on). Use the sound collage as an introduction to a performance reading of the extract.

● In small groups, the children could make a large collective drawing to illustrate the extract, incorporating chosen words and phrases from the text. Share the images and discuss significant words and phrases.

Extension/further reading

Children may like to read the complete novel *An Angel for May* (Puffin). Other books by Melvin Burgess include *Burning Issy, The Ghost Behind the Wall* and *The Earth Giant* (all Puffin).

6: 3: T1: to describe and evaluate the style of an individual writer

An Angel for May

Extract 1

The wind was beginning to whip up hard, icy drops of rain that stung his face. Tam had run out with no coat and he was frozen already but he wasn't going home, not yet, not now – not ever, the way he felt just then. He'd catch cold first and die out here where the coarse grass began to give way to the heather from the moor above. One day someone would find his skull staring down at the town, just as he had once found a sheep's skull, and they'd wonder who he was and how he got there. Tam felt that he could do anything to hurt his mother.

As he dropped down into the secret valley the wind softened. It was still hard enough. A line of Scots pines that had once been a windbreak flickered and bent in it. Now that the sheep roamed freely over the wrecked homestead they ate the young seedlings that sprouted up and the colony of trees was dying out. The line stood against the open moorland above like shattered posts. Some trees were broken off, some were still in their prime. But there were no saplings. The sheep ate everything.

If you had to be miserable the old farm was a good place to do it. There was no one there to see you except a few untidy sheep and the little brown and grey birds that flicked and chirruped over these low moorland fields.

Tam sat down in a corner of one of the rooms. The noises of the moor – the wind, a curlew calling some way off, a little bird chittering nearby – carried on above his head. It was a strange feeling, sitting in a room with the rain still speckling your skin and the wind in your hair. To one side of him was the tall wall with the chimney in it. People had come for picnics and lit fires there. A circle of stones had been laid out in front of it, and at night, staring at a blaze you could imagine that this was still a home and that behind your back the rooms still stood and people slept and talked and lived. Perhaps they did.

Annotations (left):
- sensation – touch
- incremental repetition
- Tam's thoughts
- description of setting – bleak atmosphere reflects Tam's desolation
- Tam's thoughts
- theme of time – past and present

Annotations (right):
- weather used to reflect Tam's mood
- destruction words
- time theme
- what might Tam's mother have done to make him so angry?
- seeking comfort in the secret valley
- visual image
- the wind's impact on the landscape reflects the way Tam has been affected by his mother's actions
- sounds of the moor
- sensation – sound
- sensation – touch

An Angel for May

by Melvin Burgess

Extract 2

Background

An Angel for May is a time-slip novel (characters travel backwards in time either to right some injustice in the past, to change events and influence the present or to learn something from the experience that allows them to confront problems in their own lives). Through visiting the past, Tam is able to influence the course of events so that the young girl May is cared for, and in so doing he recognises what is important to him in the present day. Here, Tam slips into the past for the first time.

Shared reading and discussing the text

● In *An Angel for May*, Tam travels through the fireplace to go back in time. Discuss any other books the children have read which involve the characters in time travel and the devices the authors use, for example a clock that strikes 13 – in *Tom's Midnight Garden* by Philippa Pearce (HarperCollins); a statue of Father Time – in *Moondial* by Helen Cresswell (OUP).

● Ask the children whether they have seen any films in which the characters travel through time. What conventions might be used to show that a character has gone back into the past? (Wavy lines or a change to black and white, for example.)

● What clues are there in the passage to suggest that Tam is in a different time? (For example, the familiar landscape and seasonal changes.) Compare the third paragraph with the second paragraph in extract 1 (*As he dropped down into the secret valley…*) What are the similarities and differences in the way the setting is described? Where does Tam think he is? What is he feeling? (Frightened, angry.) Find evidence in the text that illustrates Tam's feelings. Discuss the relationship between anger and fear. Relate the discussion back to the previous extract and Tam's feelings.

● Who do the children think Rosey is? How is she described? What does Tam think about Rosey? In this extract he shows no empathy and dismisses her as mad. Is Tam's reaction typical of the way people react to mental illness?

● Focus on the pacing of the first paragraph. In shared writing, write a paragraph, using this one as a model.

● This extract illustrates a complication in the story and poses questions that are not yet answered. Why has the old woman taken Tam back in time? What will happen to him? Will he be able to get back to his own time? When and how? Does he have a task to perform in the old time first?

Activities

● Ask the children to imagine that they are producing the film of *An Angel for May.* How will they translate the time-slip scene from written text to the visual? They should divide a piece of paper into eight, and use it to plan a storyboard of the eight shots they will use. They will need to indicate whether the shots show what Tam sees (if he is in the shot) and where they will use close-ups (head and shoulders), mid-shots (waist upwards or full body) and long shots (landscape). Encourage the children to consider the viewpoint of the shot (looking up, down or straight on) and whether they intend to use any special effects. Notes can be added about music, sound effects or dialogue to be incorporated.

● This passage is written in the third person but is focalised through the eyes of Tam. Ask the children to rewrite it in the first person, then read aloud their rewritten version to a partner. What differences do they notice? Which bits work well in the first person and which bits don't work? Let pairs share their observations with the class. This is a fairly easy passage to transpose into Tam's voice in the first person. Ask the children to rewrite it from Rosey's point of view. Guide them to see that writing from this new viewpoint requires more changes.

● Can the children extend the story by improvising in pairs the possible conversation between Tam and the old woman? They can then write down their improvisation as a scene for a play (see page 24 for the conventions of script writing).

6: 3: T1: to describe and evaluate the style of an individual writer

6: 3: S1: to revise the language conventions and grammatical features of the different types of text such as narrative (e.g. stories and novels)

An Angel for May

Extract 2

It was cold. Something seemed to be sliding over him, or through him. Then he thought he must be falling and his hands flew out to the brick wall to stop his head from bumping, but he twisted and seemed to miss the ground altogether. He cried out.

Then it stopped. He was unexpectedly on his backside on solid ground. He had his hands stretched out and his face pulled back. The wall that had been in front was now behind him. He was in a farmyard. There were chickens pecking and a strong smell of straw and manure. Tam backed into the wall; he was terrified, he felt sick. Everything had gone wrong. He had been moved out of his place – but then he saw that it was the same place. There above him was the old familiar hill, just as it had been a moment before, lying in the same secret stillness. But then he saw it was not the same, not quite. It was purple, but he had seen it like this before.

The heather was out. The leaves were turning. Spring had gone and it was autumn – a blowy autumn day with big fluffy clouds and yellow leaves scutting about the yard. And there were the Scots pines, but now in a dense thicket of shrubs with young saplings around them. Winnie was standing by his side; she barked twice and sat down. She seemed to be smiling. But Tam felt really dizzy – he was all wrong, he shouldn't be here. Had he gone mad?

He noticed Rosey standing by him. He was sure she hadn't been there before. He turned on her.

"Where are we?" he demanded. She said nothing. Her mouth was working and she was nodding her head. She had that faint smile again. For a second Tam thought she was laughing at him.

"What have you done to me?" he shouted.

The old woman looked blankly past him.

"You… What have you done?" demanded Tam in a frightened rage. He would have jumped at her and screamed, but the dog was near and watching him closely.

This was her place. He *had* gone mad – just like the old woman. She had taken him to a place where mad people go.

Annotations:

short simple sentence

pace given by variation of sentence length in 1st paragraph; symmetry in opening and closing with a very short sentence – this builds tension

contrasts with extract 1

strong speech verb

Rosey's stereotypical movements

Tam's mixed emotions (fear and anger) revealed in the vocabulary choice

longer 2nd sentence

compound sentence

paragraph ends with a short sentence

punctuation of this sentence connects together short phrases to add pace and create a staccato effect (which mirrors Tam's feelings)

recognises familiar landscape

visual clue given before explanation to give reader a chance to work out what has happened

indirect thought

italic for emphasis

Tam's view of Rosey

The Ghost Behind the Wall

by Melvin Burgess

Extracts 1 and 2

Background

The Ghost Behind the Wall is about a young boy, David, who lives with his father and is left on his own for large amounts of time. To amuse himself he sneaks about in the ventilation shafts of a block of flats and discovers that he can use the network to get into other people's homes. During one of his visits David enters the flat of Mr Alveston, an old man suffering from dementia.

There is not a clear distinction between good and bad characters in this story. In the beginning David is an unlikeable boy but he eventually becomes a good friend to old Mr Alveston. In an interview with *Achuka*, Melvin Burgess explains about his characters: 'I get a great deal of pleasure hunting out the good in the bad and the bad in the good. So, often they're not what they seem, and there's a drama in that sort of story which seems to me to be at the heart of all the best fiction.'

The extracts here reveal two key moments: the first, when David discovers that he can enter the ventilation system; and the second, his discovery of Mr Alveston in his flat.

Shared reading and discussing the text

● Provide some contextual information about *The Ghost Behind the Wall*. Read extract 1. Ask the children what they think is happening in this passage and what might happen next.
● What sort of atmosphere does the first extract have? Guide the children to notice the emphasis on darkness and horror (*It was dark in there, pitch black; to his horror; gazing into the dark heart of Mahogany Villas*). Consider how tension is built up through the depiction of David's reluctance to go into the ventilation shaft but the inner compulsion driving him to it.
● Cover the last paragraph of extract 2 and read the text aloud to *…and peered in*. Consider how Melvin Burgess builds up the suspense: David's thoughts (*Maybe it was being decorated*); in particular, look at the variation of short and long sentences in the paragraph beginning *He tried to be quiet…*;

note the movement verbs (for example, *poked, froze*), adverbs (for example, *cautiously*), nouns (*scufflings*) and the simile (*slid like a snake*); also look at the contrast between silence and noise (*banged hard on the metal*).
● Encourage the children to discuss what they think will happen next. Using clues from the passage, write the next paragraph together (or the children could do this in pairs). Now reveal the last paragraph and read it. Are the children surprised when the old man looks at David and says *'Jonathon!'*?
● Discuss what kinds of things help to build atmosphere in ghost stories. Guide children to reflect on the differences between developing suspense (leading us to expect that something will happen) and surprise (when something happens unexpectedly). These techniques are also used in films.

Activities

● Ask the children to work in pairs to annotate the passage in preparation for reading it aloud. Guide them to consider the volume, pace and pauses. Encourage them to experiment with different ways of reading. When they have a version that they are pleased with, they can record it. Share recordings with the class and talk about the choices made in deciding how to read the passage.
● Suggest that the children make a collection of words and phrases that can be used in suspense stories and keep them in their personal word books (for example, *she froze; an unearthly cry shattered the silence*).
● Using some of the techniques discussed, the children could write a suspense paragraph for a story. They can build the tension by incorporating a variety of short and long sentences. Different types of sentence can be used to achieve different effects: simple sentences to add drama; complex sentences to add detail; questions to heighten suspense; and exclamations for emphasis. The paragraph could end with a cliffhanger that makes the reader want to know what will happen next.

6: 3: T1: to describe and evaluate the style of an individual writer

6: 3: S1: to revise the language conventions and grammatical features of the different types of text such as narrative (e.g. stories and novels)

THE **GHOST BEHIND** THE **WALL**

Extract 1

He pushed the sofa up against the wall and climbed up to have a look. It was dark in there, pitch black, and he knew at once that it was big enough for him to get inside if he wanted to. Of course, he didn't want to. Why should anyone want to go creeping about like a rat in the intestines of the old building? But he was glad that grid was screwed to the wall so tightly, that was for sure, because that meant he couldn't get in even if he did want to. Then, to his horror, David saw that the grid wasn't screwed on at all. It was only the metal frame that held the grid that was screwed on. The grid itself was slid sideways into the frame.

David pushed the grid; it slid sideways with a sudden jerk and there he was, gazing into the dark heart of Mahogany Villas. His heart twisted and sank. He knew he was going to have to go in there.

Extract 2

After a little while, when there was no noise, he poked his head cautiously round to have another look.

Inside the flat it was dull. Maybe it was being decorated. He remembered how his dad had taken the grid off once when he was decorating. He waited a long time but heard nothing – no voices, no radio or television – so he plucked up his courage and slid like a snake down towards the opening to try and see inside.

He tried to be quiet, but some scufflings had to happen. At one point he forgot himself and banged hard on the metal. He froze – but there was still no noise. It must be that no one was in. He got to the lip of the vent, waited just to be sure there was no noise, then pulled himself forward on his stomach and peered in.

Right down below him was an old man sitting in an armchair. As David stared, the old man opened his eyes and looked up. David yelped. For one horrible moment they stared straight into each other's faces, and then the old man opened his mouth and said,

"Jonathon!"

Annotations (left):
- creates atmosphere
- his reaction reveals his feelings – the battle inside him between not wanting to do something but knowing that he has to do it
- adverb
- noise contrasts with silence in previous paragraph
- like a scene from a horror movie
- unexpected – why does he call David 'Jonathon'? raises questions

Annotations (right):
- David's thoughts
- simile
- 3rd person narration focalised through David's eyes
- dark wood
- effective simile to evoke image
- abrupt change after movement
- images created by movement verbs

The Ghost Behind the Wall
by Melvin Burgess

Extract 3

Background

Each time David enters the ventilation shaft to visit Mr Alveston's flat he hears strange noises which appear to grow stronger on each occasion, as though he has disturbed something that should have been left undisturbed. In this extract he discovers a ghost boy, Jonathon, crying. Later in the story it emerges that Jonathon is the boy that Mr Alveston once was. Melvin Burgess says: 'What is a ghost? The idea of it being a memory really struck me the first time I heard it years ago, and the idea of losing a part of yourself in old age… struck me very powerfully… I hope it will help readers understand something about the frailties of old age… I hope the portrayal of Mr Alveston is sympathetic, and that it penetrates; but probably, the imagery of the ghost is the most important part of the book in getting these things across.'

The character of the ghost is introduced primarily through the use of dialogue.

Shared reading and discussing the text

● Read the passage aloud. Ask the children whether they think the ghost is friendly or not and to justify their opinions by referring to the text. They may think he is friendly because he is just a boy, speaks softly, and says to David *'Come in here with me'* as though he is looking for someone to play with. On the other hand they may think he is unfriendly because he swears and hisses, and *'Come in here with me'* might be interpreted as threatening rather than playful. Allow for a variety of responses.

● Much of what we learn about the ghost in this short extract is gleaned from the dialogue. Use a highlighter pen to pick out the dialogue. Ask the children what we find out about the ghost from what he says and the way in which he says it (for example, that he is lost, that he is upset, that he is a bit prickly about being asked questions, that he is playful).

● What questions would the children like to ask about the ghost? Write the questions on the board. Review them and consider which questions are likely to be answered within the course of the story.

● From whose point of view are the events in this passage seen? Although written in the third person, the scene is focalised through David.

● Talk about David's emotions in the extract – the combination of fear and curiosity. Notice how he asks the ghost lots of questions.

● Talk about other ghost stories that the children may have read. Discuss the functions that different ghosts have in stories (for example, in *A Christmas Carol* the ghosts of Christmas Past, Present and Future show Scrooge the error of his ways; the ghosts in Helen Cresswell's *Moondial* reveal injustices of the past). In *An Angel for May* and *The Ghost Behind the Wall* the protagonists encounter children from the past who are 'ghosts' of old people living in the present. Through meeting them as children they are able to make the lives of the old people better as well as make positive changes in their own lives.

Activities

● Using the three extracts from *The Ghost Behind the Wall* as a starting point, the children could build on the clues and partial information to outline a story that explains how the ghost came to be in the ventilation shaft and the possible connection with Mr Alveston. Revise the conventions of script writing (see 'Romeo and Juliet', page 24) and ask the children to write the story as a play.

● Look at other character introductions with the children in which dialogue is important for conveying information. Suggest that they invent a character for a story and write a short character introduction using dialogue. Remind them that it is important that the dialogue does not 'run away'; every line should contribute to the build up of character and plot.

● Can the children rewrite the extract from the ghost's point of view? Why is he crying? Why does he want David to join him in the ventilation shaft?

6: 3: T1: to describe and evaluate the style of an individual writer

6: 3: S1: to revise the language conventions and grammatical features of the different types of text such as narrative (e.g. stories and novels)

THE **GHOST** BEHIND THE **WALL**

Extract 3

temporal cohesive device used in narrative

vocabulary choice emphasises childish qualities of the ghost

untagged direct speech

tagged speech

indirect thought

will David be tempted by the ghost?

That night, David heard crying again. The ghost boy was weeping in a thin, quiet way to itself, as if it didn't know or care if anyone heard it. The sound was clearer and louder than before, as if the ghost was becoming more real every time he went into the pipes. David sat up in bed to listen.

"What's wrong?" whispered David. The ghost didn't answer, but the sobbing became slightly louder. David was sure the boy had heard him.

"Where are you?" David asked again.

The ghost snuffled and a voice from nowhere said, "I'm lost."

"Lost?" David was puzzled. He looked around and tried to work out where the voice was coming from. "Where do you want to go?" he asked.

"I don't know, I'm lost."

"Well, where do you belong, then?"

"Sod that," hissed the ghost. David laughed. A swearing ghost! The ghost laughed back.

"Sod that!" said the voice, and this time David could place it. It was coming from the floor by the side of his bed, and when he turned to look, there was the ghost lying there. He was on his side towards the wall, but he had twisted his head round so that David could see his wide, tear-stained face breaking out into a laugh as he looked up at him. The face got bigger, and at first David thought he was sitting up, but it wasn't that. His face was simply getting bigger, wider, closer. Maybe it was just the ghost's way of getting closer to him, but it made David cry out in fright. Then the laugh faded, and the figure faded with it, and all David could make out was a paleness in the place where the ghost had sat.

"I'm here now," said the voice softly, and David almost jumped out of bed in fright, because suddenly the voice wasn't coming from the floor by his bed, but from behind the grid leading to the pipes. There was a pause and then the voice said clearly, "Come in here with me."

clues given to tell us what the ghost is like

shows David's emotions (curiosity and fear)

scene focused through David's eyes

clue to the ghost's character – contrasts with 'Sod that' earlier

Mum Dad and Me

by James Berry

Background

James Berry was born in Jamaica and brought up in a small seaside village. When he was 17 he went to work in America but did not like the way black people were treated there, so he returned to Jamaica. He moved to Britain in 1948. In an interview he said: 'I knew I was right for London and London was right for me. London had books and accessible libraries.' In his poems, Berry uses a mixture of standard English and Caribbean Nation language (Creole or Patwa). His collections for children, *When I Dance* (1988), for which he won the Signal Poetry Award, and *Playing a Dazzler* (1996), reflect children's experiences of growing up in Britain and in the Caribbean. He was awarded the OBE in 1990 for services to poetry. This poem and the following two represent in different ways the contrasts between life in Jamaica and England. The tone varies from the reflective comparison of London and Jamaica to the playful celebration of Jamaican independence.

The patterned text of 'Mum Dad and Me' compares life in the Caribbean with life in London. Each stanza contrasts life in two places but also tells us something about the way individuals are shaped by culture. There are shifts from past to present tense. The rhythms of natural speech are used and create the impression that the poet is talking directly to the reader.

Shared reading and discussing the text

● Give the children some contextual information about James Berry. Prior to reading the poem, ask them to close their eyes as you describe a small seaside village in Jamaica. Ask them to imagine what they can hear, see, feel, smell. Do the same for London.

● Read 'Mum Dad and Me' and ask the children for their responses. Does the poem tell a story? What do they think the speaker of the poem regrets losing from the old way of life – the life his parents had – and what does he like about his own life in London? Contrast the image of

London in the poem, the present, with the past in Jamaica.

● Ask the children if they notice any patterns in the language (for example, most stanzas create three contrasting images). Point out that there is rhythm but no rhyme, and the stanzas vary in line length and pattern.

● Look at how the punctuation can help us to read the poem aloud. For example, the use of a comma after *TV* (*We save time to eat to TV, never speaking*) helps to increase the emphasis on the last two words. Read the two lines aloud with and without a comma so that the children can hear the difference.

Activities

● Ask the children to re-read the poem in pairs, then create a concept map (spider diagram) for 'Mum Dad and Me'. They should put the title in the middle of the diagram and add notes about the poem near to lines radiating out from the centre. Notes might include thoughts about why they think the poet wrote the poem; the images created; words and phrases that they liked; language patterns, and so on. The children can then work in fours to discuss and compare each other's diagrams.

● Selecting one of the stanzas, the children could draw or paint contrasting images of London and Jamaica, captioning them with lines from the poem.

● Ask the children to talk to their parents to find out about the differences and similarities in their childhoods; even if they still live in the same place things are likely to have changed. What things would they have liked about when their parents were growing up? What things do they like about living today? Can they use the information to write a 'Then and now' poem, using 'Mum Dad and Me' as a model?

Extension/further reading

Suggestions for further reading include James Berry's *A Nest Full of Stars* (Macmillan), *When I Dance*, *Playing a Dazzler* and *The Thief in the Village and Other Stories* (all Puffin).

6: 3: T3: to describe and evaluate the style of an individual poet

6: 3: T4: to comment critically on the overall impact of a poem, showing how language and themes have been developed

poet implies what is good about life in Jamaica and what he dislikes about London

contrast makes the former seem more attractive, but would we want to wash our clothes by hand?

comma is important for emphasising 'never speaking', and line break allows for a visual pause which also gives it greater emphasis

contrast between opening and closing lines (sunshine and darkness)

Mum Dad and Me

My parents grew among palm trees,
in sunshine strong and clear.
I grow in weather that's pale,
misty, watery or plain cold,
around back streets of London.

With her friends Mum's mum washed
clothes on a river stone. Now
washing machine washes our clothes.
We save time to eat to TV,
never speaking.

Dad swam in warm sea, at my age.
I swim in a roofed pool.
Mum – she still doesn't swim.

My dad longed for a freedom in Jamaica.
I want a greater freedom.
Mum prays for us, always.

Mum went to an open village market
at my age. I go to a covered
arcade one with her now.
Dad works most Saturdays.

Mum goes to church
some evenings and Sundays.
I go to the library.
Dad goes for his darts at the local.

At my age Dad played
cricket with friends.
Mum helped her mum, or talked
shouting halfway up a hill.
Now I read or talk on the phone.

Mum walked everywhere, at my age.
Dad rode a donkey.
Now I take a bus
or catch the underground train.

James Berry

past tense (how things used to be)

present tense (the way things are now)

contrast between life in the open air and indoors

images of Jamaica focus on communal element, contrasting with images of London where activities are solitary and distant

nostalgia for Jamaica but narrator aware that his father had a reason to leave

some things are unchanged and reach back to the past

the three participants are not placed in the same order each time – this disjointed effect makes us feel that the poet is talking to us in a casual way

contrast between opening and closing lines (sunshine and darkness)

Sunny Market Song by James Berry

Background

James Berry's 'Sunny Market Song' is set in Jamaica. The items sold in the market are traditional Jamaican foods – ackee, for instance, is the national fruit introduced from West Africa used in preparing the national salt fish dish.

The poem lends itself to performance, especially to the reading of solo lines, having already been set out for different voices. The first voice represents general market voices and these lines could be further divided to include more voices; the second voice is a girl buying spices from the third voice, the stallholder (who could be voiced by the audience). Each section is punctuated by animal noises.

Shared reading and discussing the text

● Before reading the poem, make available some of the fruits and vegetables mentioned in the poem; yams, custard apples and sweet potatoes can be found in most large supermarkets. Label and display the items in the classroom with books and other resources such as travel brochures.

● Ask the children what they already know about Jamaica. Locate the West Indies and Jamaica on a globe or in an atlas. Show the children pictures from travel brochures and other sources.

● Ask pairs of children to read the poem, then tell you what it is about. Can they identify the three people speaking? Have they noticed that animal 'voices' are included as well? Encourage them to discuss any personal experiences of shopping at a street market.

● Look at the layout of the poem and compare it with the layout of a script (see 'Romeo and Juliet', pages 24 and 26). Make notes of similarities and differences.

● Read the poem to the children. Identify any items with which they are unfamiliar. Some, such as the imported spices that are used in cooking (nutmeg, cloves, ginger, allspice, pepper, annatto), are found in Britain; other items are not as available (soursop, cho-cho, callalu).

● Discuss the use of rhymes, half-rhymes, alliteration and the structure of the poem (three speakers and animal noises). Notice that the poem is patterned but the patterns vary, which makes it seem more natural when read aloud.

● Talk about the qualities of a good performance of a poem, for example, conveying the mood of the poem, varying the pace, stress, tone, volume and using pauses appropriately. Explain what each of these terms means and give examples. In the lines *Custard apple/Ripe pineapple/Sweet potatoes*, for example, the reader might want to slow down the reading of *Sw-eeeee-t* or alternatively *pot-aaa-toes*, to sound more like a market seller calling out. Experiment with reading some of the lines in a few different ways, evaluating which ways sound better.

Activities

● Organise the children into small groups in order to prepare a performance for different voices of 'Sunny Market Song'. Ask them to annotate the text to indicate the pitch, pace, tone and volume to be used. They could include a 3-D freeze-frame of the market place (3-D images should be interesting no matter what side they are viewed from; 2-D freeze-frames are intended to be seen from one side only). Share and evaluate the performances in a plenary session.

● Create a class sound collage of the market place. Use voices to create the general market noise and for the calls of the market sellers. Use instruments to imitate the sounds of the animals. Invent and record a notation for the sound collage, so that it can be followed and reproduced like a musical piece. Let the children use the piece as an introduction to a performance of the poem.

● In pairs or small groups, the children could write a poem for different voices set in a busy place (for example, a fairground or playground), using 'Sunny Market Song' as a model.

● Ask the children to make an illustrated glossary of the Jamaican words in the poem.

language patterns work visually and aurally

root of this tropical fruit is a staple food

foods that are for sale are called out

set out like a script

national fruit of Jamaica

large fruit in the fig family

used as a thickening agent in cooking

patterned language (words end in 'a')

plant extract used in fizzy drinks

repetition

repetition

patterned language (initial sounds)

polite way of addressing an older person

Jamaican word for penny-half-penny

stallholder is asking the girl what she is buying

wants to buy spices

oral patterning ('w–ks', 'w–x')

different animal noises to be used in a performance of the poem, as a 'soundscape' of the market

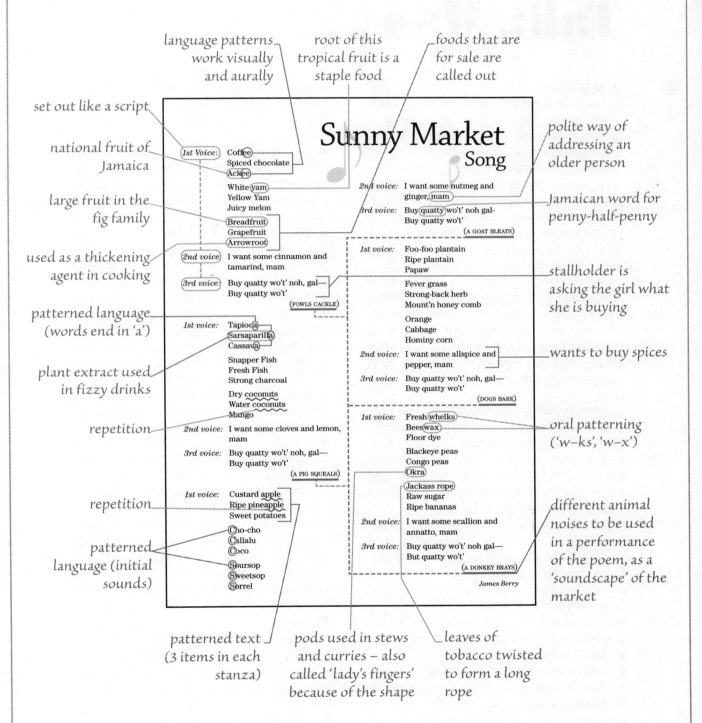

Sunny Market
Song

1st Voice: Coffee
Spiced chocolate
Ackee

White yam
Yellow Yam
Juicy melon

Breadfruit
Grapefruit
Arrowroot

2nd voice: I want some cinnamon and tamarind, mam

3rd voice: Buy quatty wo't' noh, gal—
Buy quatty wo't'
(FOWLS CACKLE)

1st voice: Tapioca
Sarsaparilla
Cassava

Snapper Fish
Fresh Fish
Strong charcoal

Dry coconuts
Water coconuts
Mango

2nd voice: I want some cloves and lemon, mam

3rd voice: Buy quatty wo't' noh, gal—
Buy quatty wo't'
(A PIG SQUEALS)

1st voice: Custard apple
Ripe pineapple
Sweet potatoes

Cho-cho
Callalu
Coco

Soursop
Sweetsop
Sorrel

2nd voice: I want some nutmeg and ginger, mam

3rd voice: Buy quatty wo't' noh gal-
Buy quatty wo't'
(A GOAT BLEATS)

1st voice: Foo-foo plantain
Ripe plantain
Papaw

Fever grass
Strong-back herb
Mount'n honey comb

Orange
Cabbage
Hominy corn

2nd voice: I want some allspice and pepper, mam

3rd voice: Buy quatty wo't' noh, gal—
Buy quatty wo't'
(DOGS BARK)

1st voice: Fresh whelks
Beeswax
Floor dye

Blackeye peas
Congo peas
Okra

Jackass rope
Raw sugar
Ripe bananas

2nd voice: I want some scallion and annatto, mam

3rd voice: Buy quatty wo't' noh gal—
But quatty wo't'
(A DONKEY BRAYS)

James Berry

patterned text (3 items in each stanza)

pods used in stews and curries – also called 'lady's fingers' because of the shape

leaves of tobacco twisted to form a long rope

Mek Drum Talk, Man

by James Berry

Background

Jamaica achieved independence from Britain on 6 August 1962. It was an occasion of great celebration; music, dancing, singing and fireworks filled the streets of Kingston, the island's capital. At midnight the lights were turned off and representatives of Britain, the Jamaican officials and 20000 Jamaicans witnessed the birth of a new nation as the Union flag was lowered for the last time. Then lights were turned on and the new black, green and gold flag of Jamaica was raised.

'Mek Drum Talk, Man' is a celebration of independence. The onomatopoeic pulsating rhythms and sounds of the hand drums require an introduction with maximum aural impact, relishing sound and rhythm. Berry also uses the natural rhythms of speech in his call for all to join him in the celebration.

Shared reading and discussing the text

● Before reading the poem do some work on rhythms. Clap the rhythm of a child's name. After listening to the rhythm, can the children work out whose name it is? Let them tap their own name rhythms, to see if they can find a 'name rhythm twin' in the class.

● Using a variety of drums, tap some rhythms. The children can then answer with the same rhythm, either by tapping drums or desks. Make up some words which imitate the sounds. Invent different onomatopoeic words for different types of drum.

● Provide a brief historical context and tell the children the title and sub-title of the poem you are going to read.

● Read the poem aloud and ask the children for their first impressions. Check any unfamiliar vocabulary. Explain that James Berry uses a combination of standard English and Jamaican Creole (Patwa) in his poems. Identify the Creole words (for example, *yu* = 'you'; *galang* = 'go on'). Encourage the children to work out the meanings. Give definitions where necessary.

● Look at the personification of the drum. Berry describes the drum as though it has been sleeping and needs waking up (*Wake skin up*). Make the connection with Jamaica, the country that is being woken up now that it has achieved independence.

● 'Mek Drum Talk, Man' is a political poem; refer to the poem's sub-title. Discuss the thoughts and feelings of the speaker of the poem. What reasons might he or she have for wanting to celebrate?

● Ask the children how they would describe the tone and mood of the poem. Draw out the playful qualities, including the humour, for example *Mek drum sey to be hit is fun*.

● Show the children the text with some annotations for a performance reading. A contrast between the first part of each stanza (call for celebration) and the second part (imitation of the drums) and the emphasis on the alliteration should be marked. The annotated text provides information about how these lines might be read but you may want to explore other ideas.

● Read the poem again, then encourage the children to evaluate your reading. Was the feeling of the poem conveyed? What improvements can they suggest? Mark the children's ideas on the text.

● Re-read the two previous poems by James Berry (see pages 84 and 86) and, together with this poem, discuss the similarities and differences, focusing on style, subject, values expressed, and appeal to the reader.

Activities

● Divide the class into eight groups, one group for each stanza. Ask each group to prepare a polished reading of their section of the poem, annotating the text as appropriate. Share and evaluate the performances.

● The children could write their own celebration poems. They can incorporate drum rhythms or alternatively invent new onomatopoeic words to imitate the sounds of other instruments.

● Ask the children to prepare a mini-dictionary of the Creole words used in the poem, then to investigate other Creole words.

6: 3: T3: to describe and evaluate the style of an individual poet

6: 3: T4: to comment critically on the overall impact of a poem, showing how language and themes have been developed

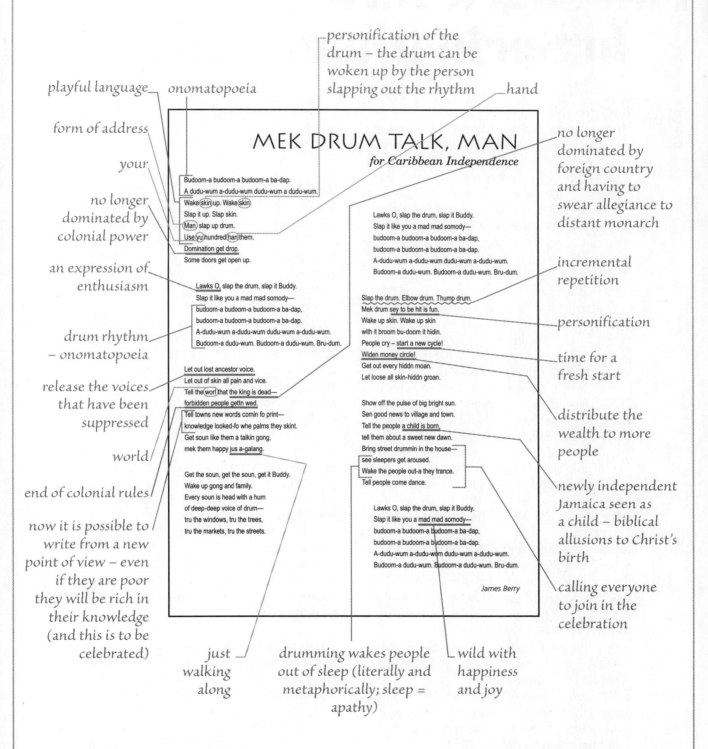

personification of the drum – the drum can be woken up by the person slapping out the rhythm

hand

playful language   onomatopoeia

form of address

your

no longer dominated by colonial power

an expression of enthusiasm

drum rhythm – onomatopoeia

release the voices that have been suppressed

world

end of colonial rules

now it is possible to write from a new point of view – even if they are poor they will be rich in their knowledge (and this is to be celebrated)

no longer dominated by foreign country and having to swear allegiance to distant monarch

incremental repetition

personification

time for a fresh start

distribute the wealth to more people

newly independent Jamaica seen as a child – biblical allusions to Christ's birth

calling everyone to join in the celebration

just walking along

drumming wakes people out of sleep (literally and metaphorically; sleep = apathy)

wild with happiness and joy

MEK DRUM TALK, MAN
for Caribbean Independence

Budoom-a budoom-a budoom-a ba-dap.
A dudu-wum a-dudu-wum dudu-wum a dudu-wum.
Wake skin up. Wake skin.
Slap it up. Slap skin.
Man, slap up drum.
Use yu hundred han them.
Domination get drop.
Some doors get open up.

Lawks O, slap the drum, slap it Buddy.
Slap it like you a mad mad somody—
budoom-a budoom-a budoom-a ba-dap,
budoom-a budoom-a budoom-a ba-dap.
A-dudu-wum a-dudu-wum dudu-wum a-dudu-wum.
Budoom-a dudu-wum. Budoom-a dudu-wum. Bru-dum.

Let out lost ancestor voice.
Let out of skin all pain and vice.
Tell the worl that the king is dead—
forbidden people gettn wed.
Tell towns new words comin fo print—
knowledge looked-fo whe palms they skint.
Get soun like them a talkin gong,
mek them happy jus a-galang.

Get the soun, get the soun, get it Buddy.
Wake up gong and family.
Every soun is head with a hum
of deep-deep voice of drum—
tru the windows, tru the trees,
tru the markets, tru the streets.

Lawks O, slap the drum, slap it Buddy.
Slap it like you a mad mad somody—
budoom-a budoom-a budoom-a ba-dap,
budoom-a budoom-a budoom-a ba-dap.
A-dudu-wum a-dudu-wum dudu-wum a-dudu-wum.
Budoom-a dudu-wum. Budoom-a dudu-wum. Bru-dum.

Slap the drum. Elbow drum. Thump drum.
Mek drum sey to be hit is fun.
Wake up skin. Wake up skin
with it broom bu-doom it hidin.
People cry – start a new cycle!
Widen money circle!
Get out every hiddn moan.
Let loose all skin-hiddn groan.

Show off the pulse of big bright sun.
Sen good news to village and town.
Tell the people a child is born,
tell them about a sweet new dawn.
Bring street drummin in the house—
see sleepers get aroused.
Wake the people out-a they trance.
Tell people come dance.

James Berry

6: 3: T12: to compare texts in writing, drawing out:
● their different styles and preoccupations
● their strengths and weaknesses
● their different values and appeal to a reader

6: 3: S2: to conduct detailed language investigations through interviews, research and reading, e.g. of proverbs, language change over time, dialect, study of headlines

The Caged Bird in Springtime
by James Kirkup

Background

Poet, translator and travel writer, James Kirkup was born in South Shields in 1918. His poetry is often found in anthologies for children. 'The Caged Bird in Springtime' is a poem that reflects on the issue of animals in captivity. It can be compared with other poems that address the theme in different ways, such as Charles Causley's 'My Mother Saw a Dancing Bear' and Ted Hughes's 'The Jaguar' (see page 92), or it can be linked to work on discussion texts (see 'Performing sea creatures', page 66).

Written in the first person and presenting a series of questions, this poem's subject is a caged bird wondering why it longs to fly and build a nest when it has only ever known life in a cage. Ironically, the reader is well aware of the bird's true nature and has greater knowledge and understanding of its predicament. The last two lines offer a shift in viewpoint, as the reader observes the young children watching the bird. The final observation is ambiguous – perhaps the children are cruel only in their innocence or perhaps they take pleasure in the power they have to restrain the bird. We are shown the scene but not told what to think about it.

Shared reading and discussing the text

● Read the poem aloud before showing it to the children. Allow time for them to jot down their personal responses. Share and discuss the children's first thoughts, then show them the text and ask them to read it silently.
● Does the poet think it is acceptable to cage birds? Ask the children to justify their opinions. What are their own views?
● Ask who is speaking the poem. What does the bird think and feel? Why is it kept in a cage? Re-read the last four lines. What do they tell us about the children's point of view?
● Read the poem aloud a second time and ask the children to identify any patterns, interesting images, words or phrases. Mark their observations on the text. Point out the high proportion of monosyllabic words and repetition of clipped sounds (*c, d, t*), reminiscent of the bird's pecking movements. And can they see how the diminutive *little cage* contrasts with *secret branches in the air*, emphasising the bird's fragility and confinement?

Activities

● Organise the children into pairs and ask one child in each pair to assume the role of the bird. The other child should use hot-seating to explore the bird's thoughts and feelings. Encourage the children to share their ideas.
● Pairs of children could also improvise a conversation between one of the children in the poem and the caged bird. What would they say to each other? Would the child empathise with the bird's situation? Would the bird be angry, sad or confused about its imprisonment? Would the child decide to set the bird free or keep it in the cage for amusement?
● Ask the children to make a list of words that relate to the poem (for example, *captivity, prisoner, sorrow, weep*). Some words may be taken from the poem and others can be generated by association. The children can use a thesaurus to extend the list. Suggest that they design a word collage surrounding key lines from the poem. They could use lettering that adds to the meaning of the word (for example, the word sorrow could be drawn with tears). Display the word collages in the class or school library. (A contrasting word collage can be designed for 'The Jaguar'.)

Extension/further reading

Ask the children to write another poem based on animal issues that they are concerned about (for example, fox-hunting, whaling or circus performances).

Further reading includes the poems 'I am a Parrot' by Grace Nichols, 'Song of the Battery Hen' by Edwin Brock and 'Captive Bird' by Boethius in *Birds, Beasts and Fishes* edited by Anne Carter (Walker Books), and Hans Christian Andersen's story *The Emperor and the Nightingale* edited by Fiona Waters (Bloomsbury Children's Classics).

6: 3: T4: to comment critically on the overall impact of a poem, showing how language and themes have been developed

patterned language – the repetition of 'c' and 't' imitates the bird's pecking movements

poses question

first-person monologue

irony

the absurdity is not that the bird wants to fly but that it has not had the opportunity to do so

instinct overrides present circumstances

high proportion of monosyllabic words

poses question again at the end of the poem (reader has been confronted with the answer in the preceding lines of the poem)

The Caged Bird in Springtime

What can it be,
This curious anxiety?
It is as if I wanted
To fly away from here.

But how absurd!
I have never flown in my life,
And I do not know
What flying means, though I have heard,
Of course, something about it.

Why do I peck the wires of this little cage?
It is the only nest I have ever known,
But I want to build my own,
High in the secret branches of the air.

I cannot quite remember how
It is done, but I know
That what I want to do
Cannot be done here.

I have all I need –
Seed and water, air and light.
Why, then, do I weep with anguish,
And beat my head and my wings
Against these sharp wires, while the children
Smile at each other, saying: "Hark how he sings"?

James Kirkup

irregular rhyming pattern

'little' cage associated with 'little' bird (emphasises the uneven power relationship between captor and captive)

rhyme

contrasts with always being on view in the cage

half-rhyme

simple needs met, but freedom – the greatest need – is denied

self-inflicted harm shows how desperate the bird is

a shift to a view of the children, who can be seen as the 'captors'; raises questions about the innocence of children; open to different interpretations

The Jaguar

by Ted Hughes

Background

Ted Hughes (1938–98) was born in Yorkshire and was greatly influenced by the natural world in his poetry for children and adults. 'The Jaguar' was not written specifically for children, but powerful language and images involve them in the drama and enable them to make their own meanings from this complex, multi-layered poem.

The poem contrasts stasis and dynamism: the first two stanzas describe the animals in the zoo, which appear largely static and passive, but in the jaguar's cage (from the third stanza onwards) there is an unpredictable, energetic animal. Hughes's jaguar transcends his imprisonment spiritually if not physically. He watches the visitors who have come to the zoo to watch him, and some of the characteristics of the jaguar we might recognise in people we know or ourselves.

Shared reading and discussing the text

● Encourage the children to recall any visits to a zoo and the animals that they have seen (this can be linked to the discursive text 'Performing sea creatures', see page 66). Briefly talk about what the animals were doing (sleeping, hiding, performing, for example). Were some animals more active and interesting to look at than others?

● Read the poem, contrasting the first two stanzas with those that describe the jaguar. Discuss the children's first responses. In what ways is the jaguar different from the other animals in the zoo?

● Enjambment at the ends of stanzas 1, 3 and 4 sustain forward momentum which contrasts with the full stop at the end of stanza 2 – this marks a change in mood. Clarify any parts of the poem that the children don't understand.

● Read the poem a second time. Look more closely at the imagery (for example, *the boa constrictor's coil/Is a fossil* contrasts with the electrical images associated with the jaguar – *the drills of his eyes/On a short fierce fuse*).

● Ask the children if they can see any language patterns in the poem. Does the poem rhyme? At first they might think that it doesn't. The rhyme scheme is irregular and subtle, using full rhyme (*strut, nut*) and half-rhyme (*sun, lion*). Discuss the effect that this has. Experiment by replacing the rhymes and half-rhymes with non-rhyming words to see what difference it makes when read aloud.

● Alliteration and the driving beat of monosyllabic words pump energy into the poem, imitating the jaguar's mood and movement (*short fierce fuse; bang of blood in the brain deaf…*). Re-read the lines *As a child at a dream… deaf the ear.* Ask the children what these lines make them feel about the jaguar.

Activities

● Ted Hughes's jaguar has some human qualities: although caged, he is free in spirit like a *visionary* in his *cell*, but at the same time he is still a realistic jaguar. Ask the children to choose another animal that they might see at a zoo; what human-like characteristics might it display? Can they write a poem that shows both animal and human qualities?

● What is the jaguar thinking? We can infer some of his thoughts from the poem but there is room for interpretation. Ask the children to write a monologue for the jaguar.

● Encourage the children to use a rhyming dictionary to generate lists of full rhymes and half-rhymes for some of the line-end words (*sun/strut, coil/straw* and so on).

● Ask the children to make notes (in two columns) on the things they think are similar and different between this poem and 'The Caged Bird in Springtime' (see page 90). In a plenary session, share the children's lists of similarities and build up a class list. Do the same for differences. After discussion, re-read each poem.

Extension/further reading

Children may like to read Ted Hughes's *The Cat and the Cuckoo* and *The Iron Wolf* (both Faber & Faber).

6: 3: T2: to discuss how linked poems relate to one another by themes, format and repetition, e.g. cycle of poems about the seasons

6: 3: T6: to look at connections and contrasts in the work of different writers

piercing – not a pleasant noise

somebody walking leisurely

most of the animals are inactive, in contrast to the jaguar's energy

The Jaguar

showy, without substance

The apes yawn and adore their fleas in the sun.
The parrots shriek as if they were on fire, or strut
Like cheap tarts to attract the stroller with a nut.
Fatigued with indolence, tiger and lion

combination of full and half rhyme

weary, tired, unable to make an effort to move

averse to activity or movement

image of lifelessness

strong verb

Lie still as the sun. The boa-constrictor's coil
Is a fossil. Cage after cage seems empty, or
Stinks of sleepers from the breathing straw.
It might be painted on a nursery wall.

subtle half-rhyme

as if hypnotised, spellbound

But who runs like the rest past these arrives
At a cage where the crowd stands, stares, mesmerized,
As a child at a dream, at a jaguar hurrying enraged
Through prison darkness after the drills of his eyes

image of the jaguar as if powered by electricity

image – looking in awe and wonder

onomatopoeic – like a burning fizzing fuse

On a short fierce fuse. Not in boredom—
The eye satisfied to be blind in fire,
By the bang of blood in the brain deaf the ear—
He spins from the bars, but there's no cage to him

enjambment sustains forward momentum

monosyllabic with repetition of sounds 'b' and 'd'

one who sees visions, is imaginative

More than to the visionary his cell:
His stride is wildernesses of freedom:
The world rolls under the long thrust of his heel.
Over the cage floor the horizons come.

like a monastic cell

emphasises energy

this jaguar does not act like a caged animal

Ted Hughes

image of jaguar walking as if he is free in the wilderness

'cage' contrasts with 'horizons' – in his imagination the jaguar is not caged

Forces

Background

This extract is an explanation text from a science book which explains what forces are and why they work. Characteristically the text opens with a definition (*A force is any push or pull on an object...*). The second stage outlines the different components of forces (those you can see and invisible forces); these are listed under the heading *Types of Forces*. This section also subsumes some of the information about the operation or description of how forces work (*A single force acting on an object will make it start to move, or move faster or slower*). The third section, *See for yourself*, gives information about when you can see forces in action.

Shared reading and discussing the text

● Before reading the text, encourage the children to think about forces, for example why does a ball move when you kick it? Why does a lump of Plasticine change shape if you squeeze it in your hand?

● Read the extract. Discuss how you can tell that it is not a piece of fiction or poetry. Ask the children what type of text they think it is. Establish that it is an explanation.

● Ask the children to read the section headed *Types of Forces*. How many different ways can a force affect an object? Note that basically there are three different ways in which a force can act on an object: 1. a force can change the speed or direction of movement of an object; 2. a force can change the shape or state of an object; 3. when two equal and opposite forces are applied an object can remain stationary. Is this expressed clearly in the extract?

● Look at the structure of the passage. Summarise what the first paragraph tells us, giving the reader an extended definition. Notice the use of headings. What information would you expect to find under these headings? Introduce the idea of a four-part explanation structure: 1. definition; 2. components; 3. operation; 4. application. Examine whether each of these elements is included in the passage 'Forces'.

● Cause-and-effect relationships are often signalled in explanation texts (*When you kick a football*; *As you catch a ball*; *If you step on a ball*). Extend the list by thinking of other examples (such as *because, as a result of*).

● Examine the complex sentences that are used in the extract. For example: *There are forces you can see such as a foot kicking a ball, and invisible forces, such as magnetism and gravity.* This example sentence can be analysed as including the following information:
  – You can see some forces.
  – Kicking a football is a visible force.
  – Some forces are invisible.
  – Magnetism and gravity are invisible forces.
Analyse some other examples from the passage.

● Summarise the main features of explanatory writing – that is, an opening definition or question about the phenomenon, logical progression/sequence to explain the process, use of simple present tense, temporal and causal connectives, verbs that describe processes and actions, technical vocabulary, inclusion of diagrams and illustrations. List the features with examples on a prompt sheet, which can be used to aid the children's writing.

Activities

● Ask the children to create a list of causal connectives found in the extract and other explanation texts, and to include the words and phrases in their personal word books. Encourage them to practise writing cause-and-effect sentences, using causal connectives.

● Can the children rewrite the passage in their own words and incorporate the features that they think would make it easier to understand (for example, more illustrative examples)?

● The children could write an explanation for a scientific concept (for example, magnetism). They could use a writing frame (definition; how it works; cause and effect; applications; any other interesting facts or special features), together with the prompt sheet created in shared reading above.

technical vocabulary emboldened

opening definition characteristic in explanation texts

cause-and-effect relationships

technical vocabulary

headings for clarity

operation; description of how forces work

technical vocabulary emboldened

testing the explanation – a feature of science books

definition in this context = 'apply'

captions explain pictures above

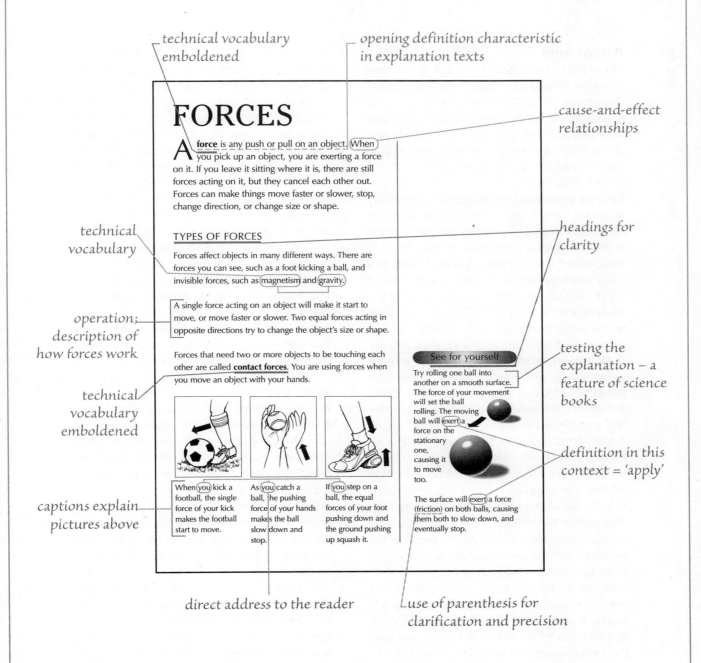

FORCES

A **force** is any push or pull on an object. When you pick up an object, you are exerting a force on it. If you leave it sitting where it is, there are still forces acting on it, but they cancel each other out. Forces can make things move faster or slower, stop, change direction, or change size or shape.

TYPES OF FORCES

Forces affect objects in many different ways. There are forces you can see, such as a foot kicking a ball, and invisible forces, such as magnetism and gravity.

A single force acting on an object will make it start to move, or move faster or slower. Two equal forces acting in opposite directions try to change the object's size or shape.

Forces that need two or more objects to be touching each other are called **contact forces**. You are using forces when you move an object with your hands.

When you kick a football, the single force of your kick makes the football start to move.

As you catch a ball, the pushing force of your hands makes the ball slow down and stop.

If you step on a ball, the equal forces of your foot pushing down and the ground pushing up squash it.

See for yourself

Try rolling one ball into another on a smooth surface. The force of your movement will set the ball rolling. The moving ball will exert a force on the stationary one, causing it to move too.

The surface will exert a force (friction) on both balls, causing them both to slow down, and eventually stop.

direct address to the reader

use of parenthesis for clarification and precision

How Things Work

Extracts 1 and 2

Background

These short explanation extracts show how scientific knowledge about forces is applied in technology. Explanations usually open with a clear statement followed by an elaboration that gives further explanation; the language is objective; the tense is the simple present; technical vocabulary is often used.

Shared reading and discussing the text

● Explain that when we describe how something works we call it an explanation. Explanations can be spoken or written. Ask the children whether they have ever been on a roller-coaster or similar theme park ride. What did it feel like? Read through both parts of the first extract.

● The writer assumes that the reader of the second part of extract 1 will already have read the explanation of the roller-coaster. Comparisons are made between the two fairground rides. It can be quite difficult to follow the explanation of a complex idea when it is compressed into a few lines. Break down extract 1 into stages. For example, focus on *a moving object will continue in a straight line unless acted on by an outside force, to change its speed or direction.* Explain that on a roller-coaster ride, the centripetal force is the tension that keeps the object moving in a circular motion. Gravity pulls the riders towards the ground, but the centripetal force exerted on them by the seat keeps them in place.

● Before reading extract 2, ask the children if they have ever wondered how a spinning top works. If you have a top, spin it and ask them to watch what happens. Can they explain why the top spins until it eventually falls over?

● Read extract 2. Ask the children how they can tell it is an explanation text. It is unusual in that it opens with an opinion: *A spinning top is a fascinating toy.* This is because the writer is seeking to engage the reader immediately. Note the use of the impersonal voice (*The spinning object converts the vertical force of gravity into horizontal motion*); causal connectives (*When*

a spinning top slows down); use of the present tense (*This happens...*); and explanation of subject specific terms (*This is known as precession*).

● Evaluate the clarity of the information presented in the extracts. Could the explanations be made easier to understand? Annotate the text with the children's observations and suggestions. Model this for them by asking your own questions, for example *What exactly is centripetal force?*

● The diagrams help us to understand how things work and make the explanations clearer. Discuss their effectiveness. Explore whether there are any other parts of the text that could have been explained through the use of diagrams.

● Highlight technical vocabulary and check the children's understanding. Use a scientific dictionary for clarification of terms.

Activities

● Ask the children to write a set of questions that can be answered by the texts, for example *What happens when a top slows down?* When they have completed their list of questions, they should swap them with a partner and see if they can find the answers in the text to each other's questions.

● Cut a copy of the text about the roller-coaster into meaningful segments (they do not have to be complete sentences). Ask the children to reconstitute the text and to note the clues they use to help them put it together. In a plenary session, ask the children to share what they have done. Reinforce the use of cohesive features (lexical and syntactic).

● Ask the children to bring in a selection of simple gadgets from home (a pencil sharpener, a nutcracker and a tin opener, for example). In pairs, they should try to explain to each other how the gadgets work. Encourage them to prompt each other by asking questions if an explanation isn't clear. Then ask each child to choose one gadget and write a paragraph of text that explains how it works.

simple present tense

technical vocabulary – a force that acts on an object moving in a circular path; the force is directed to the centre around which the object is moving

HOW THINGS WORK

Extract 1

statement

ROLLER-COASTER
The laws of physics state that a moving object will continue in a straight line unless acted on by an outside force, to change its speed or direction. As the riders in a roller-coaster loop the loop, they are moving in a circle and are therefore changing direction from a straight line. The force causing this to happen is the *centripetal* force, which acts towards the centre of the circle, continually pushing the riders inwards. The reaction to centripetal force is felt when the riders are pressed into their seats.

elaboration of opening statement

name of the ride in single speech marks to indicate that it is not actually a wall of death

WALL-OF-DEATH
The 'Wall-of-Death' works in a similar way to the roller-coaster. The motion in this case is in a horizontal circle rather than a vertical one. The centripetal force acts to make the riders go round in a circle, rather than along in a straight line. As a reaction to this force, they press up against the revolving drum wall and stay there – even when the floor is lowered from under their feet! The old term of '*centrifugal* force' is no longer used to explain these types of movements.

exclamation mark to indicate how improbable this seems if the science is not understood

connective – cause and effect

obsolete term in inverted commas

Extract 2

opening statement

elaboration

SPINNING TOPS
A SPINNING TOP is a fascinating toy. It can be made to balance on the end of a pencil, and if the pencil is moved the spinning top remains pointing in the same direction. This happens because the top has angular momentum, and this momentum does not change unless a force acts on the spinning top – angular momentum is always conserved. Spinning tops, or their more sophisticated cousins called gyroscopes, are used in compasses because they resist changes to the axis of their spin. When a spinning top slows down, it leans to one side. Gravity is pulling the spinning top down, but it does not fall. Instead it slowly circles around its balance point. The spinning object converts the vertical force of gravity into a horizontal motion. This is known as precession.

technical vocabulary – the quantity of rotation possessed by an object, which is the product of its moment of inertia and its angular velocity

connective – cause and effect

simple present tense typical in explanation texts

an imaginary line around which the object rotates

introduction of technical vocabulary for a concept that has just been introduced

Meet the Wolf

Background

'Meet the Wolf' is a factual natural history report. Characteristic features are the classification in the opening paragraph: *Grey wolves are long-legged members of the dog family...* This is followed by description of key aspects of the topic organised under the headings *Habitat, Hunting* and *Sharing the meal.* The participants are generalised; the term *wolves* is used to represent the whole class. Specific species are named in the text. There is a high proportion of 'linking verbs' that show relational processes (*But terrible over-hunting by people <u>has</u> greatly reduced their numbers; The grey wolf <u>is</u> one of only two kinds...*).

Some descriptive language is used in this text (for example, *scorching deserts of Saudi Arabia*), but the overall tone is objective. The opinions of the writer are hidden; we cannot detect whether he likes or dislikes wolves.

Shared reading and discussing the text

● Briefly discuss the children's existing knowledge about wolves. Read the text.

● After reading, ask the children why they think this format was chosen for presenting the information. Ask whether it is possible to tell what the writer feels about wolves from the way the text is written. Explain that one of the requirements of report writing is to be factually accurate and objective.

● Ask the children how the text is organised (revising work on reports, see page 40). Look at the use of headings (*Habitat* and so on) and topic sentences (for example, *Grey wolves are generally found in the wilderness areas... northern US states; Wolves hunt mainly at night... sneak up on victims in the darkness*).

● Focus on the language features of the report. Draw attention to the use of generalised participants, use of linking verbs, and so on.

● Check vocabulary – what is an *alpha pair*?

● With the class, construct a concept map about wolves, clustering areas of information (such as hunting, food, feeding patterns) for research.

Activities

● Gather and display a selection of information books about wolves in order for the children to find out more about wolves, using a KWL grid (see page 28).

● Ask the children to construct a report, using the information gathered from research. They should include headings which organise their facts about wolves into classification; description (hunting); description (family groups); and a concluding statement.

● Give the children some sentences, written in different genres, about wolves. For example, report: *The grey wolf is one of only two kinds, or species, of 'true' wolf*; recount: *Then behind the she wolf we noticed a small grey bundle; it was a cub*; narrative: *The wolves were moving steadily through the long grass*; poetry: *Then crying of a baby, in this forest of starving silences, brings the wolves running*). Ask the children to identify the sentences that they think come from reports and to write down their reasons for selecting them.

● On a blank outline map of the world, work as a class to mark the areas where wolves live today. Use the text extract as a starting point, then other reference sources, including the Internet, to find other locations where wolves live. Add some notes to the map, describing the terrain they inhabit.

Extension/further reading

Let the children watch a televised documentary about wolves, such as the video *The Return of the Wolf* (National Geographic). They can then compare it with the written report, dividing a sheet of A3 paper into two columns headed *Similarities* and *Differences.* Encourage them to compare the content, media conventions/text features, intended audience, and the effect on the viewer/reader.

Can they now rewrite 'Meet the Wolf' as a script for a television documentary?

Books about wolves include Michael Leach's *Wolf (*Hodder Wayland) and Michael Morpurgo's *The Last Wolf* (Corgi Juvenile).

6: 3: T16: to identify the key features of impersonal formal language

6: 3: T19: to review a range of non-fiction text types and their characteristics, discussing when a writer might choose to write in a given style and form

classification

Meet the Wolf

statement of being

Grey wolves are long-legged members of the dog family that live together in packs. Like all dogs, they are mainly meat-eaters, and for animals, they are quite intelligent. Grey wolves once lived in many northern parts of the world. But terrible over-hunting by people has greatly reduced their numbers.

relational verb – over-hunting is related to greatly reduced numbers

Habitat

topic sentence which is then elaborated

Grey wolves are generally found in the wilderness areas of Europe and Asia, and also in North America, where they are found in Canada, Alaska and a few northern US states. In all these places, wolves are very adaptable and occupy many different habitats.

technical vocabulary – able to adjust to new conditions

In the USA and Russia grey wolves live mainly in thick forests. In Italy and Eastern Europe their home is the mountains. In northern Canada and Siberia their habitat is the icy, windy, treeless landscape called the tundra. Yet wolves also occur in tropical places such as the scrublands of India and the scorching deserts of Saudi Arabia.

technical vocabulary

The grey wolf is one of only two kinds, or species, of 'true' wolf. The other is the red wolf. There are other types of wolf, such as the maned wolf that lives

information is factual and objective

in South America. Scientists think that maned wolves are not true wolves but distant relatives.

key aspects organised under headings

Hunting

Wolves hunt mainly at night, when it is cooler in hot regions, and they can sneak up on victims in the darkness.

topic sentence

Wolves find their prey by their main sense, smell. They can travel 30 kilometres or more in a single night to reach food. One wolf hunting by itself can catch a rabbit or hare. But when six wolves work together, they can bring down prey heavier than all of their weights added together, such as moose and elk.

generalised participants

conditional connective

North American term for 'elk' (large deer)

Sharing the meal

After a big kill, the alpha pair of grey wolves have first choice of food. They usually go for soft, nutritious parts of the victim, such as the heart and liver. The others fight for their shares. They snarl, growl and snap at each other.

dominant male and female pair of wolves

When the pack has caught a large animal, every wolf can eat its fill and there is still meat left over. This remaining food is often buried in the ground. In times when prey is scarce, the pack can always return and dig up the food.

food that has goodness

as much as it wants

single quotes indicate common term, not technically accurate

descriptive language

6: 3: S1: to revise the language conventions and grammatical features of the different types of text such as reports

6: 3: S3: to revise formal styles of writing

Walk with a wolf

by Janni Howker

Background

'Walk with a wolf' is a mixed genre text in which poetic narrative is interspersed with objective report writing. Howker wrote the book to challenge what she perceived to be the negative image and unfair stereotyping of wolves in traditional fiction.

It is interesting to compare the information given in the two types of text and how our responses are affected by the manner of telling. Meaning is created by the interrelationship of the two types of text. The poetic text provides some factual information (wolves are active in the morning, they live in forested areas, and so on), but mainly provokes an emotional response; the reader is invited to admire the wolf's agility and stealth. In contrast, the text in the 'handwritten' font has the characteristics of report writing – it is unemotional, providing factual information about wolves.

Shared reading and discussing the text

● Ask the children to read the passage in pairs, sharing the reading so that one child reads the poetic text and the other the report text.

● Gather the children's first responses. Ask them what genre the text is. Draw their attention to the mixed-genre writing. Tell them that Janni Howker uses the word *story* to describe the text in her foreword to the book. Is this extract a story? Ask why they think the author chose to write about wolves in this way. Does the author like or dislike wolves? Look at the way Janni Howker encourages the reader to empathise with the wolf. For example, *There's no meat on it now—And she's hungry*; images of a domestic dog are created by the phrases *shakes herself like a dog* and *wag of her tail*; there is the invitation to *Walk with a wolf… Run with a wolf…* and *Howl with a wolf…*

● Note the way the movement of the wolf is described in the poetic text (for example, *slides, splashes, shakes, bounds*) and how this creates a playful image of the wolf. Compare this with the movement words used in the report text (*hunt alone; catch fish*).

● Ask the children what picture they have of the setting. Pick out the words and phrases that give an indication of the time (*cold air before sunrise; Winter is coming*) and place (*spruce trees and birches; snow on the mountains*).

● Notice the unusual sentence construction that is sometimes used in the poetic text. For example, in *Howl with a wolf in the dawn, thin and icy* the adjectives are not in the usual position – that is, *thin and icy dawn*). Explain that holding the adjectives until the end of the sentence where they carry more weight means that they are given more attention.

Activities

● Ask pairs of children to identify similarities and differences in the two types of text in this extract (for example, *Similarities: both texts are about wolves; Differences: the poetic text makes a specific invitation to the reader to 'Walk with a wolf'; the report style text does not directly address the reader*).

● The full text of 'Walk with a wolf' tells the story of the wolf's year from winter through to the following winter. Ask the children to find out more about the wolf and then complete the story using the same style and tone.

● Using 'Walk with a wolf' as a model, the children could write a short illustrated book about a different animal that is generally not looked on very positively (such as a worm, pig or spider). Can they write the story in a way that invites readers to reassess their opinions?

Extension/further reading

As a class, investigate the ways in which the wolf has been portrayed in a range of traditional and contemporary fiction from European and non-European backgrounds. Different groups can look at the image of the wolf in different stories and share their findings to build up a composite picture.

Stories about wolves include Joan Aiken's *The Wolves of Willoughby Chase* (Red Fox), Colin McNaughton's *Suddenly!* (Collins Educational) and M Powell's *Wolf Tales* (Ancient City Press).

6: 3: T19: to review a range of non-fiction text types and their characteristics, discussing when a writer might choose to write in a given style and form annotations

6: 3: S1: to revise the language conventions and grammatical features of the different types of text such as:
● narrative
● reports

invitation to the reader: 'Come and walk...'

image combines the aural with the visual

not referred to as 'it' – this is a specific wolf

movement verbs

emphasises that wolves and dogs are related

means 'heap into a mass'

raises question – what will happen?

invitation to experience different aspects of the wolf's life

poetic aural image

wolves communicate with each other, display intelligent behaviour

behaviour recognisable from pet dogs

setting

playful wolf – conveys image of a dog

report-style writing in a different font

time and place

movement verb – positive, full of energy

striking visual image

develops empathy

generalised in the report style sections

unusual sentence construction: adjectives placed after the noun to which they refer

uses terms that define a relationship – familial terms normally associated with humans rather than animals

Walk with a wolf

Walk with a wolf in the cold air before sunrise.
She moves, quiet as mist,
between spruce trees and birches.
A silent grey shadow, she slides between boulders
and trots over blue pebbles to the edge of the lake.

She plunges through slush ice and laps the chill water,
snaps at a feather that drifts down from a goose wing,
then splashes to shore and
shakes herself like a dog.

Wolves were probably the first large animals to live with people, and all the kinds of dog we know today are descended from them.

There's deep snow on the mountains.
Snow clouds bank in the east.
Winter is coming, and the geese fly south.

Run with a wolf as she bounds up the steep slope.
She sniffs at a skull that stares at the lake.
Moss grows on the antlers.
The bone has turned grey,
There's no meat on it now—
And she's hungry.

During the summer months, a wolf may hunt alone and catch fish, hare, squirrels and other small animals. But these creatures go into hiding in winter to escape from the freezing cold weather.

Howl with a wolf in the dawn, thin and icy.
Deep from her chest the eerie sound comes.
Long, low music.
The song of the Arctic.

Another howl answers.

With a wag of her tail, the wolf runs to the pack.
Three sons and a daughter, cubs from the spring,
squirm on their bellies and lick at her neck.

*Mother wolves give birth in springtime.
They can have anything from one to eleven cubs each year.
Although they don't stay together all the time,
most wolves live in family groups called packs.*

Janni Howker

social aspects of wolves contrasts with solitary aspects shown earlier

Why is the Grey Wolf an endangered species?

Background

This extract from the World Wide Fund for Nature website is an explanatory text – it explains why wolves are an endangered species. It also contains some of the characteristics of report writing, specifically in paragraph 2 which provides data about the wolf's size, habitat and breeding patterns. Texts that are produced for real audiences rather than those specifically written for teaching purposes often combine genres. Year 6/Primary 7 children should be made aware of the complexity of written texts, recognising that few texts conform to a simple formula. It is the entire text that conveys the intended purpose rather than isolated paragraphs or sentences.

Shared reading and discussing the text

● Ask the children if they have heard of the World Wide Fund for Nature. If you have an example of the logo, ask whether they recognise it. What sort of work do they imagine the WWF does? Explain that you are going to read a piece about wolves from the WWF website.

● Read the title. Tell the children that in the passage that follows they are going to find the answers to some questions, such as *Why was the wolf persecuted in the 19th century? Why is the wolf sometimes seen as a threat to humans? What are the current threats to the wolf's existence?* Ask them just to listen, not to make notes, while you are reading. After reading, go through the questions and allow time for children to jot down their answers. Share and refine the answers.

● Ask the children if they can tell what sort of text it is. Recap the features of explanatory texts (see pages 94 and 96) and construct a prompt sheet to aid the children's writing. Re-read paragraph 2. Ask the children whether this is an explanatory paragraph. Explain that many texts are of mixed genre and this paragraph is providing some key factual information about wolves which is consistent with report writing. Highlight some of the language features that are found in report writing. Paragraph 2 provides some defining information about the wolf and has verbs that fill the existential function (The wolf *is* the second largest predator; It *lives* in sophisticated communities). Features of the explanation genre in this text are the posing of an opening question (*Why is the Grey Wolf an endangered species?*); causal connectives (*When man began...*) indicating cause and effect; passive sentences (*the extermination of the wolf began*); temporal connectives (*Today, however, the wolf is recovering...*), generic participants (*wolves, man*).

● Point out that because the initial question requires a historical explanation, there is a variation in the tenses (past: *At one time the Grey wolf was the farthest-flung of all land mammals*; and present: *Today, however, the wolf is recovering naturally*).

● Evaluate how well the text answers the question posed. Ask the children to summarise the reasons for the wolf being endangered and to identify the words in the text that provide the answers. (For example, *When man began tending sheep and cattle... a competitor*).

Activities

● Ask the children to read the text again and, using the prompt sheet, annotate it to highlight the characteristic features of explanatory texts.

● Suggest that the children design a page for the WWF website (or your school website) for a different endangered species (tiger, blue whale, African elephant or giant panda, for example). Using the Internet or other sources, they can learn about the specific threats to their chosen animal and what needs to be done to protect the species. Ask them to give their page the title *Why is the... an endangered species?*

Extension/further reading

Further information can be obtained in *The Atlas of Endangered Species* by Richard Mackay (Earthscan Publications) and *Planet Zoo: 100 Animals We Can't Afford to Lose* by Simon Barnes (Orion Children's Books). The World Wide Fund for Nature is at www.wwf.org.uk.

6: 3: T19: to review a range of non-fiction text types and their characteristics, discussing when a writer might choose to write in a given style and form

6: 3: S1: to revise the language conventions and grammatical features of the different types of text such as:
- reports
- explanatory texts

movement verb

poses an opening question

causal connective

'hemi' + 'sphere' = half of the Earth

victim of hostile behaviour

objective, factual information

Why is the Grey Wolf an endangered species?

generalised participant

farm animals

living off others

destroy (kill all the wolves)

cold desert

technical vocabulary – adjective relating to the study of living things ('-ical' suffix turns noun into adjective)

taking advantage of what is available

paragraph 2 – report style

leader – the head of the pack

subjective language

dash gives a pause and emphasises following phrase

Background

At one time the Grey wolf was the farthest-flung of all land mammals, loping across much of the northern hemisphere. Its prey includes livestock, which is why during the 19th century it was persecuted across central and northern European countries. Recovery started naturally in several remote parts across the continent and now the biggest populations are found in eastern countries, particularly Romania, the Balkans and Poland.

An adult male can weigh 40kg and is an average 150cm in length. The wolf is the second largest predator in Europe after the brown bear. Its main prey is moose and deer but it feeds opportunistically. It can adapt very successfully to the environment – anything from the hot central plains of Spain to the bleak tundra of Finland. It lives in sophisticated communities of family packs within clearly defined territory, with only the leading animals – the alpha male and female – breeding. The cubs are then cared for by the remainder of the pack. Wolves are intelligent and shy and prefer to avoid confrontation with people.

The wolf has been transformed in man's perception from hero to villain – and has suffered accordingly. When man was a hunter-gatherer the wolf was revered as a resourceful, powerful fellow-hunter. When man began tending sheep and cattle, the wolf remained a hunter – but became a competitor. It had to be eliminated and the extermination of the wolf began. This, together with man's encroachment upon the wolf's habitat, meant serious inroads were made on the animal's numbers. Today, however, the wolf is recovering naturally and there are between 15,500 and 18,000 in Europe.

Current threats & problems

The wolf suffers a negative image problem and despite its ability to adapt and therefore live close to man, it continues to take the blame – sometimes unfairly – for attacks on livestock. Actual figures for wolves taking domestic livestock are very low, but predatory activities, real or imagined, remain the main reason for attempting to exterminate the wolf.

The animal is hunted in some countries without restriction and in others licences to hunt are issued without biological or ecological understanding of the situation. Poaching is widespread and is the cause of the biggest losses. Although it can co-exist with humans, it needs safe areas in which to retreat. If this problem is not addressed, wolf communities will fragment as a result of moving into unsuitable habitat.

ecology – a branch of biology concerned with the ways living things relate to each other and their surroundings

statistics add authenticity

intrusion

live alongside

Dictionary of phrase and fable

Background

Young readers and writers should have access to a range of reference sources including specialist dictionaries that are not specifically written for children. A dictionary of phrase and fable is a wonderful treasury that explains the origins and meanings of the names, phrases and expressions that have been absorbed into English language usage and literature.

The extracts here show how prevalent references to the wolf are in the English language. The attitude towards the wolf is usually one of a hungry, untrustworthy enemy. This can be compared with information given in the previous extracts (see pages 98–102).

Shared reading and discussing the text

● Ask the children if they know of any expressions which include the word *wolf.* Give an example (such as *a wolf in sheep's clothing*). List them and discuss their meanings.

● Show them the text and explain where it comes from and the purpose of a dictionary of phrase and fable. Explain that the entries are organised in alphabetical order like other dictionaries. Point out that the full entry for *to cry wolf* is found under *c.*

● Ask the children to consider why there are so many sayings with wolf in them. What are the qualities of the wolf that are suggested by the phrases *to keep the wolf from the door; wolf in sheep's clothing; wolf pack; Wolf Cub*? For each of the examples, discuss whether the qualities are positive (*Wolf Cub*) or negative.

● Ask the children if they know the story of the boy who cried wolf. Summarise the story.

● Provide a set of questions to go with the text (for example, *What is the name of the squeak made by unskilled players of reed instruments? For how many years did Edgar the Peaceful reign?*). Ask pairs of children to read the entries and find the answers to the questions.

● Draw attention to the conventions that are used for presenting information in the dictionary (italic for titles of books and direct quotations, and so on).

● Brainstorm different phrases for a word such as *nail* (*to nail; nail in the coffin; nail one's colours to the mast; as hard as nails; bed of nails; fight tooth and nail; hit the nail on the head*, and so on). Demonstrate how to use a dictionary of phrase and fable to find out the origins and meanings of the expressions.

Activities

● Ask the children to brainstorm, in pairs or small groups, all the expressions they know that contain the word *fire* (for example, *no smoke without fire; line of fire*). There are many other possibilities including *water, house, king* and *jump.* The children can now use a range of specialist dictionaries to find out the origins of the expressions, then create their own entries for a dictionary of phrase and fable, using the shared text as a model.

● After they have selected one of the entries from the shared text to illustrate, ask the children to divide a sheet of paper in two. Explain that in one half they should draw the literal meaning of the phrase (for example, *a wolf in sheep's clothing*). In the second half they should draw the intended meaning (*an enemy posing as a friend*). Other well-known phrases could also be illustrated in this way.

● Devise a matching game for the children to play. Write the sayings about wolves onto strips of card. On a second set of strips write the literal meanings. Explain that the object is to match the sayings and meanings together and then check the answers by referring to the text. Expand the game by adding additional phrases and providing the children with a dictionary of phrase and fable.

Extension/further reading

Other specialist dictionaries include the *Oxford Dictionary of Proverbs*, the *Oxford Dictionary of Nursery Rhymes* and the *Oxford Dictionary of Slang.* The children may like to read Tony Ross's *The Boy Who Cried Wolf!* (Andersen Press) and Hilaire Belloc's poem 'Matilda' in *Cautionary Verses* (Red Fox).

6: 3: T17: to appraise a text quickly and effectively; to retrieve information from it; to find information quickly and evaluate its value

6: 3: T19: to review a range of non-fiction text types and their characteristics

entries organised alphabetically like a dictionary

what the phrase means

could look for different versions

name of the book

publication date

title capitalised

dates of his reign

alternative meaning

played with a bow

intestines

reference

how the phrase originated

references (in small caps) to other entries

British author who lived in India

publication dates

could research this fable

directed to reference where this phrase is explained

another animal name

eating or devouring greedily

French idiom in italic

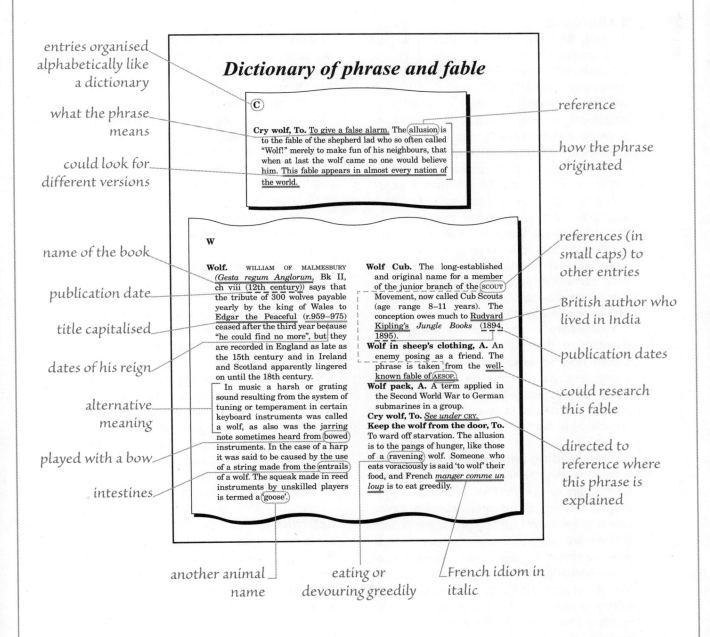

Dictionary of phrase and fable

C

Cry wolf, To. To give a false alarm. The allusion is to the fable of the shepherd lad who so often called "Wolf!" merely to make fun of his neighbours, that when at last the wolf came no one would believe him. This fable appears in almost every nation of the world.

W

Wolf. WILLIAM OF MALMESBURY (*Gesta regum Anglorum,* Bk II, ch viii (12th century)) says that the tribute of 300 wolves payable yearly by the king of Wales to Edgar the Peaceful (r.959–975) ceased after the third year because "he could find no more", but they are recorded in England as late as the 15th century and in Ireland and Scotland apparently lingered on until the 18th century.

In music a harsh or grating sound resulting from the system of tuning or temperament in certain keyboard instruments was called a wolf, as also was the jarring note sometimes heard from bowed instruments. In the case of a harp it was said to be caused by the use of a string made from the entrails of a wolf. The squeak made in reed instruments by unskilled players is termed a 'goose'.

Wolf Cub. The long-established and original name for a member of the junior branch of the SCOUT Movement, now called Cub Scouts (age range 8–11 years). The conception owes much to Rudyard Kipling's *Jungle Books* (1894, 1895).

Wolf in sheep's clothing, A. An enemy posing as a friend. The phrase is taken from the well-known fable of AESOP.

Wolf pack, A. A term applied in the Second World War to German submarines in a group.

Cry wolf, To. *See under* CRY.

Keep the wolf from the door, To. To ward off starvation. The allusion is to the pangs of hunger, like those of a ravening wolf. Someone who eats voraciously is said 'to wolf' their food, and French *manger comme un loup* is to eat greedily.

Origins of the word 'wolf'

Background

By Year 6/Primary 7, most children will be able to use independently a range of spelling strategies. An etymological dictionary gives information about the origins of English words with details of earliest recorded uses. Introducing an etymological dictionary and showing children how to access information from it can support investigations into unusual spelling patterns that do not conform to those most frequently found in English (such as *yacht*).

The unusual pronunciation of wolf (-*ulf*) is accounted for if we investigate the provenance of the word. The word is of Germanic origin and was introduced into English by the Anglo-Saxons. It would at that time have been spelled *wulf*. Sometimes a *u* was changed into an *o* in spelling because of the similarity in the formation of the letters.

The entries in the dictionary may look daunting at first sight but children can be shown how to extract the most significant information. As with the previous text, they should be encouraged to make use of adult reference materials as well as those written especially for children.

Shared reading and discussing the text

● Before reading the text, ask the children what a dictionary can be used for. Responses might include looking up the meaning of a word; checking the correct spelling of a word. Explain that you are going to show them how to use a different kind of dictionary – write *etymological* on the board and give its pronunciation. Explain that an etymological dictionary is organised alphabetically and tells us the origins of the words in English. Tell the children that they are going to learn how to become word detectives; knowing where an unusually spelled word comes from can sometimes help us understand the spelling.

● Write the word *wolf* on the board and ask the children if they can think of any other words in English with an -*olf* ending and the pronunciation '-*ulf*' (they may suggest *golf* – ask them to listen to the difference in pronunciation betwen *wolf* and *golf*).

● Prepare a copy of the text, masking all but extract 1 and the first sentence of extract 2. Read the text that can be seen. Look up *cognate* in a dictionary. Use a map to show where the other Germanic languages were spoken and why Old English was a related language.

● Ask the children for three things they have learned about the word wolf:

– The spelling of *wolf* comes from around 1300 when it was recorded in the poem 'Arthour and Merlin'.

– It was originally an Old English word spelled *wulf*.

– Other German languages had similar words. (Explain that this is the most important information.)

● On the board demonstrate how easy it was for a *u* to become an *o* (*o* is a *u* with a closed top), especially before spelling had really become standardised.

● Reveal the rest of extract 2. Explain that it tells us about the first recorded use of *to eat like a wolf* used as a verb, the noun *wolfhound* and the use of the adjective *wolfish*.

● Show other examples of animal nouns being made into adjectives by adding the suffix -*ish* (*hawk* + *ish*, *sheep* + *ish*, *bull* + *ish*). Can the children think of any others?

Activities

● Ask pairs of children to use the extracts to answer questions that they give to each other (for example, *Give the date of the earliest recorded use of the word 'wolf'*).

● Prepare some simplified etymological entries of words taken from a class novel or other curricular work and present them to the children with a list of questions to answer.

Extension/further reading

Compile a class etymological dictionary of interesting words that arise from shared, guided or independent reading. For each word, write the date of the earliest recorded usage.

6: 3: T17: to appraise a text quickly and effectively; to retrieve information from it; to find information quickly and evaluate its value

6: 3: T19: to review a range of non-fiction text types and their characteristics

Origins of the word 'wolf'

historical language period before 1100; the Anglo-Saxon Chronicles and the epic poem 'Beowulf' were written in Old English

spelling later changed to 'wolf'

the word for 'wolf' in some European languages, such as French ('loup'), is derived from Latin

family of languages derived from Sanskrit and Old Persian

❶

wolf comes from Old English *wulf,* of ancient Germanic origin. It can be traced back to an Indo-European root shared by Latin *lupus,* also meaning 'a wolf', which is where the word *lupine* 'like a wolf' comes from.

JK Rowling uses etymological knowledge in naming Professor Lupin (a werewolf)

word class information: 'wolf' is a noun

related to same ancestral language

different spelling

explains modern pronunciation

non-Germanic instances

reference book and page number

'wolfhound' first recorded in Walter Scott's novel

❷

wolf *n.* Probably before 1300 *wolf,* in *Arthour and Merlin;* developed from Old English (about 750) *wulf;* cognate with Old Frisian *wolf,* Old Saxon *wulf,* Middle Dutch and modern Dutch *wolf,* Old High German *wolf* (modern German *Wolf*), feminine *wulpa,* Old Icelandic *ulfr* (Swedish, Norwegian, and Danish *ulv*), and Gothic *wulfs* from Proto-Germanic *wulfaz* (earlier *wulHwaz*). Cognates outside Germanic are found in Latin (really Sabine) *lupus* wolf, Greek *lýkos,* Lithuaninan *vil̃kas,* Latvian *vilks,* Old Slavic *vlŭkŭ,* Avestan *vəhrkō,* and Sanskrit *vŕka-s,* from Indo-European *wl̥kwos* (Pok. 1178). —**v.** eat like a wolf, devour. 1862 in George A. Sala's *The Seven Sons of Mammon;* from the noun. —**wolfhound** *n.* (1823, in Scott's *Quentin Durward*) —**wolfish** *adj.* 1570, formed from English *wolf,* n. + *-ish.* An earlier form *wolvish* was formed in Middle English (about 1430) from *wolv-,* inflectional stem form of *wolf* + *-ish,* but became obsolete in the early 1800s.

earliest recorded date for 'wolf' and the source

shows derivation of the word

before 1100

before 1100

before 1500

1100–1500

before 1100

gives information about formation of the adjective 'wolfish' (noun + 'ish' = adjective)

Thesaurus

Background

A thesaurus is an essential reference tool for the classroom, and children should be encouraged to use one regularly to support their writing. The classroom collection should include at least one full thesaurus as well as the simpler versions produced especially for children.

These three entries from the *Longman Synonym Dictionary* feature words that the children might use when writing their suspense paragraphs (see page 80). The activities can easily be carried out with any other words appropriate to the writing that the children are doing at the time.

Shared reading and discussing the text

● Have available a small collection of thesauruses. Explain that a thesaurus is used for finding synonyms – words with a similar meaning. The word *thesaurus* is borrowed from the Latin for 'treasury' or 'storehouse', so a thesaurus is literally a treasury of words.

● Ask why a thesaurus is a useful tool. Establish that because we tend to reuse words that are very familiar in our writing a thesaurus can help us find more interesting words. We also use a thesaurus when we need help in finding exactly the right word with the precise shade of meaning for our purposes.

● Explain how a thesaurus is organised – like a dictionary, entries (headwords) are arranged alphabetically. Help the children to notice, however, that the synonyms are not organised in alphabetical order but in order of the closest match in meaning. Thus *anxiety* is considered nearer in meaning to the headword *tension* than *apprehension*. Look at the entry for *fear* and evaluate the ordering of the synonyms. Are there any changes that the children would make to this order?

● Ask what other words the children can think of that have a similar meaning to the word *fear* and list them on the board. Show the children the first entry. Compare the children's list with the thesaurus list. (*Note*: nouns are not included in this entry.)

● Explain that the headword is written in bold. In the first entry, the *v.* indicates that the following synonyms are for the verb *to fear*. The number *4.* shows that this is the fourth group of synonyms for the word *fear*. Informal vocabulary used more in oral than written language is indicated by the abbreviation *Sl.* (for *slang*) and informal words are indicated by *Inf*. These terms only apply to the word immediately following. Discuss the slang expressions for *fright*. Are there any expressions not listed that the children know for *fright*?

● Look at the second entry. What do the children think the *n.* and the *1.* following the headword mean? Point out *Archaic* written in italic and explain the meaning – language of the past no longer used in ordinary speech. Explain that *All sl.* means that all of the following words are slang synonyms. Arrange the synonyms for *fright* in order of intensity from mild fright to extreme fear, using the children's suggestions to compile a class scale. Discuss any points of disagreement.

● Explore the ways in which writers have to change words when selecting words from a thesaurus in order for sentences to make sense. Consider what sorts of changes need to be made (suffixes, syntax and so on). Use words from the third entry to demonstrate this.

Activities

● Provide the children with some sentences and ask them to supply the most appropriate synonyms for the words in brackets. (Tell them that they will need to check that the word fits the grammar as well as the meaning of the sentence.) For example:

As she entered the room she was overcome by _____. (fear)

Everyone present avoided his eyes. Milo sensed the _____ in the room. (tension)

● Using a piece of their recent writing, the children could highlight words where they think a stronger or more appropriate word could have been used. They can then use a thesaurus to look for possible alternatives and select one.

6: 3: T19: to review a range of non-fiction text types and their characteristics

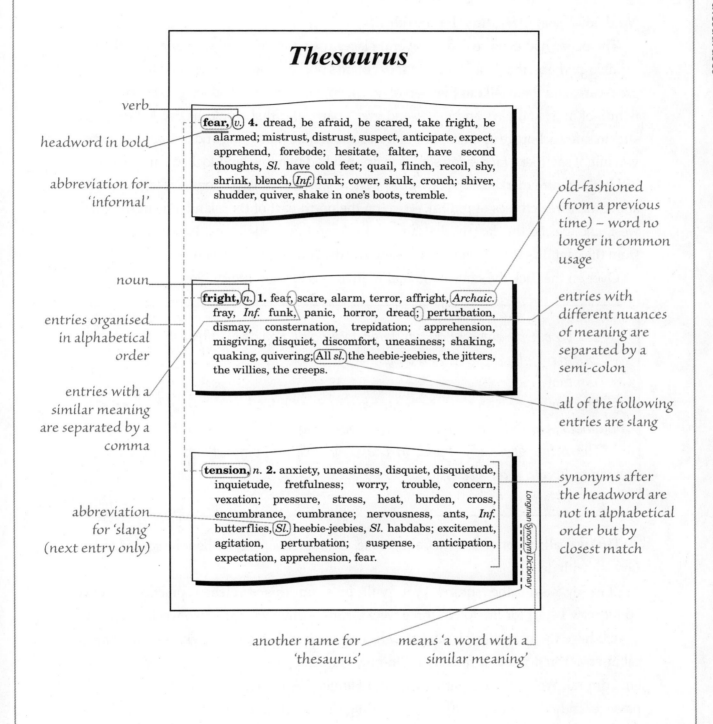

Thesaurus

verb

headword in bold

abbreviation for 'informal'

fear, *v.* **4.** dread, be afraid, be scared, take fright, be alarmed; mistrust, distrust, suspect, anticipate, expect, apprehend, forebode; hesitate, falter, have second thoughts, *Sl.* have cold feet; quail, flinch, recoil, shy, shrink, blench, *Inf.* funk; cower, skulk, crouch; shiver, shudder, quiver, shake in one's boots, tremble.

old-fashioned (from a previous time) – word no longer in common usage

noun

entries organised in alphabetical order

entries with a similar meaning are separated by a comma

fright, *n.* **1.** fear, scare, alarm, terror, affright, *Archaic.* fray, *Inf.* funk, panic, horror, dread; perturbation, dismay, consternation, trepidation; apprehension, misgiving, disquiet, discomfort, uneasiness; shaking, quaking, quivering; *All sl.* the heebie-jeebies, the jitters, the willies, the creeps.

entries with different nuances of meaning are separated by a semi-colon

all of the following entries are slang

abbreviation for 'slang' (next entry only)

tension, *n.* **2.** anxiety, uneasiness, disquiet, disquietude, inquietude, fretfulness; worry, trouble, concern, vexation; pressure, stress, heat, burden, cross, encumbrance, cumbrance; nervousness, ants, *Inf.* butterflies, *Sl.* heebie-jeebies, *Sl.* habdabs; excitement, agitation, perturbation; suspense, anticipation, expectation, apprehension, fear.

Longman Synonym Dictionary

synonyms after the headword are not in alphabetical order but by closest match

another name for 'thesaurus'

means 'a word with a similar meaning'

TREASURE ISLAND

Extract 1

THE CAPTAIN'S PAPERS

"And now," said the squire, "for the other."

The paper had been sealed in several places with a thimble by way of a seal; the very thimble, perhaps, that I had found in the captain's pocket. The doctor opened the seals with great care, and there fell out the map of an island, with latitude and longitude, soundings, names of hills, and bays and inlets, and every particular that would be needed to bring a ship to safe anchorage upon its shores. It was about nine miles long and five across, shaped, you might say, like a fat dragon standing up, and had two fine land-locked harbours, and a hill in the centre marked "The Spy-glass". There were several additions of a later date; but, above all, three crosses of red ink – two on the north part of the island, one in the south-west, and, beside this last, in the same red ink, and in a small, neat hand, very different from the captain's tottery characters, these words: "Bulk of treasure here".

Over on the back the same hand had written this further information:

> "Tall tree, Spy-glass shoulder, bearing a point to the N. of N.N.E.
> "Skeleton Island E.S.E. and by E.
> "Ten feet.
> "The bar silver is in the north cache: you can find it by the trend of the east hummock, ten fathoms south of the black crag with the face on it.
> "The arms are easy found, in the sand hill, N. point of north inlet cape, bearing E. and a quarter N.
>
> "J.F."

That was all; but brief as it was, and, to me, incomprehensible, it filled the squire and Dr. Livesey with delight.

"Livesey," said the squire, "you will give up this wretched practice at once. To-morrow I start for Bristol. In three weeks' time – three weeks! – two weeks – ten days – we'll have the best ship, sir, and the choicest crew in England. Hawkins shall come as cabin-boy. You'll make a famous cabin-boy, Hawkins. You, Livesey, are ship's doctor; I am admiral. We'll take Redruth, Joyce and Hunter. We'll have favourable winds, a quick passage, and not the least difficulty in finding the spot, and money to eat – to roll in – to play duck-and-drake with ever after."

TREASURE ISLAND

LONG JOHN SILVER

At the Sign of the "Spy-glass" *Extract 2*

As I was waiting, a man came out of a side room, and, at a glance, I was sure he must be Long John. His left leg was cut off close by the hip, and under the left shoulder he carried a crutch, which he managed with wonderful dexterity, hopping about upon it like a bird. He was very tall and strong, with a face as big as a ham – plain and pale, but intelligent and smiling. Indeed, he seemed in the most cheerful spirits, whistling as he moved about among the tables, with a merry word or a slap on the shoulder for the more favoured of his guests.

Now, to tell the truth, from the very first mention of Long John in Squire Trelawney's letter, I had taken a fear in my mind that he might prove to be the very one-legged sailor whom I had watched for so long at the old "Benbow". But one look at the man before me was enough. I had seen the captain, and Black Dog, and the blind man Pew, and I thought I knew what a buccaneer was like – a very different creature, according to me, from this clean and pleasant-tempered landlord.

The First Blow *Extract 3*

And with that this brave fellow turned his back directly on the cook, and set off walking for the beach. But he was not destined to go far. With a cry, John seized the branch of a tree, whipped the crutch out of his arm-pit, and sent that uncouth missile hurtling through the air. It struck poor Tom, point foremost, and with stunning violence, right between his shoulders in the middle of his back. His hands flew up, he gave a sort of gasp, and fell.

Whether he were injured much or little, none could ever tell. Like enough, to judge from the sound, his back was broken on the spot. But he had no time given him to recover. Silver, agile as a monkey, even without leg or crutch, was on top of him next moment, and had twice buried his knife up to the hilt in that defenceless body. From my place of ambush, I could hear him pant aloud as he struck the blows.

Robert Louis Stevenson

The story of Romeo and Juliet

In old Verona, where the streets were hot and narrow and the walls were high, where men were as bright as wasps and carried quick swords for their stings, there lived two families – the Capulets and the Montagues – who hated each other worse than death. They had but to pass in the street and they were at each other's throats like dogs in the sun. Cursing and shouting and bawling, and crashing from civil pillar to post, they filled the good people of Verona with fear and anger to have their city's peace so senselessly disturbed.

They were at it again! In the buzzing heat of a July morning, two lazy no-good servants of the Capulets had spied two strolling men of the Montagues. Looks had been exchanged, then words, and in moments the peaceful market was in uproar as the four idle ruffians set about defending their masters' honour by smashing up stalls, overturning baskets, wrecking shops and wounding passers-by, in their valiant endeavours to cut each other into pieces.

Benvolio, a sensible young Montague, came upon the scene and tried to put a stop to it; Tybalt, a young Capulet so full of fury that he sweated knives, promptly went for Benvolio; old Montague and old Capulet appeared and tried to draw their doddering swords – that surely would have shaken more like straws in the wind than lightning in the sky. Men shouted, women screamed and rushed to drag wandering infants into safety… and bloody riot threatened to swallow up all the fair city, till the Prince of Verona, with soldiers, came furiously into the square.

"Rebellious subjects, enemies to peace!" he roared; and, by dint of stern anger and sterner threats, restored some semblance of peace. The vile destructive brawling between the Montagues and the Capulets incensed him beyond measure.

"If ever you disturb our streets again," he swore, "your lives shall pay the forfeit."

Leon Garfield

Cargoes

Quinquereme of Ninevah from distant Ophir
Rowing home to haven in sunny Palestine,
With a cargo of ivory,
And apes and peacocks,
Sandalwood, cedarwood, and sweet white wine.

Stately Spanish galleon coming from the Isthmus,
Dipping through the Tropics by the palm-green shores,
With a cargo of diamonds,
Emeralds, amethysts,
Topazes, and cinnamon, and gold moidores.

Dirty British coaster with a salt-caked smoke stack
Butting through the Channel in the mad March days,
With a cargo of Tyne coal,
Road-rail, pig-lead,
Firewood, iron-ware, and cheap tin trays.

John Masefield

The Sea

The sea is a hungry dog.

Giant and grey.

He rolls on the beach all day.

With his clashing teeth and shaggy jaws

Hour upon hour he gnaws

The rumbling, tumbling stones,

And "Bones, bones, bones, bones!"

The giant sea-dog moans,

Licking his greasy paws.

And when the night wind roars

And the moon rocks in the stormy cloud,

He bounds to his feet and snuffs and sniffs,

Shaking his wet sides over the cliffs,

And howls and hollos long and loud.

But on quiet days in May or June,

When even the grasses on the dune

Play no more their reedy tune,

With his head between his paws

He lies on the sandy shores,

So quiet, so quiet, he scarcely snores.

James Reeves

SOUVENIR FROM WESTON-SUPER-MARE

Moving in a bunch like creeping hands
    the donkeys, prised from their hay,
cross the day's backdrop again: cloud, tide, mud
    cement the scene grey.

I scoop away. I build. I mould – the oil's
    good for adhesion. There, that
can do for the necessary moat,
    and look! A *sand-cat*!

Ears, nose, paws straight from Egypt. And still
    ten minutes before the bus.
We look back from the top of the wall.
    Long drawn out after us

a family comes breasting the wind –
    it'll be right in their track.
The boy spots it first, running ahead.
    He goes running back

to fetch the others. They cluster and point,
    looking up and down the strand
before the wind detaches them again.
    He waits. Their backs turned,

he drops to his knees, he strokes the sand fur.
Come on – five past the bus leaves!
Dodging the weaving cars we race the station
    clock's hands light as thieves.

Libby Houston

We'll Go To Sea No More

Oh blythely shines the bonnie sun
  Upon the Isle of May,
And blythely comes the morning tide
  Into St Andrew's Bay.
Then up, gude-man, the breeze is fair,
  And up, my braw bairns three;
There's gold in yonder bonny boat
  That sails so well the sea!

I've seen the waves as blue as air,
  I've seen them green as grass;
But I never feared their heaving yet,
  From Grangemouth to the Bass.
I've seen the sea as black as pitch,
  I've seen it white as snow:
But I never feared its foaming yet,
  Though the winds blew high or low.

I never liked the landsman's life,
  The earth is aye the same;
Give me the ocean for my dower,
  My vessel for my hame.
Give me the fields that no man ploughs,
  The farm that pays no fee:
Give me the bonny fish that dance
  Aye merrily in the sea!

The sun is up, and round Inchkeith
  The breezes softly blaw;
The gude-man has his lines aboard –
  Awa', my bairns, awa'.
An ye'll be back by gloaming grey,
  An' bright the fire will low,
An' in your tales and songs we'll tell
  How weel the boat ye row.

Anon

Romeo and Juliet

Extract 1

[ACT I SC I]

Enter two other Servingmen
[ABRAM and BALTHASAR].

Samp. My naked weapon is out. Quarrel, I will
back thee.

Greg. How, turn thy back and run?

Samp. Fear me not.

Greg. No, marry! I fear thee!

Samp. Let us take the law of our sides: let them
begin.

Greg. I will frown as I pass by, and let them take
it as they list.

Samp. Nay, as they dare. I will bite my thumb at
them, which is disgrace to them if they
bear it.

Abram. Do you bite your thumb at us, sir?

Samp. I do bite my thumb, sir.

Abram. Do you bite your thumb at us, sir?

Samp. Is the law of our side if I say ay?

Greg. No.

Samp. No sir, I do not bite my thumb at you, sir,
but I bite my thumb, sir.

Greg. Do you quarrel, sir?

Abram. Quarrel, sir? No, sir.

Samp. But if you do, sir, I am for you. I serve as
good a man as you.

Abram. No better.

Samp. Well, sir.

Enter BENVOLIO.

Greg. Say 'better', here comes one of my
master's kinsmen.

Samp. Yes, better, sir.

Abram. You lie.

Samp. Draw if you be men. Gregory, remember
thy washing blow.

They fight.

Ben. Part, fools, put up your swords, you know
not what you do.

Enter TYBALT.

Tyb. What, art thou drawn among these
heartless hinds?
Turn thee, Benvolio, look upon thy death.

Ben. I do but keep the peace, put up thy sword,
Or manage it to part these men with me.

Tyb. What, drawn, and talk of peace? I hate
the word,
As I hate hell, all Montagues, and thee:
Have at thee, coward.

They fight.

Enter three or four Citizens *with*
clubs or partisans.

Citizens. Clubs, bills and partisans! Strike! Beat
them down! Down with the Capulets!
Down with the Montagues!

Enter old CAPULET *in his gown, and*
LADY CAPULET.

Cap. What noise is this? Give me my long
sword, ho!

Lady Cap. A crutch, a crutch! Why call you for
a sword?

Enter old MONTAGUE *and* LADY MONTAGUE.

Cap. My sword I say! Old Montague is come,
And flourishes his blade in spite of me.

Mont. Thou villain Capulet! Hold me not!
Let me go!

Lady Mont. Thou shalt not stir one foot to seek
a foe.

Enter Prince ESCALUS *with his* Train.

William Shakespeare

Romeo and Juliet

Extract 2

[ACT II SC II]

[*Enter* JULIET *above.*]

Romeo. But soft, what light through yonder window breaks?
It is the east and Juliet is the sun!
Arise fair sun and kill the envious moon
Who is already sick and pale with grief
That thou her maid art far more fair than she.
Be not her maid since she is envious,
Her vestal livery is but sick and green
And none but fools do wear it. Cast it off.
It is my lady, O it is my love!
O that she knew she were!
She speaks, yet she says nothing. What of that?
Her eye discourses, I will answer it.
I am too bold. 'Tis not to me she speaks.
Two of the fairest stars in all the heaven,
Having some business, do entreat her eyes
To twinkle in their spheres till they return.
What if her eyes were there, they in her head?
The brightness of her cheek would shame those stars
As daylight doth a lamp. Her eyes in heaven
Would through the airy region stream so bright
That birds would sing and think it were not night.
See how she leans her cheek upon her hand.
O that I were a glove upon that hand,
That I might touch that cheek.

Juliet.   Ay me.

Romeo.   She speaks.
Oh speak again bright angel, for thou art
As glorious to this night, being o'er my head,
As is a winged messenger of heaven
Unto the white-upturned wondering eyes
Of mortals that fall back to gaze on him
When he bestrides the lazy-puffing clouds
And sails upon the bosom of the air.

Juliet. O Romeo, Romeo, wherefore art thou Romeo?
Deny thy father and refuse thy name.
Or if thou wilt not, be but sworn my love
And I'll no longer be a Capulet.

Romeo. Shall I hear more, or shall I speak at this?

Juliet. 'Tis but thy name that is my enemy:
Thou art thyself, though not a Montague.
What's Montague? It is nor hand nor foot
Not arm nor face nor any other part
Belonging to a man. O be some other name.
What's in a name? That which we call a rose
By any other word would smell as sweet;
So Romeo would, were he not Romeo call'd
Retain that dear perfection which he owes
Without that title. Romeo, doff thy name,
And for thy name, which is no part of thee,
Take all myself.

Charles Darwin: The Early Years

Charles Robert Darwin was born in Shrewsbury, England, on 12 February 1809. His father Robert was a doctor, and his mother Susannah was daughter of the famous potteries owner, Josiah Wedgwood. Charles' grandfather was Erasmus Darwin, well known in his time as a scientist with unusual ideas. He wrote on a range of subjects such as travel by air, exploring by submarine, and evolution.

Despite his learned father and eminent grandfather, Charles' early years were not outstanding. He attended Shrewsbury School, where the main lessons were in the classics, such as Latin. Many years later, he wrote: "I believe that I was considered by all my masters and by my father as a very ordinary boy, rather below the common intelligence."

In 1825 Charles went to Edinburgh Medical School. He soon realized that medicine was not for him. He found the lectures dull, and he had to leave the operating theatre because he could not stand the horrors of surgery. (This was a few years before the first pain killer, chloroform, came into use.) So he gave up medicine, to the great disappointment of his father, who arranged the next best career. In 1828 Darwin went to Cambridge University, to study the Bible and become a priest. Later, he wrote: "I did not then in the least doubt the strict and literal truth of every word in the Bible."

Despite being keener on shooting partridges than attending lectures, Darwin gained a Bachelor of Arts degree at Cambridge in 1831. He became friendly with two of the professors, geologist Adam Sedgewick and botanist John Henslow, and he continued to develop his interest in rocks, fossils, animals and plants.

Darwin then read *Personal Narrative* by the explorer Alexander von Humboldt. Rather than become a priest straight away, he decided to organize a natural history expedition to the Canary Islands. By chance at the same time the Royal Navy was arranging a round-the-world survey expedition under Captain Robert Fitzroy. Fitzroy asked Professor Henslow to recommend a naturalist for the expedition.

Henslow, knowing of Darwin's interest, recommended him for the job. At first Darwin's father refused to provide the money needed, but was eventually persuaded that this was an excellent opportunity for his son. On 27 December 1831, Charles Darwin set sail on the 235-ton sloop-brig HMS *Beagle*.

Steve Parker

A letter from Charles Darwin

The Voyage: South America

My dear Father

I am writing this on the 8th of February one day's sail past St. Jago, (Cape de Verd), & intend taking the chance of meeting with a homeward bound vessel somewhere about the Equator.— The date however will tell whether this opportunity occurs.— I will now begin from the day of leaving England & give a short account of our progress.—

We sailed as you know on the 27th of December & have been fortunate enough to have had from that time to the present a fair & moderate breeze: It afterward proved that we escaped a heavy gale in the Channel, another at Madeira & another on coast of Africa.— But in escaping the gale, we felt its consequence—a heavy sea: In the Bay of Biscay there was a long & continued swell & the misery I endured from sea-sickness is far far beyond what I ever guessed at.— I believe you are curious about it. I will give all my dear-bought experience.— Nobody who has only been to sea for 24 hours has a right to say that sea-sickness is even uncomfortable.— The real misery only begins when you are so exhausted—that a little exertion makes a feeling of faintness come on.— I found nothing but lying in my hammock did me any good.— I must especially except your receipt of raisins, which is the only food that the stomach will bear:— On the 4th of January we were not many miles from Madeira: but as there was a heavy sea running, & the Island lay to Wind ward it was not thought worth while to beat up to it.— It afterwards has turned out it was lucky we saved ourselves the trouble: I was much too sick even to get up to see the distant outline.— On the 6th in the evening we sailed into the harbour of Santa Cruz.— I now first felt even moderately well, & I was picturing to myself all the delights of fresh fruit growing in beautiful valleys, & reading Humboldt's descriptions of the Island's glorious views.— When perhaps you may nearly guess at our disappointment, when a small pale man informed us we must perform a strict quarantine of 12 days…

…The conviction that I am walking in the new world, is even yet marvellous in my own eyes, & I daresay it is little less so to you, the receiving a letter from a son of yours in such a quarter: Believe me, my dear Father Your most affectionate son

Charles Darwin

LIVINGSTONE DISCOVERS VICTORIA FALLS, 1855

After twenty minutes' sail from Kalai we came in sight, for the first time, of the columns of vapour appropriately called 'smoke' rising at a distance of five or six miles, exactly as when large tracts of grass are burned in Africa. Five columns now arose, and, bending in the direction of the wind, they seemed placed against a low ridge covered with trees; the tops of the columns at this distance appeared to mingle with the clouds. They were white below, and higher up became dark, so as to simulate smoke very closely. The whole scene was extremely beautiful; the banks and islands dotted over the river are adorned with sylvan vegetation of great variety of colour and form… no one can imagine the beauty of the view from any thing witnessed in England. It had never been seen before by European eyes; but scenes so lovely must have been gazed upon by angels in their flight. The only want felt is that of mountains in the background. The falls are bounded on three sides by ridges 300 or 400 feet in height, which are covered with forest, with the red soil appearing among the trees.

When about half a mile from the falls, I left the canoe by which we had come down thus far, and embarked in a lighter one, with men well acquainted with the rapids, who, by passing down the centre of the stream in the eddies and still places caused by many jutting rocks, brought me to an island situated in the middle of the river, and on the edge of the lip over which the water rolls. In coming hither there was danger of being swept down by the streams which rushed along on each side of the island; but the river was now low, and we sailed where it is totally impossible to do when the water is high. But, though we had reached the island, and were within a few yards of the spot, a view from which would solve the problem, I believe that no one could perceive where the vast body of water went; it seemed to lose itself in the earth, the opposite lip of the fissure into which it disappeared being only 80 feet distant. At least I did not comprehend it until, creeping with awe to the verge, I peered down into a large rent which had been made from bank to bank of the broad Zambesi, and saw that a stream of a thousand yards broad leaped down a hundred feet, and then became suddenly compressed into a space of fifteen or twenty yards.

David Livingstone

Kensuke's Kingdom

Ship's log

December 25

Christmas Day at sea. Dad found some carols on the radio. We had crackers, all of them a bit soggy so none of them cracked, and we had the Christmas pudding Gran made for us. I gave them a drawing each – my flying fish for Dad and one of the skipper, in her hat, at the wheel for Mum. They gave me a really neat knife they'd bought in Rio. So I gave a coin back. You're supposed to do that. It's for luck.

When we were in Rio we gave the *Peggy Sue* a good scrub down. She was looking a bit manky inside and outside, but she's not anymore. We took on a lot of stores and water for the long haul to South Africa. Mum says we're doing fine, just so long as we keep south, so long as we stay in the west-to-east South Atlantic current.

We passed south of an island called St Helena a few days ago. No need to stop. Nothing much there, except it's the place where Napoleon was exiled. He died there. Lonely place to die. So, of course, I had to do a history project on Napoleon. I had to look him up in the encyclopaedia and write about him. It was quite interesting, really, but I didn't tell them that.

Stella's sulking on my bunk. Maybe it's because no one gave her a Christmas present. I offered her a taste of Gran's Christmas pudding, but she hardly gave it a sniff. Can't say I blame her.

I saw a sail today, another yacht. We shouted Happy Christmas and waved, and Stella barked her head off, but they were too far away. When the sail disappeared, the sea felt suddenly very empty.

Mum won the chess this evening. She's ahead now, twenty-one games to twenty. Dad said he let her win because it was Christmas. They joke about it, but they both want to win.

Michael Morpurgo

A Tiptoe Down Memory Lane

Extract 1

Once on the beach, my sisters ran off to get muddy and sticky and wet (and they say I am weird!) and left me sitting on a towel working out bits of mental arithmetic to keep myself occupied. Mum was busy with Joe who was only about four and very little but she interspersed this with the occasional "Go and play with your sisters, Luke" or "Just give it a go, you may like it". I sat and thought "Yeah, about as much as reclining in a vat full of acid", but eventually I dutifully got up and wandered in the direction of my sisters, trying to tiptoe to avoid as much of the sand as possible, whilst casting mournful faces at a smiling, applauding Mum.

As I walked and tolerated the disgusting feeling of wet sand between my toes, the attraction of the warm grass and the reed-type plants sticking out of the grass was too much for me and I turned and wandered to a particular big patch of grass, never giving anyone else a second thought.

One second I was there, the next, poof – I was gone, or so it seemed to them. In actual fact, I was picking all the little seeds off this piece of grass and then trying to fold it and blow between it. Have you ever tried that? Be careful though, because grass is like paper and can cut you. If you get it right, it makes a really cool squealing noise. I never can quite manage it.

Extract 2

Meanwhile, Mum had got every single person on the beach looking for me. Coastguards, police, a pack of Brownies and every available person were all shouting my name over a loudspeaker. I didn't hear a thing! I have a strange kind of hearing and can only concentrate on listening to things if I know I am meant to. Distinguishing between background and foreground noise has always been a problem, so however loud they shouted I would have presumed that it was background noise. This is a difficulty of AS because I get told off so many times for being an ignorant pig when I genuinely do not recognize that I am being spoken to. Joe has this problem a lot, lot worse than I do.

I wasn't really looking for anyone when I was found. I just stumbled across them. It was very strange because my sisters and brothers were crying and Mum grabbed me and a big fuss was made over what seemed to me like nothing. Sometimes it is very hard to understand exactly what I have done wrong.

© Luke Jackson 2002

The Village School

The morning came, without any warning, when my sisters surrounded me, wrapped me in scarves, tied up my bootlaces, thrust a cap on my head and stuffed a baked potato in my pocket.

"What's this?" I said.

"You're starting school today."

"I ain't. I'm stopping 'ome."

"Now come on, Loll. You're a big boy now."

"I ain't."

"You are."

"Boo-hoo."

They picked me up bodily, kicking and bawling, and carried me up to the road.

"Boys who don't go to school get put into boxes, and turn into rabbits, and get chopped up Sundays."

I felt this was overdoing it rather, but I said no more after that. I arrived at the school just three feet tall and fatly wrapped in my scarves. The playground roared like a rodeo, and the potato burned through my thigh. Old boots, ragged stockings, torn trousers and skirts, went skating and skidding around me. The rabble closed in; I was encircled; grit flew in my face like shrapnel. Tall girls with frizzled hair, and huge boys with sharp elbows, began to prod me with hideous interest. They plucked at my scarves, spun me round like a top, screwed my nose, and stole my potato.

I was rescued at last by a gracious lady – the sixteen-year-old junior-teacher – who boxed a few ears and dried my face and led me off to The Infants. I spent that first day picking holes in paper, then went home in a smouldering temper.

"What's the matter, Loll? Didn't he like it at school, then?"

"They never gave me the present!"

"Present? What present?"

"They said they'd give me a present."

"Well, now, I'm sure they didn't."

"They did! They said: 'You're Laurie Lee, ain't you? Well, just you sit there for the present.' I sat there all day but I never got it. I ain't going back there again!"

But after a week I felt like a veteran and grew as ruthless as anyone else. Somebody had stolen my baked potato, so I swiped somebody else's apple.

Laurie Lee

THE SOURCES OF ROMEO AND JULIET

By 1594 or 1595 when *Romeo and Juliet* was most probably written, Shakespeare had already begun to make his mark in the London theatre. Since about 1590 he had been working there as an actor and playwright. Back home in Stratford upon Avon he had left behind a wife, whom he had married when he was eighteen, and three children. His eldest child Susannah, was thirteen, around the age of Juliet. Shakespeare himself was 30 years old. He was an experienced man, poised for success in what was still an exciting new form of entertainment: the theatre.

Shakespeare had a shrewd understanding of the subjects which would be popular with audiences and the theme of tragic young love was no exception. A version of *Romeo and Juliet*, printed and sold in London in 1599, was described as 'an excellent and lamentable tragedy…'. Romeo and Juliet was a success right from the start.

The story of Romeo and Juliet was well known in several forms before Shakespeare made it his own. There had been poems, plays and stories in Italian and French. In 1567, borrowing from these European originals, William Painter had included 'The goodly history of Rhomeo and Julietta' in a volume of short stories. Even earlier, in 1562, another writer, Arthur Brooke, had turned the story into a long poem, 'The Tragical History of Romeus and Juliet'. There are many similarities between Brooke's poem and Shakespeare's play, and it is likely that Shakespeare had the poem in front of him as he wrote.

It was quite normal for Elizabethan playwrights to use existing stories as the basis for their plays. Shakespeare was a master at choosing the most interesting ideas and developing them into something more complex than the originals. In *Romeo and Juliet* we find a wider range of attitudes to love than in any of the stories on which it was based…

…Shakespeare's use of language, too, is much more interesting. The contrasts in the play are expressed in many different styles. These range from formal poetry to witty puns, from the angry outbursts of Juliet's father to the passionate idealism of the lovers. We feel the atmosphere of the play through its language.

Wendy Greenhill

News

Power of the Ring too strong for boy wizard

Thursday December 19, 2002

The second instalment in Peter Jackson's Lord of the Rings trilogy has broken the UK box office record for advance ticket sales.

The Two Towers, which went on general release yesterday, racked up a mammoth £1.7m in advance sales, well ahead of the likes of Harry Potter and the Chamber of Secrets and the recent Bond outing, Die Another Day. The figure also trumps the £1.2m in advance sales amassed by its predecessor, The Fellowship of the Ring.

The figures have prompted the Odeon cinema chain to predict that The Two Towers will go on to beat Harry Potter over the long run at the box office. Last year, The Fellowship of the Ring grossed $860m worldwide, yet lost out to Harry Potter and the Philosopher's Stone, on $965m. Odeon predicts the positions will reverse this time round.

In the meantime, The Two Towers opened yesterday to rave reviews in North America. The New York Daily News hailed it as "a masterpiece of epic film-making", while Newsday dubbed it a "stirring epic and an adventure of old-fashioned substance and eye-popping visuals".

The general consensus was that The Two Towers was both better than the current Harry Potter excursion and an improvement on the first film in Jackson's trilogy. The Boston Globe said that chapter two was "better: tighter, smarter, funnier". The Toronto Star added that "the movie plays like a true blockbuster follow-up: the action is bigger, the characters far more numerous and the stakes are much higher".

THE HOBBIT *Extract 1*

In a hole in the ground there lived a hobbit. Not a nasty, dirty, wet hole, filled with the ends of worms and an oozy smell, nor yet a dry, bare, sandy hole with nothing in it to sit down on or to eat: it was a hobbit-hole, and that means comfort.

It had a perfectly round door like a porthole, painted green, with a shiny yellow brass knob in the exact middle. The door opened on to a tube-shaped hall like a tunnel: a very comfortable tunnel without smoke, with panelled walls, and floors tiled and carpeted, provided with polished chairs, and lots and lots of pegs for hats and coats – the hobbit was fond of visitors. The tunnel wound on and on, going fairly but not quite straight into the side of the hill – The Hill, as all the people for many miles round called it – and many little round doors opened out of it, first on one side and then on another. No going upstairs for the hobbit: bedrooms, bathrooms, cellars, pantries (lots of these), wardrobes (he had whole rooms devoted to clothes), kitchens, dining-rooms, all were on the same floor, and indeed on the same passage. The best rooms were all on the lefthand side (going in), for these were the only ones to have windows, deep-set round windows looking over his garden, and meadows beyond, sloping down to the river.

This hobbit was a very well-to-do hobbit, and his name was Baggins. The Bagginses had lived in the neighbourhood of The Hill for time out of mind, and people considered them very respectable, not only because most of them were rich, but also because they never had any adventures or did anything unexpected; you could tell what a Baggins would say on any question without the bother of asking him. This is a story of how a Baggins had an adventure, and found himself doing and saying things altogether unexpected. He may have lost the neighbours' respect, but he gained – well, you will see whether he gained anything in the end.

JRR Tolkien

THE HOBBIT   *Extract 2*

On the table in the light of a big lamp with a red shade he spread a piece of parchment rather like a map.

"This was made by Thror, your grandfather, Thorin," he said in answer to the dwarves' excited questions. "It is a plan of the Mountain."

"I don't see that this will help us much," said Thorin disappointedly after a glance. "I remember the Mountain well enough and the lands about it. And I know where Mirkwood is, and the Withered Heath where the great dragons bred."

"There is a dragon marked in red on the Mountain," said Balin, but it will be easy enough to find him without that, if we ever arrive there."

"There is one point that you haven't noticed," said the wizard, "and that is the secret entrance. You see that rune on the West side, and the hand pointing to it from the other runes? That marks a hidden passage to the Lower Halls." (Look at the map at the beginning of this book, and you will see there the runes.)

"It may have been secret once," said Thorin, "but how do we know that it is secret any longer? Old Smaug has lived there long enough now to find out anything there is to know about those caves."

"He may – but he can't have used it for years and years."

"Why?"

"Because it is too small. 'Five feet high the door and three may walk abreast' say the runes, but Smaug could not creep into a hole that size, not even when he was a young dragon, certainly not after devouring so many of the dwarves and men of Dale."

"It seems a great big hole to me," squeaked Bilbo (who had no experience of dragons and only of hobbit-holes). He was getting excited and interested again, so that he forgot to keep his mouth shut. He loved maps, and in his hall there hung a large one of the Country Round with all his favourite walks marked on it in red ink. "How could such a large door be kept secret from everybody outside, apart from the dragon?" he asked. He was only a little hobbit you must remember.

"In lots of ways," said Gandalf. "But in what way this one has been hidden we don't know without going to see. From what it says on the map I should guess there is a closed door which has been made to look exactly like the side of the Mountain."

THE HOBBIT

Extract 3

I suppose hobbits need some description nowadays, since they have become rare and shy of the Big People, as they call us. They are (or were) a little people, about half our height and smaller than the bearded Dwarves. Hobbits have no beards. There is little or no magic about them, except the ordinary everyday sort which helps them to disappear quietly and quickly when large stupid folk like you and me come blundering along, making a noise like elephants which they can hear a mile off. They are inclined to be fat in the stomach; they dress in bright colours (chiefly green and yellow); wear no shoes, because their feet grow natural leathery soles and thick warm brown hair like the stuff on their heads (which is curly); have long clever brown fingers, good-natured faces, and laugh deep fruity laughs (especially after dinner, which they have twice a day when they can get it).

Extract 4

Deep down here by the dark water lived old Gollum, a small slimy creature. I don't know where he came from, nor who or what he was. He was Gollum – as dark as darkness, except for two big round pale eyes in his thin face. He had a little boat, and he rowed about quite quietly on the lake; for lake it was, wide and deep and deadly cold. He paddled it with large feet dangling over the side, but never a ripple did he make. Not he. He was looking out of his pale limp-like eyes for blind fish, which he grabbed with his long fingers as quick as thinking. He liked meat too. Goblin he thought good, when he could get it; but he took care they never found him out. He just throttled them from behind, if they ever came down alone anywhere near the edge of the water, while he was prowling about. They very seldom did, for they had a feeling that something unpleasant was lurking down there, down at the very roots of the mountain.

JRR Tolkien

The Eagle of the Ninth

Extract 1

On the Road

From the Fosseway westward to Isca Dumnoniorum the road was simply a British trackway, broadened and roughly metalled, strengthened by corduroys of logs in the softest places, but otherwise unchanged from its old estate, as it wound among the hills, thrusting further and further into the wilderness.

It was a busy road and saw many travellers: traders with bronze weapons and raw yellow amber in their ponies' packs; country folk driving shaggy cattle or lean pigs from village to village; sometimes a band of tawny-haired tribesmen from further west; strolling harpers and quack-oculists, too, or a light-stepping hunter with huge wolf-hounds at his heel; and from time to time a commissariat wagon going up and down to supply the Roman frontier post. The road saw them all, and the cohorts of the Eagles for whom all other travellers must make way.

There was a cohort of leather-clad auxiliaries on the road today, swinging along at the steady Legion's pace that had brought them down from Isca Silurium at twenty miles a day; the new garrison coming to relieve the old one at Isca Dumnoniorum. On they went, following the road that now ran out on a causeway between sodden marsh and empty sky, now plunged into deep boar-hunted forest, or lifted over bleak uplands where nothing grew save furze and thorn-scrub. On with never a halt nor a change of rhythm, marching century by century, the sun bright on the Standard at their head, and the rolling dust-cloud kicked up over the pack-train behind.

At the head of the column marched the Pilus Prior Centurion, the cohort Commander, the pride that shone from him showing clearly that this was his first command. They were, he had long since decided, a command worthy of anyone's pride; six hundred yellow-haired giants recruited from the tribes of Upper Gaul, with the natural fighting power of mountain cats, drilled and hammered into what he firmly believed to be the finest auxiliary cohort ever to serve with the Second Legion. They were a newly joined cohort; many of the men had not yet proved themselves in action, and the spearshaft of their Standard had no honours on it, no gilded laurel wreath nor victor's crown. The honours were all to win – perhaps during his command.

Rosemary Sutcliff

The Eagle of the Ninth

Extract 2

Gladiators

The roar which greeted the pair of fighters had fallen to a breathless hush. In the centre of the arena the two men were being placed by the captain of the gladiators; placed with exquisite care, ten paces apart, with no advantage of light or wind allowed to either. The thing was quickly and competently done, and the captain stepped back to the barriers. For what seemed a long time, neither of the two moved. Moment followed moment, and still they remained motionless, the centre of all that great circle of staring faces. Then, very slowly, the swordsman began to move. Never taking his eyes from his adversary, he slipped one foot in front of the other; crouching a little, covering his body with the round buckler, inch by inch he crept forward, every muscle tensed to spring when the time came.

The Fisher stood as still as ever, poised on the balls of his feet, the trident in his left hand, his right lost in the folds of the net. Just beyond reach of the net, the swordsman checked for a long, agonising moment, and then sprang in. His attack was so swift that the flung net flew harmlessly over his head, and the Fisher leapt back and sideways to avoid his thrust, then whirled about and ran for his life, gathering his net for another cast as he ran, with the young swordsman behind him. Half round the arena they sped, running low; the swordsman had not the other's length and lightness of build, but he ran as a hunter runs – perhaps he had run down deer on the hunting trail, before ever his ear was clipped – and he was gaining on his quarry now. The two came flying round the curve of the barrier towards the Magistrates' benches, and just abreast of them the Fisher whirled about and flung once more. The net whipped out like a dark flame; it licked round the running swordsman, so intent on his chase that he had forgotten to guard for it; the weight carried the deadly folds across and across again, and a howl burst from the crowd as he crashed headlong and rolled over, helplessly meshed as a fly in a spider's web.

Rosemary Sutcliff

The Eagle of the Ninth

Extract 3

Esca's Freedom

When Marcus, with Cub at his heels, entered his sleeping-quarters that night, Esca, who was waiting for him as usual, laid down the belt whose clasps he had been burnishing, and asked: "When do we start?"

Marcus closed the door and stood with his back against it. "Probably the morn's morning – that is, for myself, at least. The details can wait awhile; but first you had best take this," and he held out a slim papyrus roll he had been carrying.

Esca took it with a puzzled glance at his face, and unrolling it, he held it to the lamplight. And watching him, Marcus remembered suddenly and piercingly the moment that afternoon when he had taken off Cub's collar. Cub had come back to him; but Esca?

Esca looked up from the papyrus, and shook his head. "Capitals are one thing," he said, "but I can make nothing of this script. What is it?"

"Your manumission – your freedom," Marcus said. "I made it out this evening, and Uncle Aquila and the Legate witnessed it. Esca, I ought to have given it to you long ago; I have been a completely unthinking fool, and I am sorry."

Esca looked down at the thing in his hands once more, and again back to Marcus, as though he was not sure that he understood. Then he let the roll spring back on itself, and said very slowly: "I am free? Free to go?"

"Yes," Marcus said. "Free to go, Esca."

There was a long dragging silence. An owl cried somewhere afar off, with a note that seemed at once desolate and mocking. Cub looked from one to the other, and whined softly in his throat.

Then Esca said, "Is it that you are sending me away?"

"No! It is for you to go, or stay, as you wish."

Esca smiled, the slow grave smile that always seemed to come a little unwillingly to his face. "Then I stay," he said, and hesitated. "It is perhaps not only I who think foolish thoughts because of the Tribune Placidus."

"Perhaps." Marcus reached out and set both hands lightly on the other's shoulders. "Esca, I should never have asked you to come with me into this hazard when you were not free to refuse. It is like to prove a wild hunt, and whether or not we shall come back from it lies on the knees of the gods. No one should ask a slave to go with him on such a hunting trail; but – he might ask a friend." He looked questioningly into Esca's face.

Riddles

On the way a miracle: water become bone.

(A: ɘɔi)

KEVIN CROSSLEY-HOLLAND (Anglo-Saxon)

This thing all things devours:
Birds, beasts, trees, flowers;
Gnaws iron, bites steel;
Grinds hard stones to meal;
Slays kings, ruins town,
And beats high mountains down.

(A: ɘɯiʇ)   JRR TOLKIEN

Riddle me this, and riddle my that—
Guess my riddle or perhaps not.
What is it you pass going to town
that faces you, and coming from town it
faces you and hasn't moved?

(A: ɘɘɹʇ ɐ)   JAMES BERRY

Light fingered, invisible
A thief through and through
He'll steal your hat, he'll whip your scarf
And your newspaper too.
He'll hang around street corners
And pounce as you go by
Or hover at your window
And slip in with a sigh.

(A: puiʍ)   GEORGE SZIRTES

Limericks

There was a Young Lady of Ryde,
Whose shoe-strings were seldom untied;
　　She purchased some clogs,
　　And some small spotty dogs,
And frequently walked about Ryde.

There was a Young Lady from Norway
Who casually sat in a doorway;
　　When the door squeezed her flat,
　　She exclaimed, "What of that?"
This courageous Young Lady of Norway.

There was an old man in a tree,
Who was horribly bored by a bee.
　　When they said, "Does it buzz?"
　　He replied, "Yes it does!
It's a regular brute of a bee."

Edward Lear

A fly and a flea in a flue
Were imprisoned, so what could they do?
　　Said the fly, "Let us flee!"
　　"Let us fly!" said the flea,
So they flew through a flaw in the flue.

PL Mannock

There was an old man of St. Bees,
Who was stung in the arm by a wasp,
　　When asked, "Does it hurt?"
　　He replied, "No it doesn't,
I'm so glad it wasn't a hornet."

WS Gilbert

January to December

The warm cows have gone
From the fields where grass stands up
Dead-alive like steel.

Unexpected sun
Probes the house as if someone
Had left the lights on.

Novel no longer
Snowdrops melt in the hedge, drain
Away into spring.

The heron shining
Works his way up the bright air
Above the river.

Earth dries. The sow basks
Flat out with her blue-black young,
Ears over their eyes.

The early lambs, still
Fleecy, look bulkier now
Than their shorn mothers.

In this valley full
Of bird song, the gap closes
Behind the cuckoo.

Fields of barley glimpsed
Through trees shine out like golden
Windows in winter.

Though nothing has changed –
The sun is even hotter –
Death is in the air.

Long shadows herald
Or dog every walker
In the cut-back lanes.

A crop of mist grows
Softly in the valley, lolls
Over the strawsacks.

Meadows filmed across
With rain stare up at winter
Hardening in the hills.

Patricia Beer

Sonnets

OZYMANDIAS

I met a traveller from an antique land
Who said: Two vast and trunkless legs of stone
Stand in the desert… Near them, on the sand,
Half sunk, a shattered visage lies, whose frown
And wrinkled lip, and sneer of cold command,
Tell that its sculptor well those passions read
Which yet survive, stamped on these lifeless things,
The hand that mocked them, and the heart that fed:
And on the pedestal these words appear:
'My name is Ozymandias, king of kings:
Look on my works, ye Mighty, and despair!'
Nothing beside remains. Round the decay
Of that colossal wreck, boundless and bare
The lone and level sands stretch far away.

PB SHELLEY

Sonnet composed upon Westminster Bridge, 3rd September 1802

Earth has not anything to show more fair:
Dull would he be of soul who could pass by
A sight so touching in its majesty:
This City now doth, like a garment, wear
The beauty of the morning; silent, bare,
Ships, towers, domes, theatres and temples lie
Open unto the fields, and to the sky;
All bright and glittering in the smokeless air.
Never did sun more beautifully steep
In his first splendour, valley, rock or hill;
Ne'er saw I, never felt, a calm so deep!
The river glideth at his own sweet will:
Dear God! The very houses seem asleep;
And all that mighty heart is lying still!

WILLIAM WORDSWORTH

Rules – are they there to be broken?

The media often describes a new band or fashion as 'breaking all the rules'. This means they think it is exciting, refreshing and rebellious. The word 'rules' suggests boring and restricting regulations, but a healthy society needs some rules and laws so that citizens can live harmoniously together. Citizens over the age of 18 are responsible for voting in the government, whose job it is to create the laws.

Why have any rules at all?

Are rules at home and school just adults' way of bossing children about and stopping them from being individuals? Or can rules be helpful? Do you agree with this young person's opinion, which comes from the National Children's Bureau's *Young Opinions, Great Ideas* survey: "I think that the children should have a say in the rules and it shouldn't just be the parents' point of view of what you should and shouldn't do. I think that children should put down some rules for them as well."

Keeping you safe

Both in school and outside, rules and laws are intended to protect you from yourself and others. Sometimes they are really a warning, for example shops are not allowed to sell cigarettes to anyone under the age of sixteen because they are so bad for your health. There are always big lists of rules at swimming pools, which aim to prevent accidents. Speed restrictions on roads and rules about not driving if you have drunk alcohol are there to save lives and avoid accidents.

If everybody had enough money, and everything they needed to have a good quality of life, do you think we would still need laws? The only thing that seems to stop some people from breaking the rules and committing crimes is a fear of going to prison. Can you think of a situation where you think more rules or laws are needed?

FACTS
- *75% of 12–25 year-olds are afraid of being physically attacked, and boys are more worried about it than girls.*
- *39% of 11–16 year-olds declare disruptive classmates as the most common cause of problems at school.*

2020 Vision survey by the Industrial Society, 1997

Katrina Dunbar

Performing sea creatures

A new trend in animal entertainment is the growth of centres and theme parks devoted to sea life. These twenty-first century aquaria attract the same type of criticism as zoos because they use captive animals, but they defend themselves by pointing out the high standard of care that they provide for their animals.

Sea life centres in Britain are very popular with schools and young people. The 'walk through' layout takes visitors past and even under glass tanks that allow them to see marine animals in a version of their natural habitat. The centres are primarily for entertainment but they also offer a great deal of information and education. The sea life centres do not keep larger marine animals captive as they feel that this would be cruel.

The sea world adventure parks in the USA are much larger. Sea World Florida covers 81 hectares and is home to some of the largest marine mammals including the famous orca (killer whale) Shamu. Sea World focuses on entertainment, offering rides, shows and attractions that star 800 different creatures including whales, walruses, seals, polar bears, sea lions, otters, dolphins and many others.

Critics of this kind of park say that it is cruel to keep large marine animals captive; they need more space than the park can offer. Sea World says that its animals enjoy what they do, they are looked after well by experts and are happy living in the company of others in large tanks. In addition, Sea World is actively involved in education, rescue rehabilitation and captive breeding work.

> **• case study • case study •**
>
> Catharine Mason and her Brownie group visited her local sea life centre in Tynemouth, UK for a sleepover.
>
> "It was great, we slept in the hotel next to the centre and were allowed in to the centre at night. They switched all the lights off except in the tanks – it was beautiful. We learned a lot about fish and they even let us stroke the rays."
>
> **• case study • case study •**

Chris Mason

50 Shared texts • Year 6

Why conservation?

What does conservation have to do with us?

It is not always easy to see why we should get involved in conservation. After all, in the UK most people have enough food, computers are everywhere and most homes have a television, washing machine and telephone. What are the links between our standard of living and events in other parts of the world?

Our standard of living depends on using resources taken from the environment. The resources may not be from our immediate environment – indeed many of the goods we need and want are made from metals that come from the world's poorest countries. For example:

- only two of the top ten copper-producing countries use large amounts of copper, the rest is exported to other countries
- only four of the top ten lead-producing countries use large amounts of lead
- of the ten top tin-producing countries, five are not leading tin users.

So, what do the figures mean? Developing countries that need resources (in this case, metals) for their own development are selling the resources to other countries that already have a far higher standard of living than their own. At the same time, the large-scale mining operations to extract the metals cause wide-scale damage to their environment. Developing countries cannot afford to put the damage right and very often mining companies extracting the metals think that the environmental damage is not their responsibility. They argue that the economy of the countries concerned benefit from mining activities.

In fact, the money a country earns from sending its resources to other countries to be turned into manufactured goods is rarely enough to improve the living standards of its people. The people living near mines are actually exposed to increased pollution which can lead to health problems such as lead poisoning and **respiratory diseases.** In addition, turning resources into goods uses up valuable fuel energy.

Although this may seem far removed from you, the copper wires that carry electricity to your house to power your television could well have come form a developing country. That is just one of many examples. What can you do to make a difference? By recycling your can of cola you are helping reduce the amount of new aluminium that needs to be mined. Can you think of other ways to make a difference? Every small action helps.

Richard Spilsbury

Packaging guidelines

Dos	Don'ts
Do check on any prohibitions or restrictions on goods.	Don't send dangerous or prohibited goods as you may be liable to prosecution.
Do use a strong outer container such as a corrugated fibreboard carton with a good quality kraft outer liner.	Don't use substandard or damaged cartons.
Do put protective wrapping around each individual item.	Don't allow movement of contents.
Do use expanded polystyrene chips, polyethylene foam, bubble plastic or shredded paper to cushion fragile items.	Don't allow fragile items inside parcel to touch each other.
Do seal cartons top and bottom with an 'H' seal using 38mm or 50mm wide plastic or reinforced carton sealing tape.	Don't use domestic adhesive tape.
Do strap (with non metallic strapping if possible) and tape large or heavy items, use an outer carton strong enough to withstand fully tensioned strapping.	Don't use string around boxes (it can be used around other wrapping).
Do include the sender's address on the outer carton/wrapper, as well as inside the parcel.	Don't send consignments without the full address, the postcode or zip code, or telephone number of the addressee.

Suggested content and carton grades

It is important that the outer packaging is of sufficient grade in relation to the weight of the contents. Please see table:

Weight of Contents (up to)	Grade of Carton
5kg	200gsm
10kg	300gsm
15kg	150gsm double wall
20kg	200gsm double wall
25kg	200gsm double wall
30kg	300gsm double wall

Please note: gsm (grammes per square metre) is a standard measure for the weight of paper.

Suitable cushioning material, of which a minimum thickness of 50mm is recommended, should be used for inner packaging to protect contents from damage.

Claims for compensation in the event of damage will be refused if the contents are inadequately packaged and may be refused if the packaging is not retained. For further information and guidance about packaging, please phone the Parcelforce Worldwide Enquiry Centre free on **08708 50 11 50**.

Living well with allergies

A quarter of the UK population will experience an allergic reaction at some point in their lives. This number is increasing by 5% every year, and children now make up half the total number of sufferers.

While hayfever is probably the most common condition, there are many more, each with a wide range of effective treatments. So, once you've found the best way to manage your allergy, it needn't stop you from leading a full, comfortable and enjoyable life.

What is an allergy?

An allergy or allergic reaction is caused when your body's immune system reacts to a particular 'allergen' or trigger. This trigger gets into your body through your skin or eyes, but you can also eat it or breathe it in.

The most common allergies are: hayfever, with 9 million sufferers; eczema, 6 million; asthma, 5.1 million; and year round hayfever-like symptoms, triggered by dust mites, known as perennial rhinitis. They tend to run in the family so if one of your parents has an allergy you have a one in three chance of being affected too. This rises to a two in three chance if both your parents have allergies.

What causes an allergic reaction?

The most common triggers are pollen, the house dust mite and pets. Others include:

- Bee and wasp stings
- Latex
- Mould spores
- Particular foods, e.g. nuts and shellfish

Why are so many people suffering from allergies today?

Modern lifestyles may have an effect on our immune systems:

- Warm, well-sealed homes encourage common triggers like the house dust mite.
- We now spend on average 90% of our time indoors.
- Most people's diets are high in fat and low in fruit and vegetables.
- Fluctuating levels of air pollution.

Further information and advice
British Allergy Foundation
Deepdene House
30 Bellegrove Road
Welling
Kent DA16 3PY

FIRE INSTRUCTIONS

1. **IF YOU DISCOVER A FIRE:**

    a. Immediately press the nearest fire alarm button – causing the fire alarm bells to ring.

    b. Pick up the nearest telephone and dial 999 – the operator will ask you which service you require. Say:

    # "Fire Brigade"

    Give this telephone number:

    # 01234 56789

    Then say distinctly:

    ### FIRE AT **NAME OF BUILDING AND STREET**.

    c. Try to extinguish the fire by using the nearest suitable fire extinguishers but DO NOT take any personal risks.

2. **EVACUATION OF THE BUILDING**

    On the sounding of the alarm leave the building and assemble away from the building leaving all approach roads clear to enable the fire brigade to reach the building.

    * Act quietly.
    * Use the nearest available exit.
    * Do not use lifts or elevators.

3. **ADVICE FOR DEALING WITH A FIRE**

    a. If a person's clothing is on fire, use an overcoat, rug or other similar article and wrap it around the person, who should be laid on the ground to prevent the flames reaching the head.

    b. If electrical fittings are involved in a fire, be sure that the current is switched off before touching them or dealing with the fire.

    c. Shut the doors and, if possible, the windows of the room in which the fire is discovered. This will prevent draughts and reduce the risks of the fire spreading.

Nikki Gamble

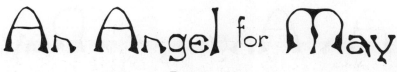

An Angel for May

Extract 1

The wind was beginning to whip up hard, icy drops of rain that stung his face. Tam had run out with no coat and he was frozen already but he wasn't going home, not yet, not now – not ever, the way he felt just then. He'd catch cold first and die out here where the coarse grass began to give way to the heather from the moor above. One day someone would find his skull staring down at the town, just as he had once found a sheep's skull, and they'd wonder who he was and how he got there. Tam felt that he could do anything to hurt his mother.

As he dropped down into the secret valley the wind softened. It was still hard enough. A line of Scots pines that had once been a windbreak flickered and bent in it. Now that the sheep roamed freely over the wrecked homestead they ate the young seedlings that sprouted up and the colony of trees was dying out. The line stood against the open moorland above like shattered posts. Some trees were broken off, some were still in their prime. But there were no saplings. The sheep ate everything.

If you had to be miserable the old farm was a good place to do it. There was no one there to see you except a few untidy sheep and the little brown and grey birds that flicked and chirruped over these low moorland fields.

Tam sat down in a corner of one of the rooms. The noises of the moor – the wind, a curlew calling some way off, a little bird chittering nearby – carried on above his head. It was a strange feeling, sitting in a room with the rain still speckling your skin and the wind in your hair. To one side of him was the tall wall with the chimney in it. People had come for picnics and lit fires there. A circle of stones had been laid out in front of it, and at night, staring at a blaze you could imagine that this was still a home and that behind your back the rooms still stood and people slept and talked and lived. Perhaps they did.

Melvin Burgess

Term 3: Comparison of work by significant children's author

An Angel for May

Extract 2

It was cold. Something seemed to be sliding over him, or through him. Then he thought he must be falling and his hands flew out to the brick wall to stop his head from bumping, but he twisted and seemed to miss the ground altogether. He cried out.

Then it stopped. He was unexpectedly on his backside on solid ground. He had his hands stretched out and his face pulled back. The wall that had been in front was now behind him. He was in a farmyard. There were chickens pecking and a strong smell of straw and manure. Tam backed into the wall; he was terrified, he felt sick. Everything had gone wrong. He had been moved out of his place – but then he saw that it was the same place. There above him was the old familiar hill, just as it had been a moment before, lying in the same secret stillness. But then he saw it was not the same, not quite. It was purple, but he had seen it like this before.

The heather was out. The leaves were turning. Spring had gone and it was autumn – a blowy autumn day with big fluffy clouds and yellow leaves scutting about the yard. And there were the Scots pines, but now in a dense thicket of shrubs with young saplings around them. Winnie was standing by his side; she barked twice and sat down. She seemed to be smiling. But Tam felt really dizzy – he was all wrong, he shouldn't be here. Had he gone mad?

He noticed Rosey standing by him. He was sure she hadn't been there before. He turned on her.

"Where are we?" he demanded. She said nothing. Her mouth was working and she was nodding her head. She had that faint smile again. For a second Tam thought she was laughing at him.

"What have you done to me?" he shouted.

The old woman looked blankly past him.

"You… What have you done?" demanded Tam in a frightened rage. He would have jumped at her and screamed, but the dog was near and watching him closely.

This was her place. He *had* gone mad – just like the old woman. She had taken him to a place where mad people go.

Melvin Burgess

THE GHOST BEHIND THE WALL

Extract 1

He pushed the sofa up against the wall and climbed up to have a look. It was dark in there, pitch black, and he knew at once that it was big enough for him to get inside if he wanted to. Of course, he didn't want to. Why should anyone want to go creeping about like a rat in the intestines of the old building? But he was glad that grid was screwed to the wall so tightly, that was for sure, because that meant he couldn't get in even if he did want to. Then, to his horror, David saw that the grid wasn't screwed on at all. It was only the metal frame that held the grid that was screwed on. The grid itself was slid sideways into the frame.

David pushed the grid; it slid sideways with a sudden jerk and there he was, gazing into the dark heart of Mahogany Villas. His heart twisted and sank. He knew he was going to have to go in there.

Extract 2

After a little while, when there was no noise, he poked his head cautiously round to have another look.

Inside the flat it was dull. Maybe it was being decorated. He remembered how his dad had taken the grid off once when he was decorating. He waited a long time but heard nothing – no voices, no radio or television – so he plucked up his courage and slid like a snake down towards the opening to try and see inside.

He tried to be quiet, but some scufflings had to happen. At one point he forgot himself and banged hard on the metal. He froze – but there was still no noise. It must be that no one was in. He got to the lip of the vent, waited just to be sure there was no noise, then pulled himself forward on his stomach and peered in.

Right down below him was an old man sitting in an armchair. As David stared, the old man opened his eyes and looked up. David yelped. For one horrible moment they stared straight into each other's faces, and then the old man opened his mouth and said,

"Jonathon!"

Melvin Burgess

THE GHOST BEHIND THE WALL

Extract 3

That night, David heard crying again. The ghost boy was weeping in a thin, quiet way to itself, as if it didn't know or care if anyone heard it. The sound was clearer and louder than before, as if the ghost was becoming more real every time he went into the pipes. David sat up in bed to listen.

"What's wrong?" whispered David. The ghost didn't answer, but the sobbing became slightly louder. David was sure the boy had heard him.

"Where are you?" David asked again.

The ghost snuffled and a voice from nowhere said, "I'm lost."

"Lost?" David was puzzled. He looked around and tried to work out where the voice was coming from. "Where do you want to go?" he asked.

"I don't know, I'm lost."

"Well, where do you belong, then?"

"Sod that," hissed the ghost. David laughed. A swearing ghost! The ghost laughed back.

"Sod that!" said the voice, and this time David could place it. It was coming from the floor by the side of his bed, and when he turned to look, there was the ghost lying there. He was on his side towards the wall, but he had twisted his head round so that David could see his wide, tear-stained face breaking out into a laugh as he looked up at him. The face got bigger, and at first David thought he was sitting up, but it wasn't that. His face was simply getting bigger, wider, closer. Maybe it was just the ghost's way of getting closer to him, but it made David cry out in fright. Then the laugh faded, and the figure faded with it, and all David could make out was a paleness in the place where the ghost had sat.

"I'm here now," said the voice softly, and David almost jumped out of bed in fright, because suddenly the voice wasn't coming from the floor by his bed, but from behind the grid leading to the pipes. There was a pause and then the voice said clearly, "Come in here with me."

Melvin Burgess

Mum Dad and Me

My parents grew among palm trees,
in sunshine strong and clear.
I grow in weather that's pale,
misty, watery or plain cold,
around back streets of London.

Dad swam in warm sea, at my age.
I swim in a roofed pool.
Mum – she still doesn't swim.

Mum went to an open village market
at my age. I go to a covered
arcade one with her now.
Dad works most Saturdays.

At my age Dad played
cricket with friends.
Mum helped her mum, or talked
shouting halfway up a hill.
Now I read or talk on the phone.

With her friends Mum's mum washed
clothes on a river stone. Now
washing machine washes our clothes.
We save time to eat to TV,
never speaking.

My dad longed for a freedom in Jamaica.
I want a greater freedom.
Mum prays for us, always.

Mum goes to church
some evenings and Sundays.
I go to the library.
Dad goes for his darts at the local.

Mum walked everywhere, at my age.
Dad rode a donkey.
Now I take a bus
or catch the underground train.

James Berry

Sunny Market
Song

1st Voice: Coffee
Spiced chocolate
Ackee

White yam
Yellow Yam
Juicy melon

Breadfruit
Grapefruit
Arrowroot

2nd voice: I want some cinnamon and
tamarind, mam

3rd voice: Buy quatty wo't' noh, gal—
Buy quatty wo't'

(FOWLS CACKLE)

1st voice: Tapioca
Sarsaparilla
Cassava

Snapper Fish
Fresh Fish
Strong charcoal

Dry coconuts
Water coconuts
Mango

2nd voice: I want some cloves and lemon,
mam

3rd voice: Buy quatty wo't' noh, gal—
Buy quatty wo't'

(A PIG SQUEALS)

1st voice: Custard apple
Ripe pineapple
Sweet potatoes

Cho-cho
Callalu
Coco

Soursop
Sweetsop
Sorrel

2nd voice: I want some nutmeg and
ginger, mam

3rd voice: Buy quatty wo't' noh gal-
Buy quatty wo't'

(A GOAT BLEATS)

1st voice: Foo-foo plantain
Ripe plantain
Papaw

Fever grass
Strong-back herb
Mount'n honey comb

Orange
Cabbage
Hominy corn

2nd voice: I want some allspice and
pepper, mam

3rd voice: Buy quatty wo't' noh, gal—
Buy quatty wo't'

(DOGS BARK)

1st voice: Fresh whelks
Beeswax
Floor dye

Blackeye peas
Congo peas
Okra

Jackass rope
Raw sugar
Ripe bananas

2nd voice: I want some scallion and
annatto, mam

3rd voice: Buy quatty wo't' noh gal—
But quatty wo't'

(A DONKEY BRAYS)

James Berry

MEK DRUM TALK, MAN

for Caribbean Independence

Budoom-a budoom-a budoom-a ba-dap.

A dudu-wum a-dudu-wum dudu-wum a dudu-wum.

Wake skin up. Wake skin.

Slap it up. Slap skin.

Man, slap up drum.

Use yu hundred han them.

Domination get drop.

Some doors get open up.

Lawks O, slap the drum, slap it Buddy.

Slap it like you a mad mad somody—

budoom-a budoom-a budoom-a ba-dap,

budoom-a budoom-a budoom-a ba-dap.

A-dudu-wum a-dudu-wum dudu-wum a-dudu-wum.

Budoom-a dudu-wum. Budoom-a dudu-wum. Bru-dum.

Let out lost ancestor voice.

Let out of skin all pain and vice.

Tell the worl that the king is dead—

forbidden people gettn wed.

Tell towns new words comin fo print—

knowledge looked-fo whe palms they skint.

Get soun like them a talkin gong,

mek them happy jus a-galang.

Get the soun, get the soun, get it Buddy.

Wake up gong and family.

Every soun is head with a hum

of deep-deep voice of drum—

tru the windows, tru the trees,

tru the markets, tru the streets.

Lawks O, slap the drum, slap it Buddy.

Slap it like you a mad mad somody—

budoom-a budoom-a budoom-a ba-dap,

budoom-a budoom-a budoom-a ba-dap.

A-dudu-wum a-dudu-wum dudu-wum a-dudu-wum.

Budoom-a dudu-wum. Budoom-a dudu-wum. Bru-dum.

Slap the drum. Elbow drum. Thump drum.

Mek drum sey to be hit is fun.

Wake up skin. Wake up skin

with it broom bu-doom it hidin.

People cry – start a new cycle!

Widen money circle!

Get out every hiddn moan.

Let loose all skin-hiddn groan.

Show off the pulse of big bright sun.

Sen good news to village and town.

Tell the people a child is born,

tell them about a sweet new dawn.

Bring street drummin in the house—

see sleepers get aroused.

Wake the people out-a they trance.

Tell people come dance.

Lawks O, slap the drum, slap it Buddy.

Slap it like you a mad mad somody—

budoom-a budoom-a budoom-a ba-dap,

budoom-a budoom-a budoom-a ba-dap.

A-dudu-wum a-dudu-wum dudu-wum a-dudu-wum.

Budoom-a dudu-wum. Budoom-a dudu-wum. Bru-dum.

James Berry

The Caged Bird in Springtime

What can it be,
This curious anxiety?
It is as if I wanted
To fly away from here.

But how absurd!
I have never flown in my life,
And I do not know
What flying means, though I have heard,
Of course, something about it.

Why do I peck the wires of this little cage?
It is the only nest I have ever known.
But I want to build my own,
High in the secret branches of the air.

I cannot quite remember how
It is done, but I know
That what I want to do
Cannot be done here.

I have all I need –
Seed and water, air and light.
Why, then, do I weep with anguish,
And beat my head and my wings
Against these sharp wires, while the children
Smile at each other, saying: "Hark how he sings"?

James Kirkup

The Jaguar

The apes yawn and adore their fleas in the sun.
The parrots shriek as if they were on fire, or strut
Like cheap tarts to attract the stroller with a nut.
Fatigued with indolence, tiger and lion

Lie still as the sun. The boa-constrictor's coil
Is a fossil. Cage after cage seems empty, or
Stinks of sleepers from the breathing straw.
It might be painted on a nursery wall.

But who runs like the rest past these arrives
At a cage where the crowd stands, stares, mesmerized,
As a child at a dream, at a jaguar hurrying enraged
Through prison darkness after the drills of his eyes

On a short fierce fuse. Not in boredom—
The eye satisfied to be blind in fire,
By the bang of blood in the brain deaf the ear—
He spins from the bars, but there's no cage to him

More than to the visionary his cell:
His stride is wildernesses of freedom:
The world rolls under the long thrust of his heel.
Over the cage floor the horizons come.

Ted Hughes

FORCES

A **force** is any push or pull on an object. When you pick up an object, you are exerting a force on it. If you leave it sitting where it is, there are still forces acting on it, but they cancel each other out. Forces can make things move faster or slower, stop, change direction, or change size or shape.

TYPES OF FORCES

Forces affect objects in many different ways. There are forces you can see, such as a foot kicking a ball, and invisible forces, such as magnetism and gravity.

A single force acting on an object will make it start to move, or move faster or slower. Two equal forces acting in opposite directions try to change the object's size or shape.

Forces that need two or more objects to be touching each other are called **contact forces**. You are using forces when you move an object with your hands.

When you kick a football, the single force of your kick makes the football start to move.

As you catch a ball, the pushing force of your hands makes the ball slow down and stop.

If you step on a ball, the equal forces of your foot pushing down and the ground pushing up squash it.

See for yourself

Try rolling one ball into another on a smooth surface. The force of your movement will set the ball rolling. The moving ball will exert a force on the stationary one, causing it to move too.

The surface will exert a force (friction) on both balls, causing them both to slow down, and eventually stop.

50 Shared texts ● **Year 6**

Alastair Smith and Corinne Henderson

HOW THINGS WORK

Extract 1

ROLLER-COASTER

The laws of physics state that a moving object will continue in a straight line unless acted on by an outside force, to change its speed or direction. As the riders in a roller-coaster loop the loop, they are moving in a circle and are therefore changing direction from a straight line. The force causing this to happen is the *centripetal* force, which acts towards the centre of the circle, continually pushing the riders inwards. The reaction to centripetal force is felt when the riders are pressed into their seats.

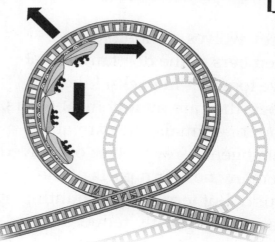

WALL-OF-DEATH

The 'Wall-of-Death' works in a similar way to the roller-coaster. The motion in this case is in a horizontal circle rather than a vertical one. The centripetal force acts to make the riders go round in a circle, rather than along in a straight line. As a reaction to this force, they press up against the revolving drum wall and stay there – even when the floor is lowered from under their feet! The old term of '*centrifugal* force' is no longer used to explain these types of movements.

Steve Parker

Extract 2

SPINNING TOPS

A SPINNING TOP is a fascinating toy. It can be made to balance on the end of a pencil, and if the pencil is moved the spinning top remains pointing in the same direction. This happens because the top has angular momentum, and this momentum does not change unless a force acts on the spinning top – angular momentum is always conserved. Spinning tops, or their more sophisticated cousins called gyroscopes, are used in compasses because they resist changes to the axis of their spin. When a spinning top slows down, it leans to one side. Gravity is pulling the spinning top down, but it does not fall. Instead it slowly circles around its balance point. The spinning object converts the vertical force of gravity into a horizontal motion. This is known as precession.

Peter Lafferty

Meet the Wolf

Grey wolves are long-legged members of the dog family that live together in packs. Like all dogs, they are mainly meat-eaters, and for animals, they are quite intelligent. Grey wolves once lived in many northern parts of the world. But terrible over-hunting by people has greatly reduced their numbers.

Habitat

Grey wolves are generally found in the wilderness areas of Europe and Asia, and also in North America, where they are found in Canada, Alaska and a few northern US states. In all these places, wolves are very adaptable and occupy many different habitats.

In the USA and Russia grey wolves live mainly in thick forests. In Italy and Eastern Europe their home is the mountains. In northern Canada and Siberia their habitat is the icy, windy, treeless landscape called the tundra. Yet wolves also occur in tropical places such as the scrublands of India and the scorching deserts of Saudi Arabia.

The grey wolf is one of only two kinds, or species, of 'true' wolf. The other is the red wolf. There are other types of wolf, such as the maned wolf that lives in South America. Scientists think that maned wolves are not true wolves but distant relatives.

Hunting

Wolves hunt mainly at night, when it is cooler in hot regions, and they can sneak up on victims in the darkness.

Wolves find their prey by their main sense, smell. They can travel 30 kilometres or more in a single night to reach food. One wolf hunting by itself can catch a rabbit or hare. But when six wolves work together, they can bring down prey heavier than all of their weights added together, such as moose and elk.

Sharing the meal

After a big kill, the alpha pair of grey wolves have first choice of food. They usually go for soft, nutritious parts of the victim, such as the heart and liver. The others fight for their shares. They snarl, growl and snap at each other.

When the pack has caught a large animal, every wolf can eat its fill and there is still meat left over. This remaining food is often buried in the ground. In times when prey is scarce, the pack can always return and dig up the food.

Michael Leach

Walk with a wolf

Walk with a wolf in the cold air before sunrise.
She moves, quiet as mist,
  between spruce trees and birches.
A silent grey shadow, she slides between boulders
and trots over blue pebbles to the edge of the lake.

She plunges through slush ice and laps the chill water,
snaps at a feather that drifts down from a goose wing,
  then splashes to shore and
    shakes herself like a dog.

*Wolves were probably the first large animals to live with people,
and all the kinds of dog we know today are descended from them.*

There's deep snow on the mountains.
Snow clouds bank in the east.
Winter is coming, and the geese fly south.

Run with a wolf as she bounds up the steep slope.
She sniffs at a skull that stares at the lake.
Moss grows on the antlers.
The bone has turned grey,
There's no meat on it now—
And she's hungry.

*During the summer months, a wolf may hunt alone
  and catch fish, hare, squirrels and other small animals.
      But these creatures go into hiding in winter
        to escape from the freezing cold weather.*

Howl with a wolf in the dawn, thin and icy.
Deep from her chest the eerie sound comes.
  Long, low music.
    The song of the Arctic.

Another howl answers.

With a wag of her tail, the wolf runs to the pack.
Three sons and a daughter, cubs from the spring,
squirm on their bellies and lick at her neck.

*Mother wolves give birth in springtime.
They can have anything from one to eleven cubs each year.
  Although they don't stay together all the time,
    most wolves live in family groups called packs.*

Janni Howker

Why is the Grey Wolf an endangered species?

Background

At one time the Grey wolf was the farthest-flung of all land mammals, loping across much of the northern hemisphere. Its prey includes livestock, which is why during the 19th century it was persecuted across central and northern European countries. Recovery started naturally in several remote parts across the continent and now the biggest populations are found in eastern countries, particularly Romania, the Balkans and Poland.

An adult male can weigh 40kg and is an average 150cm in length. The wolf is the second largest predator in Europe after the brown bear. Its main prey is moose and deer but it feeds opportunistically. It can adapt very successfully to the environment – anything from the hot central plains of Spain to the bleak tundra of Finland. It lives in sophisticated communities of family packs within clearly defined territory, with only the leading animals – the alpha male and female – breeding. The cubs are then cared for by the remainder of the pack. Wolves are intelligent and shy and prefer to avoid confrontation with people.

The wolf has been transformed in man's perception from hero to villain – and has suffered accordingly. When man was a hunter-gatherer the wolf was revered as a resourceful, powerful fellow-hunter. When man began tending sheep and cattle, the wolf remained a hunter – but became a competitor. It had to be eliminated and the extermination of the wolf began. This, together with man's encroachment upon the wolf's habitat, meant serious inroads were made on the animal's numbers. Today, however, the wolf is recovering naturally and there are between 15,500 and 18,000 in Europe.

Current threats & problems

The wolf suffers a negative image problem and despite its ability to adapt and therefore live close to man, it continues to take the blame – sometimes unfairly – for attacks on livestock. Actual figures for wolves taking domestic livestock are very low, but predatory activities, real or imagined, remain the main reason for attempting to exterminate the wolf.

The animal is hunted in some countries without restriction and in others licences to hunt are issued without biological or ecological understanding of the situation. Poaching is widespread and is the cause of the biggest losses. Although it can co-exist with humans, it needs safe areas in which to retreat. If this problem is not addressed, wolf communities will fragment as a result of moving into unsuitable habitat.

WWF website

Dictionary of phrase and fable

C

Cry wolf, To. To give a false alarm. The allusion is to the fable of the shepherd lad who so often called "Wolf!" merely to make fun of his neighbours, that when at last the wolf came no one would believe him. This fable appears in almost every nation of the world.

W

Wolf. WILLIAM OF MALMESBURY (*Gesta regum Anglorum,* Bk II, ch viii (12th century)) says that the tribute of 300 wolves payable yearly by the king of Wales to Edgar the Peaceful (r.959–975) ceased after the third year because "he could find no more", but they are recorded in England as late as the 15th century and in Ireland and Scotland apparently lingered on until the 18th century.

In music a harsh or grating sound resulting from the system of tuning or temperament in certain keyboard instruments was called a wolf, as also was the jarring note sometimes heard from bowed instruments. In the case of a harp it was said to be caused by the use of a string made from the entrails of a wolf. The squeak made in reed instruments by unskilled players is termed a 'goose'.

Wolf Cub. The long-established and original name for a member of the junior branch of the SCOUT Movement, now called Cub Scouts (age range 8–11 years). The conception owes much to Rudyard Kipling's *Jungle Books* (1894, 1895).

Wolf in sheep's clothing, A. An enemy posing as a friend. The phrase is taken from the well-known fable of AESOP.

Wolf pack, A. A term applied in the Second World War to German submarines in a group.

Cry wolf, To. *See under* CRY.

Keep the wolf from the door, To. To ward off starvation. The allusion is to the pangs of hunger, like those of a ravening wolf. Someone who eats voraciously is said 'to wolf' their food, and French *manger comme un loup* is to eat greedily.

Origins of the word 'wolf'

wolf comes from Old English *wulf,* of ancient Germanic origin. It can be traced back to an Indo-European root shared by Latin *lupus,* also meaning 'a wolf', which is where the word lupine 'like a wolf' comes from.

wolf *n.* Probably before 1300 *wolf,* in *Arthour and Merlin;* developed from Old English (about 750) *wulf;* cognate with Old Frisian *wolf,* Old Saxon *wulf,* Middle Dutch and modern Dutch *wolf,* Old High German *wolf* (modern German *Wolf*), feminine *wulpa,* Old Icelandic *ulfr* (Swedish, Norwegian, and Danish *ulv*), and Gothic *wulfs* from Proto-Germanic *wulfaz* (earlier *wulHwaz*). Cognates outside Germanic are found in Latin (really Sabine) *lupus* wolf, Greek *lýkos,* Lithuaninan *vilkas,* Latvian *vìlks,* Old Slavic *vlŭkŭ,* Avestan *vəhrkō,* and Sanskrit *vŕka-s,* from Indo-European *wḷkwos* (Pok. 1178). **—v.** eat like a wolf, devour. 1862 in George A. Sala's *The Seven Sons of Mammon;* from the noun. **—wolfhound** *n.* (1823, in Scott's *Quentin Durward*) **—wolfish** *adj.* 1570, formed from English *wolf,* n. + *-ish.* An earlier form *wolvish* was formed in Middle English (about 1430) from *wolv-,* inflectional stem form of *wolf* + *-ish,* but became obsolete in the early 1800s.

❶ *Oxford Dictionary of Word Origins* ❷ *Chambers Dictionary of Etymology*

Thesaurus

fear, *v.* **4.** dread, be afraid, be scared, take fright, be alarmed; mistrust, distrust, suspect, anticipate, expect, apprehend, forebode; hesitate, falter, have second thoughts, *Sl.* have cold feet; quail, flinch, recoil, shy, shrink, blench, *Inf.* funk; cower, skulk, crouch; shiver, shudder, quiver, shake in one's boots, tremble.

fright, *n.* **1.** fear, scare, alarm, terror, affright, *Archaic.* fray, *Inf.* funk, panic, horror, dread; perturbation, dismay, consternation, trepidation; apprehension, misgiving, disquiet, discomfort, uneasiness; shaking, quaking, quivering; All *sl.* the heebie-jeebies, the jitters, the willies, the creeps.

tension, *n.* **2.** anxiety, uneasiness, disquiet, disquietude, inquietude, fretfulness; worry, trouble, concern, vexation; pressure, stress, heat, burden, cross, encumbrance, cumbrance; nervousness, ants, *Inf.* butterflies, *Sl.* heebie-jeebies, *Sl.* habdabs; excitement, agitation, perturbation; suspense, anticipation, expectation, apprehension, fear.

Longman Synonym Dictionary

Acknowledgements

The publishers gratefully acknowledge permission to reproduce the following copyright material:

Andersen Press Ltd for extracts from *The Ghost Behind the Wall* by Melvin Burgess © 2000, Melvin Burgess (2000, Andersen Press) and for extracts from *An Angel for May* by Melvin Burgess © 1992, Melvin Burgess (1992, Andersen Press). **Boots Group plc** for an extract from 'Living with hayfever and other allergies' © 2002, Boots Group plc (2002, Boots Group plc). **Cambridge University Press** for an extract from *Charles Darwin's Letters: A Selection 1825–1859* by Charles Darwin © 1998, Cambridge University Press (1998, CUP). **Laura Cecil Literary Agency** on behalf of the James Reeves Estate for 'The Sea' from *Complete Poems for Children* by James Reeves © 1973, James Reeves (1973, Heinemann). **Chrysalis Books Ltd** for an extract from *Science Discoveries: Charles Darwin and Evolution* by Steve Parker, text © 1992, Steve Parker © Chrysalis Children's Books (1992, Belitha Press). **Consignia plc** for 'Packaging guidelines' by Parcelforce Worldwide © 2002, Consignia. **The Controller of HMSO** for extracts from the National Literacy Strategy: *Framework for Teaching* © Crown copyright 1998. **Kevin Crossley-Holland** for 'A Riddle' from *The Exeter Book of Riddles* translated by Kevin Crossley-Holland © 1993, Kevin Crossley-Holland (1993, Penguin). **Faber & Faber** for 'Riddle 21' from *The Red-All-Over Riddle Book* by George Szirtes © 1997, George Szirtes (1997, Faber & Faber) and for 'The Jaguar' from *The Hawk in the Rain* by Ted Hughes © 1982, Ted Hughes (1982, Faber & Faber). **Guardian Newspapers** for 'Power of the Ring too strong for boy wizard' from the *Guardian Unlimited* website, Thursday 19th December 2002 © 2002, The Guardian (2002, www.guardian.co.uk). **Harcourt Education** for an extract from *The Shakespeare Library: Romeo and Juliet* by Wendy Greenhill © 1995, Wendy Greenhill (1995, Heinemann Library); for an extract from *What's At Issue? Making a Difference* by Richard Spilsbury © 2001, Richard Spilsbury (1991, Heinemann Library) and for an extract from *What's At Issue? Citizenship and You* by Katrina Dunbar © 2001, Katrina Dunbar (2001, Heinemann Library). **HarperCollins Publishers** and Frank Richard Williamson and Christopher Reuel Tolkien, executors of the estate of the late John Ronald Reuel Tolkien, for extracts from *The Hobbit* by JRR Tolkien © 1937, JRR Tolkien (1937, George Allen & Unwin Ltd). **David Higham Associates** for an extract from *Kensuke's Kingdom* by Michael Morpurgo © 1999, Michael Morpurgo (1999, Heinemann). **Hodder & Stoughton** for an extract from *Why Do People Harm Animals?* by Chris Mason © 2001, Chris Mason (2001, Hodder Wayland) and for extracts from *Natural World: Wolf* by Michael Leach © 2002, Hodder Wayland (2002, Hodder Wayland). **Libby Houston** for

'Souvenir from Weston-Super-Mare' from *All Change* by Libby Houston © 1993, Libby Houston (1993, Oxford University Press). **John Johnson (Authors' Agents) Ltd** on behalf of the Estate of Leon Garfield for extracts from *Shakespeare's Stories* by Leon Garfield © 1985, The Estate of Leon Garfield (1985, Victor Gollancz). **Kingfisher** for an extract from *Chambers Dictionary of Etymology* © 1988, Larousse (1988, The HW Wilson Company) and for extracts from *How Things Work* by Steve Parker © 1990, Steve Parker (1990, Kingfisher). **Jessica Kingsley Publishers** for extracts from *Freaks, Geeks and Asperger Syndrome* by Luke Jackson © 2002, Luke Jackson (2002, Jessica Kingsley Publishers). **James Kirkup** for 'The Caged Bird in Springtime' from *Collected Shorter Poems, Volume 1* © 1996, James Kirkup (1996, Salzburg University Press). **Julius Kovac** for extracts from *Romeo and Juliet* by William Shakespeare using the text from the website www.shakespeare.sk. **Orion Children's Books** for an extract from *Brewer's Dictionary of Phrase and Fable* ©1959, Cassell Publishers Ltd (1959, Cassell). **Oxford University Press** for extracts from *The Eagle of the Ninth* by Rosemary Sutcliff © 1954, Anthony Lawton (1954, Oxford University Press) and for an extract from *Oxford Dictionary of Word Origins* by John Ayto © 2002, John Ayto (2002, Oxford University Press). **Penguin Group UK** for an extract from *Eyewitness Guides: Force and Motion* © 1992, Peter Lafferty (1992, Dorling Kindersley Ltd). **The Peters Fraser & Dunlop Group** on behalf of James Berry for 'Riddle Poem', 'Mum Dad and Me', 'Sunny Market Song' and 'Mek Drum Talk, Man' from *When I Dance* by James Berry © 1988, James Berry (1988, Hamish Hamilton Children's Books); and on behalf of the Estate of Laurie Lee for an extract from *Cider with Rosie* © 1959, Laurie Lee (1959, Hogarth Press). **Rodale Press** for an extract from the *Longman Synonym Dictionary* © 1979, Rodale (1979, Rodale Press). **The Society of Authors** as the literary representative of the Estate of John Masefield for 'Cargoes' by John Masefield from *Ballads and Poems* © 1910, John Masefield (1910, Elkin Mathews). **Usborne Publishing Ltd** for an extract from *Usborne Internet-linked Library of Science: Energy, Forces and Motion* © 2001, Alastair Smith & Corinne Henderson (2001, Usborne Publishing Ltd). **Walker Books** for an extract from *Walk with a Wolf* by Janni Howker © 1997, Janni Howker, illustrations by Sarah Fox-Davies © 1997, Janni Howker (1997, Walker Books). **WWF-UK Ltd** for an extract from *Grey Wolf* on www.wwf.org.uk © 2002, WWF-UK Ltd.

Every effort has been made to trace copyright holders for the works reproduced in this book, and the publishers apologise for any inadvertent omissions.